HITLER'S
INTERPRETER

HITLER'S
INTERPRETER
THE MEMOIRS OF PAUL SCHMIDT

PAUL SCHMIDT

The
History
Press

Title of the original German edition: *Statist auf diplomatischer Bühne*
© 1949, 1984 by AULA-Verlag GmbH, Wiebelsheim.

This edition published 2016

The History Press
The Mill, Brimscombe Port
Stroud, Gloucestershire, GL5 2QG
www.thehistorypress.co.uk

British Library Cataloguing in Publication Data.
A catalogue record for this book is available from the British Library.

ISBN 978 0 7509 6505 7

Typesetting and origination by The History Press
Printed and bound in Malta by Melita Press

CONTENTS

FOREWORD

When Paul Schmidt was training as an interpreter in the German foreign office in Berlin in the early 1920s, he would scarcely have imagined the role that he would one day play in some of the most central events of the twentieth century. Schmidt, a Berliner and a veteran from the First World War, studied modern languages in the early 1920s in Berlin. He briefly moonlighted as a journalist before enrolling in 1921 on the training course that would change his life. He was evidently a brilliant student, proficient in French, English, Dutch, Spanish, Russian, Czech, Polish, Slovak and Romanian, and able – by his own account – to commit as much as twenty minutes of speech to memory before giving his translation.

Interpreting was quite a new field and was the result of a paradigm shift in diplomacy in the aftermath of the First World War. Before 1914, French had served as the *lingua franca* of international dialogue, with every diplomat expected to be proficient in the language. However, after 1918, the rejection of the perceived 'secret' methods of diplomacy meant that the old Francophone norms had to be abandoned. Suddenly, the need arose for a trained cadre of professional interpreters to aid communication in the international arena; Schmidt would be one of the most famous examples.

Employed in the German foreign ministry from 1923, Schmidt already had over a decade of experience before he first interpreted for Hitler in 1935. It was the start of a relationship that would propel him to the very heart of the story of the Third Reich and of the Second World War.

Paul Schmidt's memoir is a remarkable account of a remarkable career. He was simply everywhere. He acted as interpreter in discussions between Hitler and Mussolini, with the Duke and Duchess of Windsor, with British Foreign Minister Lord Halifax, with Prime Minister Neville Chamberlain, and with Lloyd George. He was called on to interpret at the Nuremberg Rallies, at the 1936 Olympics, in the Reich Chancellery in Berlin and at Hitler's residence in Berchtesgaden. He interpreted at the Munich Conference in 1938, travelled to Moscow for the negotiations that led to the infamous Nazi-Soviet Pact in 1939, and accompanied Hitler to Hendaye to meet Generalissimo Franco in 1940. Even when he was not directly interpreting, Schmidt was usually present within the entourage to make detailed records of conversations for the German foreign office.

Later in the war, in 1942, he was brought in to interrogate Canadian prisoners captured in the Dieppe Raid. He even interpreted for the Allies in the preparation of the Nuremberg tribunal.

As a result of his apparent ubiquity, Schmidt's recollections are of tremendous value both to those interested in pre-war and wartime diplomacy, and those interested in the inner workings of the Nazi state. Though he was intimately involved in many of the discussions that he describes, there is nonetheless a curious 'fly on the wall' quality to his memoir. He comes across as detached and objective, dryly observing events and the individuals concerned.

That detachment and objectivity, Schmidt suggests, is an essential part of the interpreter's art. The greatest mistake an interpreter can make, he says, is to assume that he or she is 'the leading actor on the stage'. Instead, he claims that the primary quality of a good interpreter, paradoxically, is the ability to remain silent.

Of course, Schmidt is less than entirely silent about his former employers. About Hitler, for instance, he was sometimes complimentary, impressed by his master's clear and skilful mode of expression. Hitler was, he said, 'a man who advanced his arguments intelligently and skilfully, observing all the conventions of such political discussions, as though he had done nothing else for years.'

On other occasions, however, he spied what he described as 'the other Hitler', brooding, distracted and non-committal. Utilising the racist vocabulary of the age, Schmidt even saw fit to question Hitler's genealogy, criticising his 'untidy Bohemian appearance', his 'coarse nose' and 'undistinguished mouth' – all of which led him to believe that Hitler might be the product of some 'miscegenation from the Austro-Hungarian Empire'.

Others fare little better. Goebbels is described, pithily, as 'a wolf in exceptionally well-tailored sheep's clothing'; Ribbentrop was arrogant, vain and suspicious in equal measure. Only Göring emerges from Schmidt's account with even a modicum of praise.

He could be similarly candid in describing other salient figures. Franco, for instance, was so short, stout and dark skinned that 'he might be taken for an Arab'. About Mussolini, he was relatively positive, praising the Italian Duce's laugh – 'free and whole-hearted' – and his speaking style: 'he never said a word too many, and everything he uttered could have been sent straight to the printers.'

Schmidt was himself no Nazi; rather he was an old-fashioned, conservative nationalist. He was given an SS rank in 1940 and joined the Nazi Party in 1943 but these were more formalities than acts of ideological commitment, and he was duly exonerated by the denazification court after 1945. As this memoir demonstrates, Schmidt tended to view his Nazi masters with the haughty disdain that is typical of a senior civil servant. They were simply beneath him. He described them, rightly, as 'fanatics' and 'enemies of mankind'; his friends and colleagues at the German Foreign Office viewed them, he claims, as a 'transitory phenomenon' – and yet he served them loyally for over a decade.

Indeed, what might surprise readers is that – apart from that aside – Schmidt is strangely uncritical of his former masters and is seemingly unrepentant about the work that he did for them. Of course, as interpreter, he had no hand in formulating policy, and was restricted solely to facilitating communications between parties, at which – evidently – he was an expert.

But it is nonetheless disconcerting how Schmidt appears to render the Third Reich almost completely harmless. He makes no mention of the

Holocaust, for instance, despite the fact that when this book was first published in 1951 knowledge of the Nazis' genocide against the Jews was already well advanced and was being widely discussed. Surely it would have merited a mention, if only to state – perhaps mendaciously – that he had known nothing of it?

Schmidt had the opportunity, with the publication of this memoir, to wipe the slate clean; to set some distance between himself and his former masters. But, he said nothing, and recalled his time serving Hitler with only the aloof hauteur of the inveterate snob. Hitler's greatest crime, one might conclude from Schmidt's account, was to have neglected to pass the port.

So it is that Schmidt references the fall of the Third Reich in 1945 with only the laconic comment, 'thus ended my work as an interpreter.' There is no evident remorse for his 'not unimportant role' in wartime diplomacy, just the dry, rather amoral detachment of the bureaucrat blindly following his instructions. This, I think, is instructive.

Schmidt comes across as urbane, cultured and thoughtful; he seems to belong to a very different class from most of the other members of Hitler's entourage. The Führer's drivers, valets, cooks and secretaries were, on the whole, rather uncomplicated individuals who had not enjoyed the benefits of a university education or a more cosmopolitan, liberal world view. Schmidt was different. He had studied at Berlin's prestigious Humboldt University; he had been awarded a doctorate; he spoke numerous foreign languages. Yet, for all those differences, Schmidt shared one essential trait with his less advantaged fellows; what one might call 'moral myopia'. Like the valets and the secretaries – most of whom adored Hitler as an avuncular 'boss' and a man of perfect Viennese manners – Schmidt was unable to see beyond his immediate environment, unable to recognise the moral squalor of the Nazi Reich and unable to discern the hideous, misanthropic character of the endeavour in which he played his 'not unimportant role'.

The primary difference between Paul Schmidt and his fellows, therefore, is that – like so many educated Germans of his generation – he really could, and should, have known better.

Roger Moorhouse
2016

EXTRACTS FROM THE EDITOR'S PREFACE, 1951 EDITION

Although we think inevitably of Paul Schmidt as 'Hitler's Interpreter', he had in fact been interpreting for a whole series of German Chancellors and Foreign Ministers during the decade before Hitler and Ribbentrop entered the international scene.

The first half of the German edition of Dr Schmidt's book is devoted to his reminiscences of that earlier period. I decided, in preparing a book of reasonable size and closely sustained interest for the ordinary British reader, to leave out the pre-Hitlerian part altogether.

Schmidt is at pains to make it clear that he places the Nazis — especially Hitler and Ribbentrop — in the category of 'fanatics, the real enemies of mankind, in whatever camp they may be'. He is damning and often contemptuous in his judgments of the men for whom he worked so loyally for so long – and has been criticised on that account. He claims that he was never a Nazi sympathiser, that he merely did his job as a civil servant and expert technician, that he made no secret of his independent outlook and that this was duly noted against him in his dossier.

His account of himself seems to be borne out by the impression he made, among others, on Sir Neville Henderson, British Ambassador in Berlin until the outbreak of war. He certainly showed considerable courage of a negative kind in that, despite his very special position, he resisted pressure to join the Nazi Party until 1943. On the other hand he makes no concession to the view that the German people as a whole were in any way responsible for Hitler. He attributes the triumph of the nationalist extremists in Germany to the economic crisis of 1930–32 and to what he described as the mistakes on the part of the Allies in making their concessions to Germany too late and too grudgingly. I think Schmidt might fairly be described as an enlightened, cosmopolitanised German nationalist, and find it a little hard on him that we have to hand him down to posterity as 'Hitler's Interpreter' and not, perhaps more aptly, as 'Stresemann's Interpreter' – a title to which he has at least an equal claim.

R.H.C. Steed
1951

INTRODUCTION

'Archduke Franz Ferdinand Assassinated at Sarajevo!' With these words I became acquainted for the first time with current affairs when the Special Editions appeared on the streets of Berlin in June 1914. I was still at school then, knew nothing about politics and in my history classes had not yet studied beyond Karl V. Therefore at that moment in time I did not have the slightest presentiment of the event's significance and how it would mark the turning point not only of my own life, but also the future history of Germany, Europe and the whole world.

'First mobilisation second of August!' the village crier informed the farming families of the small Mark Brandenburg town where I was staying with relatives, thereby announcing officially the outbreak of the First World War. Shortly afterwards, as a 15-year-old auxiliary policeman, I wore a white armband, carried an unloaded rifle on my shoulder and played at 'railway protection' below a railway bridge. In 1915 I helped usher in the 'age of food rationing' as later historians were to call it, when I distributed ration books. In 1916, I studied for my school-leaving certificate while working at a munitions factory known as BAMAG (Berlin-Anhaltischer Maschinenbau A.G.) in the Huttenstrasse.

In 1917 I was called up. By then Berlin had already experienced its first food riots. Beneath the surface there was growing unrest amongst the masses: we Berlin recruits were therefore sent for training to the farthest possible regions of the Reich. So I came to the Black Forest and was provided with my basic training on the Hornisgrinde and at the Mummelsee as a mountain infantryman together with others from Berlin, most of whom had never seen a hill higher than the Berlin Kreuzberg in their lives.

One day, we were issued with field-grey uniforms to replace the old blue ones so that we looked like 'real' soldiers if one didn't look too closely at our schoolboy faces. We were trained … in street fighting! We learnt how to force back masses of people energetically but without violence using the rifle at an angle, how to prevent a Socialist grabbing it, how to blockade streets and protect businesses. It was a strange beginning to a 'heroic career'. We were used operationally in Mannheim, blockading streets against the hungry masses in revolt. There were no incidents. The Mannheim workers teased us mainly for our youthful appearance, but at the insistence of our officers made their way quietly home so that we forgot very quickly our 'local police' training tactics.

A few days later we were sent off to the real war just in time to take part in the great offensives of the spring of 1918. As a machine gunner I fought mainly in the 'first wave', as it was called, against the French, British, Americans and Portuguese, who bore the brunt of the March 1918 offensive defending a position the Allies had thought would remain quiet.

On 15 July 1918 I experienced for the first time a turning point in history. It was the first link in the chain of those historical events, beginning with me as a private soldier manning a machine gun, which would continue link by link to my close involvement with political leaders in my later career at the Foreign Office. That day Foch's counter-offensive began, which would seal the fate of the German armies in the First World War.

As the German offensive proceeded, my company was in the first wave scattered behind the curtain of artillery fire and making its way through the cratered land at Reims. Suddenly we noticed the eerie silence and quiet withdrawal by the French. We had the distinct feeling that we were making a stab in the dark. The riddle was solved within a few hours when Foch, with his reserve army, embarked on a well-thought-through surprise counter-attack that threw us into total confusion at this most critical moment of our advance.

That morning as I sat in the shell craters at Reims I knew nothing of the decisive extent of the moment. I could never have dreamed that afterwards I would be closely involved time and again in the varied fates of Germany and Europe, that as future years passed I would witness at first hand, on the diplomatic and political battlefronts, the gradual resurrection of Germany to the height of its greatest power and then watch the wheel of history turn full circle. Almost a quarter of a century later, it would be at Reims that the unconditional surrender of the Third Reich became fact.

As a supernumerary private soldier I could never have thought it possible then that in 1936 at Obersalzberg I would have an in-depth talk with the British Prime Minister of the First World War, Lloyd George, and relate to him my experiences at the front. Even less so that twenty-two years later, in the historic dining car in the woods at Compiègne where the 1918 armistice was signed, I would sit opposite the French delegation as they signed another armistice. I knew nothing then of Locarno and the League of Nations; of the conversations between Briand and Stresemann; of the optimistic efforts to achieve peace in Europe in which I was involved in the 1920s as an interpreter; of reparations and conferences on the world economy; of Brüning and MacDonald; of Hitler and Chamberlain. At Reims in 1918 I was just happy that we had narrowly escaped the advancing Allies and embarked upon an orderly retreat. Later, positioned at a listening post in the American lines by night for my knowledge of English, I was wounded during the Argonnes offensive.

I came to Berlin during the chaos of the German Revolution. Wounded and walking with a crutch, I witnessed the Spartacus Uprising in the Friedrichstrasse and saw the front line that ran through the centre of Berlin and later divided the communist East from the anti-communist West.

As a *Frontschwein* I had been wounded and awarded the Iron Cross. In my future study of languages this gave me many advantages. I came into close and friendly contact with many British and Americans during the hyperinflation, worked as a student for an American newspaper agency in Berlin and as a result got to know international politics in the very intensive way that the Americans practised it.

After the Genoa Conference of 1921, the German Foreign office introduced special courses to train conference interpreters. It was without precedent because in earlier times diplomatic exchanges had mostly been handled by career diplomats, who all spoke French as a matter of course. French had been the common language of diplomacy before the First World War. After 1918 these circumstances underwent a major change. 'Secret diplomacy', considered to have been the principal cause of the war, would have to cease. There were now fewer diplomatic meetings and more great international conferences. Individual nations were no longer represented mainly by ambassadors but by statesmen − even the Prime Minister or Minister-President and the Foreign Minister − because it was believed that direct, personal contact would lead quicker to the achievement of goals than the old methods. These new representatives of nations were rarely competent in a language other than their own and thus a completely new calling came into being.

The interpreter who translated the speeches and conversations at such conferences owed his role in international politics to this democratisation of the methods of political negotiation. As of necessity he took part in the most secret discussions between two people, which of course entailed himself as the third. It was expected of him that if possible he would neither intrude nor undermine the atmosphere of confidence or the flow of discourse by too frequent interruptions to translate. This led to the new technique of conveying whole speeches or large extracts of conversation in a single delivery. In this way the interpreter as a disturbance faded into the background. Naturally it lengthened the time necessary to develop the negotiations, but on the other hand it gave his work the advantage that during his delivery the negotiating partners could formulate their questions and answers in a relaxed manner.

This new technique obviously required that the translator made memory notes while listening to the talk he had to translate. These notes were a major aid to the preparation of a reliable precis of the content. From them today the course of a negotiation can be reconstructed very accurately and they are therefore valuable materials for the historian engaged in research into the background and connections of the confused times after 1918.

The German Foreign Office courses taught this new technique with great thoroughness. Those participating were selected from amongst the students at Berlin University. Some were studying law, others languages. I received an offer to join and completed the entire course.

Meanwhile I had concluded my studies and in July 1923 was making my last feverish preparations for the oral exam. One evening, with an anxious eye on the approaching Romance test, poring over a huge tome on the troubadours of old Provence, fate came knocking in the truest sense of the word. A messenger from the Foreign Office arrived bearing an express letter from the head of the Languages Division instructing me to attend a small restaurant on the Savigny Platz in Charlottenburg that same evening for a conversation with him.

INTRODUCTION

Over a glass of wine, my later chief of office, Privy Councillor Gautier, disclosed, to my boundless surprise, that difficulties had arisen with the interpreter at the International Court in The Hague and that it was his intention to substitute me on an experimental basis. 'If you do well,' he concluded, 'maybe you can be transferred into the Foreign Office in the not too distant future.'

The ground seemed to tremble beneath my feet, and this was not due to the wine with which the all-powerful departmental head of the Foreign Office Languages Section had provided me to cushion the shock. After all, I had been simply tossed into an undertaking that to me looked like some crazy adventure. I would have to leave next evening, postpone my examinations and appease my course lecturers who would obviously view with great disfavour such an activity in the despised practice by a young student.

I made the decision to accept the offer and next evening, equipped with passports, visas, Dutch guilders and a ticket for a couchette, sat waiting at the Friedrichstrasse station. It was the first time in my life that I had ever got into a sleeper coach, and as I lay in the beautiful Mitropa bed it all seemed like a dream. Had I known then the journey that I was beginning, I would scarcely have slept a wink. Had I been able to foresee how many thousands of kilometres I would journey across Europe over subsequent years, how often in due course ever larger and more comfortable aircraft would fly me between Berlin, London, Paris and Rome, so that even today I could show a pilot the route, I would still have been wide awake as the train drew into The Hague.

As the train rolled out towards the Netherlands and my unsuspected destiny, world affairs ceased to be a private matter for me. From that evening on they would be part of my life.

Upon my arrival in The Hague on the Saturday, at the hotel I was approached by the outgoing chief interpreter for the Reich government Georg Michaelis. He had won his spurs at the Versailles peace conference after his predecessor had broken down when he saw the conditions being imposed on Germany and could not continue. Michaelis had seized his opportunity and impressed even Clemenceau and Lloyd George. President Wilson had declared that Michaelis must have been born and bred in Chicago, his American English was so good. Michaelis was a language genius. He was the master of eleven of them, and not 'on crutches' with the aid of dictionaries and grammars as is the case with many, but fluently, as though each language were his mother tongue. I can confirm that personally, having heard his English, French, Spanish and Italian, and the Dutch told me that his Amsterdam accent was faultless. Michaelis had the allure of a world-famous star and that was his downfall, for an interpreter is not the leading actor on the stage as he often seemed to assume. He is at the centre of an event and speaks for the greats but must remain mindful of the fact that he is only a small cog in the great clockwork of international affairs. His failure to remember this latter rule caused him constant problems with the German delegations, and in this case finally with the former Justice Minister, Schiffer.

'Can you take shorthand? Have you ever acted as an interpreter before anywhere?' When I answered no to all his questions, Michaelis forecast that it would not be possible for me to handle the complicated legal material before the court and my ship would definitely founder. With that he took his leave.

I had one day's grace to acquaint myself with the material before the court, which would reconvene on the Monday. Knowledge of the subject matter is actually an indispensable precondition for the interpreter. Over the years I have become ever more convinced by my experiences that a good diplomatic interpreter must have three qualities in this order: first, and paradoxical though it may seem, he must be able to keep silent; secondly, he must be expert to a certain extent in the matters he will have to translate, and thirdly, strange to say, comes command of the language. The best translating ability will not avail the interpreter who does not know the subject. A bilingual layman will never be able to put over what a professor of chemistry is explaining, but a chemistry student with reasonable language skill will be able to make himself understood to a foreign chemist. For this reason, when I reported to the delegation heads I boned up on the subject and then went off with the files to read in peace.

The case was later to become famous in international law. The British steamer *Wimbledon* had been chartered by a French concern to transport artillery and other war materiel from Salonica to the Polish naval depot at Danzig. The German authorities had refused to allow the ship to transit the Kiel Canal on the grounds that Poland and the Soviet Union were at war, and that Germany as a neutral was obliged under the conventions of neutrality to refuse passage of war materiel destined for either belligerent through German territory. On 23 March 1923, a few days after the incident, the French Ambassador in Berlin had called upon the German government to lift the ban on passage by virtue of Article 380 of the Treaty of Versailles, which stated that 'the Kiel Canal must remain open for passage to the warships and merchant ships of all nations at peace with Germany'. The German Reich contended that the obligations of neutrality under international law overrode the provisions of individual treaties, especially since Soviet Russia was not a signatory to the Versailles treaty.

This relatively simple but highly significant case for the times had now been garbed in a mass of complicated legal argument, but at least I had grasped the main points. On the Monday the court and public galleries were packed. The session began when Justice Minister Schiffer delivered his thirty-minute long statement from the witness box. I scribbled my notes in great haste as I had been taught on the Foreign Office courses and had practised hundreds of times. I filled page after page in large capitals and also added where appropriate important figures of speech and meaningful subordinate clauses. When Schiffer stepped down the President of the Court said, 'Translation.'

Because French and English were the working languages in the court, Schiffer's original pleading in German had no official value and was not even taken down by a shorthand writer. What the court would accept in evidence was my translation into French of what Schiffer had said in German.

I gathered up my notes and went into the witness box. Total silence had fallen except for some coughs and rustling from the public galleries. The judges looked at me expectantly. I took a deep breath and began. Suddenly all my tensions and anxieties fell away. Noticing after the first few minutes that the German pleading was not as difficult to put over as I had thought it would be, I began to feel almost at home in the witness box. One had to render the delivery to the President of the Court directly and my translation developed almost into personal advocacy to him. After half an hour I returned satisfied and relieved to my seat. Equally relieved was our small delegation. I was given to understand that its two head delegates, Schiffer and Martius, were very pleased with me.

What gave me pleasure was the courtesy with which we Germans were treated not only in court but also in the breaks outside it, when British, French, Italians and other Allied personalities conversed with us in the friendliest manner as though there were no *Wimbledon* case nor international tensions.

So I had come through my baptism of fire. Michaelis had gone with the remark that he could not understand how I had done it. On 17 August 1923, by a majority verdict, it was ruled that the German Reich had acted illegally in preventing the passage of the *Wimbledon* through the Kiel Canal and a fine of 140,000 francs was imposed.

After returning from The Hague, I sat my oral examinations at Berlin University. I received my doctorate on 1 August 1923 and was then recruited into the Languages Division of the German Foreign Office.

ONE

1935

The first time I interpreted for Hitler was on 25 March 1935, when Sir John Simon and Mr Anthony Eden came to the Reich Chancellery in Berlin for a round-table conference on the European crisis caused by German rearmament. Simon was then Foreign Secretary and Eden Lord Privy Seal. Also present were von Neurath, German Foreign Minister, and Ribbentrop, at that time special commissioner for disarmament questions.

I was surprised when I received the order to attend. It was true that I was chief interpreter at the German Foreign Office and had worked for practically every German Chancellor and Foreign Minister in the ten years up to the advent of the Hitler government in 1933. Then things had changed. Germany had dropped out of the small, man-to-man international discussions and had adopted the method of notes, memoranda and public pronouncements.

Furthermore, Hitler disliked the German Foreign Office and everyone connected with it. In the previous conversations between him and foreigners, the interpreting had been done by co-opting Ribbentrop, Baldur von Schirach or some other National Socialist as interpreter. Our Foreign Office officials were horrified when they heard that Hitler would not even allow State Secretary von Bülow to be present at these highly important discussions with Simon and Eden. In an attempt to ensure that at least one member of the Foreign Office should attend in addition to von Neurath, they decided to put me forward as interpreter. On being told that I had done good work at Geneva for a long time, Hitler remarked, 'If he was at Geneva he's bound to be no good – but so far as I'm concerned we can give him a trial.' I was told this many years later by the English girl Unity Mitford, a supporter of the British Union of Fascists leader Sir Oswald Mosley, her brother-in-law. She was often invited as a guest of Hitler and overheard this remark by chance in assessment of my probable abilities.

The developments leading up to this Anglo-German meeting had been just as unexpected as the conference itself. Both France and Great Britain had been watching developments in Germany with growing concern. The British government was becoming alarmed at German rearmament, particularly the growth of the Luftwaffe. 'Britain's frontier lies on the Rhine,' Baldwin had told the House of Commons in July 1934, and in November he had pointed openly to German rearmament as the most important factor for general unease.

While the French adhered to her established policy of a comprehensive system of security pacts to protect herself against Germany, the British had decided to seek clarification of the German intentions through talks. This idea was expressed in a joint Anglo-French communiqué of 3 February 1935: 'Great Britain and France are agreed that nothing would contribute more to the restoration of confidence and the prospects for peace between the nations than a general settlement freely concluded between Germany and the other Powers.'

In mid February the German answer was given in a note I was required to translate into French and English and whose peaceful tone surprised me: 'The German government welcomes the spirit of friendly discussions between the individual governments expressed in the communications from HM government and the French government. It would therefore be very acceptable ... if HM government ... was prepared to enter into an immediate exchange of views with the German government.'

With surprising alacrity and readiness, the British government offered to send Foreign Minister Sir John Simon to Berlin at the beginning of March. Then an unexpected development intervened. Shortly before Simon's scheduled visit, the British government issued a White Paper intended to justify its own rearmament to Parliament:

Germany is not only rearming openly and on a large scale contrary to the provisions of the Treaty of Versailles, but has also given notice of withdrawal from the League of Nations and the disarmament conference ... HM Government has obviously not declared itself to be in agreement with the breach of the Treaty of Versailles ... German rearmament, if continuing uncontrolled at its present rate, will reinforce the concerns of Germany's neighbours and could endanger peace ... Moreover the spirit in the which the people and especially the youth of Germany is being organised justifies the feeling of unease which has indisputably arisen.

The National Socialist press was indignant, and Sir John Simon's visit was postponed on the grounds that Hitler had a cold. Within the Foreign Office it was being said that it was not a diplomatic lie, Hitler really was *verschnupft*, a word that means both to have a cold and to be in a huff.

Events now followed one another apace. On 6 March the French government introduced two years' national service; on 7 March the Franco-Belgian military agreement of 1921 was extended. On 16 March Hitler replied by reintroducing conscription. Military parity, permitted to Germany in December 1932 by negotiated agreement 'in a system of security for all nations', had become reality by a unilateral decision of the Reich 'outside a system of security'. My friends in the Foreign Office commented that this could have been achieved more quickly and cheaply by negotiation, as in the evacuation of the Rhineland and in the case of reparations. In the light of my experience of the way in which Stresemann and Brüning conducted negotiations, I thought that the methods of the latter pair would have obtained the objective faster had it not been for the adverse developments before and after 1933. That it would have been cheaper for Germany and the whole world is known only too well today.

Two days later, on 18 March, HM Government protested '... against the introduction of conscription and increasing the standing peacetime Army to

36 divisions. After the setting up of the German Luftwaffe, the declaration of 16 March is a further example of unilateral proceedings ... which, quite apart from the issue of principle, are seriously increasing unrest in Europe.' To our astonishment the note concluded: 'HM Government wishes to be assured that the Reich Government still wishes the visit (of Simons) to take place within the terms of reference previously agreed.' This last sentence came as a surprise to us translators, for we had never imagined that the British would finish off a diplomatic protest with a polite enquiry whether, despite all the foregoing, they were still welcome to come to Berlin.

'As far as I am concerned,' François-Poncet, then French Ambassador in Berlin, wrote in his memoirs, 'I suggested immediately after 16 March that the powers should recall their ambassadors forthwith and set up a common defensive front against Germany by speedily concluding the Eastern and Danubian Pacts. Great Britain should naturally make it quite clear that in the future any negotiations would be superfluous, and that Sir John Simon had finally abandoned his plan to visit Berlin. My suggestion was regarded as too radical and therefore not considered.'

It was not until 21 March that M. François-Poncet handed us the French protest, which I translated for Hitler as follows:

> These decisions [conscription, standing army of 36 divisions, creation of the Luftwaffe] clearly conflict with Germany's obligations under the treaties she has signed. They also conflict with the statement of 11 December 1932 [Military parity within a security system] ... The Reich Government has deliberately breached the fundamental principles of international law ... The Government of the French Republic considers it to be its duty to deliver the most emphatic protest and to take all necessary precautions for the future.

Half an hour later our future Axis allies, the Italians, entered the fray. In his note, which we had to translate very quickly, the Italian Ambassador spoke only of taking 'unrestricted precautions', and in his final sentence stated that the Italian government could accept no *fait accompli* resulting from a 'unilateral decision annulling international obligations.'

A mere comparison of the texts of these three notes showed me that the isolation of Germany had begun to loosen. Cracks were apparent in the united front. It was with this thought in mind after the dramatic to-and-fro of the previous week that I sat, two days later on the morning of 25 March, between Hitler and Simon as interpreter in the Reich Chancellery.

Hitler welcomed von Neurath and myself quite pleasantly that morning in his office, in the extension that had been completed under Brüning. It was the first time I ever saw Hitler in person. I had never attended any of his public meetings. I was surprised to find that he was only of medium height – photographs and newsreels always made him appear tall.

Then Sir John Simon and Anthony Eden were shown in. There were friendly smiles and handshakes all round despite the very recent protests and the warning that 'unilateral action had seriously aggravated anxiety abroad'. Hitler's smile was especially friendly – for the very good reason that the presence of the British guests was a triumph for him.

'I had the military sovereignty of the Reich restored a few days ago,' Hitler began, 'because the Reich is under great threat from all sides. The danger lies principally in the East.' There followed an indictment of Bolshevism lasting about thirty minutes. In contrast to his public utterances on the subject – especially in radio broadcasts when his voice would tend to be as harsh as that of a market crier, his words issuing from the loudspeakers in a distorted form – he did not get himself particularly worked up in the presence of the British. All the same, from time to time he did speak more emotionally: 'I believe that National Socialism has saved Germany, and thereby perhaps all Europe, from the most terrible catastrophe of all times … We have experienced Bolshevism in our own country … We are only safe against the Bolshevists if we have armaments that they respect.' He spoke occasionally with some passion, but never went beyond the limits of what I had heard in the more excited moments of other international discussions.

His phraseology was perfectly conventional. He expressed himself clearly and skilfully, was clearly very sure of his arguments, easily understood, and not difficult to translate into English. He appeared to have everything he wanted to say very clear in his mind. On the table before him lay a fresh writing block, which remained unused throughout the negotiations. He had no notes with him.

I watched him closely when from time to time he paused to think over what he was about to say, which gave me an opportunity to look up from my notebook. He had clear blue eyes, which gazed penetratingly at the person to whom he was speaking. As the discussion proceeded, he addressed his remarks increasingly to me – while interpreting I have often noticed this tendency in a speaker to turn instinctively to the man who understands exactly what he is saying. In the case of Hitler, I felt that although he looked at me, he did not see me. His mind was busy with his own thoughts and he was unaware of his surroundings.

When he spoke about a matter of special importance his face became very expressive; his nostrils quivered as he described the dangers of Bolshevism for Europe. He emphasised his words with jerky, energetic gestures of his right hand, sometimes clenching his fist.

He was certainly not the raging demagogue I had half expected from hearing him on the radio, from his ruthless measures or his supporters in brown shirts and riding breeches 'in action' on the streets of Berlin. That morning, and during all these conversations with the British, he impressed me as a man who advanced his arguments intelligently and skilfully, observing all the conventions of such political discussions, as though he had done nothing else for years. The only unusual thing about him was the length at which he spoke. During the whole morning session he was practically the only speaker, Simon and Eden only occasionally interjecting a remark or asking a question. Hitler seemed able to divine when their interest was flagging – after all, they did not understand much of what he was saying – and he would then, at intervals of fifteen or twenty minutes, call on me to translate.

Simon looked at Hitler with by no means unsympathetic interest as he listened to him. His face had a certain paternally benevolent look about it. I had noticed it in Geneva when I heard him stating his country's views in his well-modulated voice with all the clarity of an English jurist, though perhaps with too much emphasis on the purely formal aspects. Watching him now, as he listened attentively to Hitler, I had the feeling that his expression of fatherly understanding was deepening. Perhaps he was pleasantly surprised to find, instead of the wild Nazi of British propaganda, a man who was emotional and emphatic but not unreasonable or ill-natured. In later years, when foreign visitors spoke to me almost with enthusiasm of the impression Hitler made on them, I often suspected that this effect was produced by a reaction against the somewhat crude anti-Hitler propaganda.

On the other hand I occasionally noticed a rather more doubting expression flit over the face of Eden, who understood enough German to be able to follow Hitler roughly. Some of Eden's questions and observations showed he had considerable doubts about Hitler and what he was saying. 'There are actually no indications,' he once observed, 'that the Russians have any aggressive plans against Germany.' And in a slightly sarcastic tone he asked, 'On what are your fears actually based?'

'I have rather more experience in these matters than is general in England,' Hitler parried, and added heatedly, throwing out his chin, 'I began my political career just when the Bolshevists were launching their first attack in Germany.' Then he went off again into a monologue on Bolshevists in general and in particular, which with translation lasted until lunch.

This first meeting, lasting from 10.15 a.m. until 2 p.m., passed off in a very pleasant atmosphere. Such at least was Hitler's impression. 'We have made good contact with each other,' he said to one of his trusties as he left his office. Turning to me and shaking me by the hand, he added, 'you did your job splendidly. I had no idea that interpreting could be done like that. Until now I have always had to stop after each sentence for it to be translated.'

'You were in good form today,' Eden said when I met him in the hall; we knew each other from many a difficult session in Geneva. I too was very satisfied with the first round of the Anglo-German talks.

The British party lunched with von Neurath, after which the discussion was resumed. On the German side, von Neurath and Ribbentrop remained silent. Simon opened the session by advancing, in a very mild and friendly way, the British reservations regarding Germany's unilateral denunciation of the Treaty of Versailles, while Eden reverted to German fears of Russia's aggressive intentions. 'Here the Eastern Pact could be of great service,' he stated, thereby indicating the subject for the first part of the afternoon session. He outlined briefly the nature of such a treaty. Germany, Poland, Soviet Russia, Czechoslovakia, Finland, Estonia, Latvia and Lithuania were envisaged as signatories. The treaty states should pledge themselves to mutual assistance in the event of one of the partners attacking another.

At the mention of Lithuania, Hitler showed anger for the first time. 'We want nothing to do with Lithuania,' he exclaimed, his eyes alight with anger. Suddenly he seemed to be a different person. I was often to see such unexpected outbursts in the future. Almost without transition, he would suddenly fly into a rage; his voice would become hoarse, he would roll his r's and clench his fists while his eyes blazed. 'In no circumstances would we enter a pact with a state that is crushing the German minority in Memel underfoot.' Then the storm subsided as suddenly as it had begun, and Hitler was again the quiet, polished negotiator as he had been before the Lithuanian outburst. His excitement was explained by the fact that for months 126 citizens of Memel had been on trial for treason before a Kovno court martial, and the case was now nearing its end.

Speaking more quietly, Hitler refused an Eastern Pact on further and weightier grounds. 'Between National Socialism and Bolshevism,' he stated emphatically, 'any association is completely out of the question.' He added with almost passionate excitement, 'Hundreds of my party members have' been murdered by Bolshevists. German soldiers and civilians have fallen in the fight against Bolshevist risings. Between Bolshevists and ourselves there will always be these sacrificial victims preventing any common participation in a pact or other agreement.' Moreover there was a third objection to the Eastern Pact – Germany's justifiable mistrust of all collective agreements: 'They do not prevent war but encourage it and promote its extension.' Bilateral treaties were preferable and Germany was prepared to conclude such non-aggression pacts with all her neighbours. 'Except Lithuania, of course,' he said vehemently, but added more quietly, 'as long as the Memel question remains unsettled.'

Eden put in another word for the Eastern Pact, asking whether this could not be combined with a system of bilateral non-aggression pacts or agreements of mutual assistance. But Hitler rejected this suggestion too, saying that one could not have two different groups of members within the framework of a general agreement. He was wholly averse to the idea of mutual assistance. Significantly he suggested instead that the individual countries should confine themselves to an undertaking not to assist an aggressor. 'That would localise wars instead of making them more general,' he said with apparent logic – but it was the logic of a man whose plan was to deal with his opponents one by one and who wanted to avoid having anyone standing in his way. At that time the motive behind his argument was not evident; it was to be revealed by his manner of proceeding later.

By some clever questions, Simon passed from the Eastern to the Danubian Pact, which was to be directed against interference in the affairs of the Danubian States. This proposal was based on a French scheme that aimed at preventing the annexation of Austria to Germany and putting up a barrier of treaties to impede the extension of Reich influence over the Balkans. I had been told at our Foreign Office that Hitler was particularly opposed to this idea for obvious reasons, and I therefore expected that he would give the British an emphatic 'No', but to my surprise he did not do so. 'Fundamentally, Germany has no objection to such a Pact,' he said in seeming agreement. I was rather surprised to hear him use the word 'fundamentally'. At Geneva, when a delegate agreed *en principe* one knew that he would oppose the proposal in practice. Was Hitler using this old international device? His very next words confirmed my assumption; he observed almost casually, 'but it would have to be stated quite clearly how so-called non-interference in the affairs of the Danube countries should be most accurately defined'. Simon and Eden exchanged a quick look when I translated these words, and I felt suddenly as though I were back at Geneva.

That afternoon the British also raised the question of the League of Nations. 'A final settlement of European problems,' Simon said quietly but emphatically, 'is unthinkable unless Germany becomes a member of the League of Nations again. Without the return of the Reich to Geneva the necessary confidence cannot be restored amongst the peoples of Europe.'

On this matter too Hitler was by no means as intransigent as I had expected. Indeed, he stated that a return of Germany to the League was well within the bounds of possibility. The ideals of Geneva were thoroughly praiseworthy, but the manner in which they had been put into practice to date had given occasion for far too many justified complaints by Germany. The Reich could return to Geneva only as a completely equal partner in every respect, and that was impossible so long as the Treaty of Versailles was linked with the League covenant. 'Moreover, we would have to be given a share somehow in the system of colonial mandates if we are really to consider ourselves as a power having equal rights,' he added quickly, but immediately avoided any further discussion of the colonial question with the remark that Germany had at that time no colonial demands to bring forward.

This conversation was continued until 7 p.m., half of the time being naturally taken up with my translation and Hitler, as was his wont, constantly repeating himself on matters about which he felt strongly. Moreover, in the absence of both chairman and agenda, discussion tended to ramble. On the whole, however, it passed off better than I had at first expected, although after the cordial atmosphere of the morning I felt that the British had cooled off a little, no doubt owing to the fact that, despite his marked friendliness and his skilful recourse to Geneva formulas, Hitler had actually said 'No' to every point.

Von Neurath gave a dinner in honour of the British visitors, which was attended by about eighty guests, including Hitler, all the ministers of the Reich, many Secretaries of State, leading figures of the Nazi Party, Sir Eric Phipps the British Ambassador and the senior members of his embassy.

I sat next to Hitler, but most of the delectable dishes were whisked away untouched while I was delivering my translation, with the result that I left the table hungry. I had not yet devised the technique of eating and working at the same time – while my client stopped eating to give his text I would eat, and then deliver my translation while he ate. This procedure came to be recognised by *chefs de protocole* as an ingenious solution for interpreters at banquets.

The following morning was devoted to a detailed discussion of German armaments. At first there was some tension between Simon and Hitler as Simon propounded once again the principles governing the British position, emphasising especially that a discussion of the level of German armaments did not imply that Britain had departed from her original position. She adhered strictly to the view that treaties could be altered only by mutual agreement and not by unilateral denunciation. Hitler replied with his well-known thesis that it was not Germany but the other powers that had first broken the disarmament provisions of the Treaty of Versailles 'by failing to carry out the clearly expressed undertaking to disarm themselves'. He added with a laugh, 'Did Wellington, when Blücher came to his assistance, first enquire of the legal experts at the British Foreign Office whether the strength of the Prussian forces matched what had been agreed under existing treaties?'

Both sides advanced their arguments without any acerbity, the British obviously taking pains to avoid any antagonism on this fundamental question. Such was my impression from the very cautious, almost deprecatory manner in which Simon expressed the British reservation. Hitler too was extremely moderate in his tone, compared with that of his public statements on disarmament, though he was not lacking in clarity. 'We are not going to let ourselves be rattled on conscription,' he stated, 'but we are prepared to negotiate regarding the strength of armed forces. Our only condition is parity on land and in the air with our most strongly armed neighbour.'

When Simon asked him at what strength he estimated the armaments requirements of Germany under prevailing conditions, Hitler replied, 'we could content ourselves with thirty-six divisions, that is, an army of 500,000 men.' This, with one SS division and the militarised police, would satisfy all his requirements. The point was somewhat confused by the fact that Hitler, while naming the SS, denied almost in the same breath that the party organisations in general had any military value, as Heydrich had done before him at Geneva. No doubt remembering the Geneva discussions on this question, in which he had taken part as British delegate, Eden expressed doubt as to whether the party organisations could be considered as having no military value and said that they should be regarded at least as reserves.

Wishing to avoid lengthy debate on this very controversial point, Simon immediately steered the discussion to the matter that at that time interested the British above everything: the question of the Luftwaffe. 'In your opinion, *Herr Reichskanzler*,' he asked, 'What should the strength of the Luftwaffe be?'

Hitler avoided making any precise statement. 'We need parity with Great Britain and with France,' he said, adding immediately, 'of course, if the Soviet Union were to augment its forces materially, Germany would have to increase the Luftwaffe to match.'

Simon wanted more information: 'May I ask how great Germany's air strength is at the present time?'

Hitler hesitated, and then said, 'we have already achieved parity with Great Britain.' Simon made no comment. For a while nobody said anything. I thought the two British delegates looked surprised and also dubious at Hitler's statement. This impression was later confirmed by Lord Londonderry, Minister for Air, at whose conversations with Göring I was almost always present as interpreter. The subject of Germany's strength in the air in 1935 cropped up constantly, as well as the question of whether Hitler's statement on that occasion had not, after all, been exaggerated.

Hitler and Simon also discussed briefly the conclusion of an air pact between the Locarno powers. Under such an agreement the signatories to the Locarno Treaty would immediately render mutual assistance with their air forces in the event of an attack. 'I am prepared to join such a pact,' Hitler said, repeating an assent given previously. 'But of course I can only do so if Germany herself has the necessary air force available,' he added with a logic to which the British had no reply.

Hitler himself introduced the question of naval strength, making the demand, later to become famous through the Naval Agreement, for a ratio of 35 per cent of the British fleet. The British did not say how they stood with regard to this proposal, but since they raised no objection it could well be assumed that inwardly they agreed.

At noon, a lunch was taken at the British Embassy, at which Hitler made an appearance; this was the first time he had ever been seen at a foreign embassy. Göring and other members of the government were present. In the reception room, the British Ambassador Sir Eric Phipps lined up his children to give the Hitler salute and, so far as I recall, they even greeted Hitler with a rather bashful 'heil'.

Immediately afterwards discussions were resumed at the chancellery, but no new points came up on the main subjects. Hitler took up much time with his favourite theme, Soviet Russia. He was particularly vehement about Soviet attempts to push westwards, and in that connection he called Czechoslovakia 'Russia's arm reaching out'. Hitler's second obsession at this discussion was German military equality. The Reich must of course have all the classes of armaments that other countries possessed, but he was prepared to cooperate in agreements whereby armaments defined at Geneva as offensive weapons would be prohibited. Similarly, Germany could agree to supervision of armaments, but of course only on the basis of parity and on the assumption that such supervision were simultaneously exercised over all the other countries concerned.

Simon and Eden listened patiently to all this, with its many repetitions. I often thought of the disarmament negotiations at Geneva. Only two years ago the skies would have fallen in had German representatives put forward such demands as Hitler was making now as though they were the most natural thing in the world. I couldn't help wondering whether Hitler had not got further with his method of *fait accompli* than would have been possible with the Foreign Office method of negotiation. I was especially inclined to think this when I observed how placidly Simon and Eden listened. Naturally they had their reservations and had evidently maintained the line of fidelity to agreements and of security guarantees in the familiar Geneva manner. Indeed, they had been emphatic to Hitler on these matters. Nevertheless, the mere fact of their presence and of this discussion about things that for years had been completely taboo at Geneva greatly impressed me.

These memorable days were concluded by an evening reception given by Hitler to a select company in the old Brüning chancellery. The furniture, carpets, paintings and even the flower arrangements in the reception rooms were harmonious and tasteful, the colours and the lighting not brash. The host himself was unassuming, sometimes almost shy, although without being awkward. During the day he had worn a brown tunic with a red swastika-armband. Now he was wearing tails, in which he never looked at ease. Only on rare occasions did I see him in his 'plutocratic' rig and then he gave the impression that the tails were hired for the occasion. That evening, in spite of his frock coat, Hitler was a charming host, moving amongst his guests as easily as if he had grown up in the atmosphere of a great house. During the concert items – I think Schlusnus, Patzak and the Ursuleac sang, mainly Wagner – I had ample opportunity of observing the British. Simon's friendly interest in Hitler struck me even more than during the negotiations; his gaze would rest on him for a while with a friendly expression, and he would then look at the paintings, the furniture and the flowers. He seemed to feel happy in the German Chancellor's house.

Eden also took in his surroundings with obvious interest and liking, but his expression indicated a sober, keen observation of men and things. I did not see the friendly warmth in his eyes that I believed present in Simon's. His deprecation was clearly evident, except with regard to the musical entertainment, which he followed with unqualified admiration.

Of the Germans present, Foreign Minister von Neurath alone was unconstrained and natural in his demeanour. All the others, especially Ribbentrop, at the time Commissioner for Disarmament Questions, were vague and colourless, like subsidiary figures indicated by an artist in the background of an historical picture.

Towards 11 p.m., Eden left for Warsaw and Moscow. In Hitler's entourage this visit to Stalin was taken much amiss, and an old National Socialist at the chancellery said to me, 'It is sheer tactlessness of Eden to go on to the Soviet chieftain immediately after his visit to the Führer.' Somewhat later Simon went back to the Hotel Adlon and then flew to London next morning.

As I left next morning for trade negotiations in Rome, I learnt nothing further of the direct impression that the British had made on Hitler. Hitler had spoken very appreciatively about Simon in the short intervals during the negotiations, and I heard him say to Ribbentrop, 'I have the impression that I would get on well with him if we came to a serious discussion with the British.' His opinion of Eden was more reserved, mainly because of the questions that Eden had put during the negotiations in order to elicit Hitler's intentions on particular matters. Hitler disliked definite questions, particularly in negotiations with foreign politicians, as I often had occasion to note when working for him. He preferred general surveys on broad lines, historical perspectives and philosophical speculation, evading any concrete details, which would reveal his real intentions too clearly.

My portable wireless, a constant companion on my travels, informed me that Simon had informed the House of Commons of substantial differences of opinion emerging in the Berlin talks. In those days a portable wireless was a great sensation. I had acquired one for use for professional reasons so that every evening I could listen in to French and English language news broadcasts for information on significant political and other events from their point of view. This kind of thing is extraordinarily important for the interpreter. He does not translate the material but remembers the word construction in the other language for later reuse to a foreign conversation partner. The aim is most effectively achieved by listening to radio broadcasts and reading foreign newspapers. Every morning, as I dressed and breakfasted, I would tune in to those programmes relating the leading articles from

European newspapers in London, Paris and Berlin, and could thus begin my day well updated, which gave me greater confidence.

During my stay in Rome, I was aware from Parisian broadcasters of the indignation of the French press at the British visit to Germany. I was able to follow Eden's route to Moscow via Prague and Warsaw; the names of these cities alone showed me without need for commentary that the Lord Privy Seal was apparently taking pains to close the circle around Germany, if not to say against Hitler. My own impression of the Berlin talks and the atmosphere in Rome convinced me that the solidarity of opposition to National Socialist Germany was not too far off.

On 11 April the British and French Prime Ministers, Ramsay MacDonald and Laval, their Foreign Ministers Sir John Simon and Flandin, and Mussolini met for a conference at Stresa on Lake Maggiore. In the final resolution, Britain, France and Italy stated that they were agreed 'to oppose with all suitable means any unilateral denunciation of treaties.' That was a clear answer by the three great powers of Western Europe to Hitler's resumption of German armed sovereignty. This declaration would indeed have seemed far less menacing to us had we known then what we know now from Churchill's memoirs – that at the very beginning of the negotiations the British Foreign Minister had emphasised that he was not in a position to consider the imposition of sanctions against a treaty breaker. At that time only the optimists among us guessed that the common front against us was so flimsy.

A few days later, on 17 April, a second blow followed when Germany's action was condemned by the Council of the League of Nations. Through her 'arbitrary action' she had 'broken the Treaty of Versailles and threatened the security of Europe'.

A third blow was the treaty of alliance concluded by Laval with the Soviet Union on 2 May. When I got back to Berlin, I found people at the Foreign Office very depressed. Germany seemed to be completely isolated. In reply to Hitler's methods of foreign policy, an anti-German coalition had been formed of all the great powers of Europe including the Soviet Union. However, I was soon to learn in Poland and in London that this coalition had little cohesion.

To my surprise I received instructions to go with Göring to Warsaw and Kraków for the funeral of Marshal Piłsudski, as it was possible that an opportunity might arise for political discussions with Laval. Accordingly on the evening of 16 May I left the Friedrichstrasse station with Göring and a small delegation in his saloon coach. At that time the later *Reichsmarschall* did not travel by special train but contented himself with having his coach attached to the scheduled train. I had just settled down comfortably in my compartment to hear the evening news on my indispensable portable radio when the massive Göring suddenly stood at my door. To my extreme astonishment he said, 'I must apologise to you for your accommodation in this confined sleeping compartment. I am usually a better host, but my people have been careless. The culprit will be admonished for this.'

I answered that I hadn't the slightest complaint to make about my accommodation, and would certainly sleep splendidly. With a laugh he pointed out that I had been put in the kitchen of his coach. I hadn't noticed this kitchen, skilfully screened behind a sliding panel.

Von Moltke, the German Ambassador, was waiting for us in the early morning at the station and took us to the embassy, from where we went straight to the funeral service at Warsaw Cathedral.

The ceremony lasted almost two hours, and my thoughts went back to Geneva where I had known Piłsudski years before, when the dispute between Poland and Lithuania came before the League Council. 'I have come here to hear the word peace,' he had said. 'Anything else is nonsense, which I leave for my Foreign Minister to handle.'

After the service Pilsudski's coffin was borne on a gun carriage through the whole of Warsaw to the Mokotów parade ground. The funeral procession was most impressive and took four hours to pass through the streets of the Polish capital. It was May and already very warm, almost oppressive, so that the slow march, followed by the long period of standing at the memorial parade, was an exceptionally severe strain on visitors unaccustomed to such exertions. Göring marched panting beside me with heavy steps, but he stuck it to the end, whereas the aged Marshal Pétain after a while got into a carriage for the remainder of the ceremony. Huge crowds stood on either side of the streets through which the procession moved.

We returned to our saloon coach dead tired for the journey to Kraków. The coffin was transported on an open wagon and lit by two searchlights. In the dark we saw the faces of Polish farmers who had turned out at the side of the tracks to pay their last respects to the marshal.

Next morning there was another three-hour procession in Kraków, followed by the final lowering of the coffin into the prepared grave in Wawel Castle. Polish Foreign Minister Beck gave the foreign delegations a breakfast at the Hôtel de France, at which I assisted Göring in some short conversations with Pétain, Laval and the British. Laval and Göring arranged for a long talk during the afternoon.

It was evident that not only Göring desired this discussion but that Laval also gladly availed himself of the opportunity to talk to us. He brought only *chef de cabinet* Rochat, and I alone accompanied Göring. The discussion, which lasted over two hours, was a compressed form of the talks between Hitler and Simon. Exactly the same subjects were dealt with, and for that reason the differences between the British and the French were the more noticeable.

Göring showed little of the considered tactics of Hitler. He went in for forthright utterance, no beating about the bush or diplomatic niceties. 'I trust you got on well with the Bolsheviks in Moscow, Monsieur Laval,' he said, launching immediately into the most sensitive subject, the Franco-Russian mutual assistance pact. 'We know the Bolsheviks better in Germany than you do in France,' he continued. 'We know that in no circumstances can one have anything to do with them if one wants to avoid trouble. You will find that out in France. Watch out and see what difficulties your Paris communists will cause you.' He followed this up with an indictment of the Russians in which he used much the same terms as Hitler had used when talking to Simon. This was my first experience of what later always struck me about leading National Socialists in their dealings with foreigners – the almost verbatim repetition of Hitler's arguments. As interpreter naturally I had to pay the closest attention to individual phrases, and could therefore ascertain how closely Hitler's henchmen followed their master. Sometimes it seemed as though the same gramophone record were being played, though the voice and temperament were different.

I also observed this in other points touched upon by Göring at Kraków: disarmament, or rather German re-armament; bilateral pacts in place of collective security; reservations with regard to the League of Nations but without excluding the possibility of Germany re-entering it; an air force pact and much besides. In the short time available, Göring could not go into details, even to the extent that Hitler had done at Berlin. Neither did he ever do so on later occasions, adhering even more than Hitler to generalities and basic ideas. He liked precision even less than did the Führer, and would dismiss technical difficulties with a wave of the hand. Nevertheless he was not wanting in diplomatic skill. I saw him later handling very delicate situations with a finesse that the German public who knew and loved him as a robust blusterer might not have believed possible.

He showed this skill for the first time at Kraków in the discussion of Franco-German relations, naturally the main theme of the conversation with Laval. With very convincing words, Göring succeeded in persuading Laval of Germany's desire to achieve a general settlement with France. Concrete details were never mentioned: it was more the impression of his words and personality on Laval that did the trick. An unprejudiced person could not fail to be convinced that Göring, who had just made a raucous condemnation of the Russians and the League of Nations, was speaking sincerely when he said:

> You may rest assured, Monsieur Laval, that the German people have no keener desire than to finally end the strife of centuries with their French neighbour and bury the hatchet. We esteem your fellow countrymen as brave soldiers, we are full of admiration for the achievements of the French spirit. The old apple of discord about Alsace-Lorraine no longer exists. What then is still keeping us from becoming really good neighbours?

These words did not fail in their effect on Laval, who emphasised how strongly he had always advocated a Franco-German rapprochement, and invited me to testify to the efforts he had made in 1931 during the Berlin conversations with Brüning in the cause of Franco-German understanding. I could confirm this with a clear conscience, for I had got the impression both during the Six-Power Conference at Paris and also at Berlin in the autumn of the same year that Laval's intentions were sincere and that he was striving sincerely for a good-neighbour relationship between the two countries. He did not go into details about the sort of Franco-German settlement he envisaged, although it seemed to me that this was just what was needed. From innumerable discussions in Geneva and Paris I knew how difficult it was to reach results when one really got down to details.

I was also interested to note that Laval, like Eden in Berlin, sought to reassure us about the Soviet intentions. 'I found nothing in Moscow,' he said, in language almost identical to that of the Lord Privy Seal, 'that could suggest that the Soviet Union harbours any warlike intentions against Germany.' He described Stalin as a man easy to get on with, a man with whom one could talk. Ribbentrop described Stalin to me in similar terms in August 1939 when I accompanied him to Moscow for the conclusion of the sensational German-Soviet pact shortly before the outbreak of war. Roosevelt too, after his first meeting with Stalin at Yalta, expressed a similar opinion to his son and later to some of his colleagues. When I reflect on what I have heard foreigners say after talking to Hitler, I am almost tempted to believe that dictators somehow exercise a special magic on their listeners.

Laval also represented the signing of the Franco-Soviet alliance as a necessity imposed by France's internal politics. 'Certain events in Germany,' he said, 'and much that has been written and said in your country against France – in conjunction with German rearmament – has caused such apprehension amongst my countrymen that anything calculated to mitigate it will contribute indirectly to Franco-German understanding.' This line of argument was typical of Laval's method of conducting negotiations. He was always the skilled, polished French lawyer. In Kraków I found my earlier impressions of Laval confirmed. He seemed to me to belong to the category of *hommes de bonne volonté* who advocated peace out of conviction. At that time I would have put him on a par with Herriot and Briand without question.

The main impression I brought back with me to Berlin from this conversation was that it should be possible at any time for Germany, by pursuing a more or less intelligent foreign policy, to emerge from the isolation into which Hitler's psychological errors had landed the country.

Following the surprise turn that the British visit in March seemed to have brought to the international situation of the Reich, in my opinion the talks between Göring and Laval were a definite move away from that isolation of the Reich that had been expressed in April by the Stresa meeting, and in May by the Franco-Soviet Pact. In the Berlin and Kraków conversations I saw clear indications that Britain and France wished to avoid a final breach with Germany, and to lead the Reich back from its isolation into the community of nations.

Göring, with whom I had a long talk about the general situation during our journey back to Berlin, shared this impression. In contrast to Hitler, he was amenable to suggestion and argument. He questioned me in detail about my earlier impressions of Laval. He asked about the relations between Briand and Stresemann, and listened carefully when I expressed the view that Stresemann had set some kind of a diplomatic record by liberating the Rhineland from foreign troops without an army of his own. 'Looking at it like that,' Göring replied thoughtfully, 'there's truth in what you say.' But he was contemptuous of our Foreign Office and its staff. 'They spend the morning sharpening pencils and the afternoon at tea parties,' he said.

Being a member of staff at the Foreign Office, I reminded him that as a result of the feverish rate at which I had to make my notes I blunted one pencil after another, and Laval had kept sharpening them for me personally. Göring laughed and replied, 'I didn't mean you, only the real diplomats.'

Immediately on my return to Berlin I received my next assignment. Although Germany had been condemned officially by the Council of the League on 17 April, a month later the British sent an invitation to the 'treaty breaker' for naval talks. Ribbentrop was appointed 'Ambassador Extraordinary' and entrusted by Hitler with the conduct of these negotiations. I was to go with him as interpreter. We flew to London by special plane at the beginning of June. This was the first of many air trips I was to make to European capitals in that three-engined Ju 52. In the next few years I made the trip between London Croydon airport and Berlin on countless occasions.

The negotiations opened at the Foreign Office. Sir John Simon was present and Ribbentrop laid his cards on the table in one of the first sessions. Germany demanded the right for a fleet up to 35 per cent of the British naval strength. With a somewhat exaggerated display of forcefulness, he declared, 'if the British government does not immediately accept this condition, there is no point at all in continuing these negotiations. We must insist upon an immediate decision.' If this principle were conceded, all technical details regarding the programme of naval construction and the ship types (i.e. battleships, cruisers, destroyers, submarines, etc.) could be easily settled.

I must confess that I did not consider these tactics very intelligent. It was obvious, in view of the fact that the Reich had just been condemned officially for a breach of the Treaty of Versailles that the British could not suddenly reverse their position and give official approval to a breach of the naval provisions of the same treaty. At that time I did not know Ribbentrop very well, and wondered why he brought up the most difficult question of all so undiplomatically right at the start, thereby risking the collapse of the negotiations before they had properly begun. Was it lack of experience of international conferences? Was it a typical National Socialist attempt to be unconventional at all costs? Or was he blindly following instructions without using his own imagination? Later I realised that his conduct was that of the terrier of the 'His Master's Voice' gramophone trademark. Just as the terrier listens fascinated to the voice coming out of the horn, Ribbentrop absorbed Hitler's words and then repeated them. On this account he gave the impression both home and abroad of being stupid – an impression that he strengthened by his arrogance, vanity and extreme suspiciousness. I must say that in the innumerable negotiations at which I was to interpret for him he was never at a loss for counter-arguments. He could formulate his ideas with some clarity, and had the relevant facts and details firmly in his head. But it never occurred to me to consider him a statesman or a Foreign Minister. At Nuremberg he described himself as Hitler's Foreign Political Secretary, which I think fairly well describes his position. His relationship to Hitler was one of extreme dependency. If Hitler was displeased with him, Ribbentrop went sick and took to his bed like a hysterical woman. He was indeed nothing but his master's voice and thus seemed to many of us a dangerous fool.

During this London visit my opinion that Ribbentrop had made a mistake by his 'bull in a china shop' technique seemed confirmed by Sir John Simon's reaction. He flushed with anger and replied with some heat, 'it is not usual to make such conditions at the very beginning of negotiations,' and concluded brusquely by saying, 'I can, of course, make no statement on the matter.' He then left the session with a frigid bow. I was already wondering what the weather would be like on our return flight to Berlin. I felt sure from previous experience that even if the negotiations did not break down completely, the conference would be adjourned long term. But here I was mistaken.

For one or two days nothing was heard from the British, and then another session was arranged, not at the Foreign Office, but at the Admiralty. The discussion took place in the historic Board Room where, as were told, many an important decision affecting the Royal Navy had been taken. It was a large, panelled room, in the centre of which was a long table with red leather chairs on either side. My chair as interpreter at the head of the table was normally occupied by the First Lord of the Admiralty and was particularly comfortable. If it be true that clothes make the man, it may also be said that the position of the chair makes the interpreter. In the forthcoming naval negotiations I had a dominating position between the two parties, and thanks to my vantage point I never lost the thread even in the most complicated technical questions regarding ship types, displacement and so on.

On my left was the German delegation, headed by Ribbentrop and Admiral Schuster assisted by naval attaché Kapitän Wasner, Korvettenkapitän Kiderlen; the diplomats Kordt and Woermann were also present. On my right were Sir Robert Craigie, Under Secretary of State at the Foreign Office, Admiral Little and Captain Danckwerts. On the wall behind the British delegation was a wind indicator connected to a weather vane on the roof. 'When the Royal Navy still consisted of sailing ships,' Admiral Little explained to us, 'wind direction was of decisive significance for the operational decisions taken by the admirals in this room.' Pointing to a particular spot on the wind indicator he added with a laugh, 'When the wind was blowing from this quarter, the French fleet could not leave Brest and we had the Channel completely at our disposal.' The days of sailing ships were long over, but in this venerable room the wind indicator still swung to the changing wind. For our scheduled return to Berlin for the Whitsun break we took more than a passing interest in this wind indicator, for the wind direction determined whether our flight over the North Sea in a Ju 52 would be comfortable or difficult. Another object of interest was a little mark on the wall, which, the admiral told us, indicated Nelson's height. We were rather surprised to see that the British naval hero was so short a man.

In contrast to the cool reserve caused by the clash between Ribbentrop and Simon at the start of negotiations, a very friendly mood now prevailed on the British side. To my astonishment Sir Robert Craigie opened with a statement to the effect that the British government was prepared to agree to Ribbentrop's demand subject to the condition that it would only have effect if agreement were achieved in all other matters. I scarcely believed my ears when I heard Craigie make this wholly unexpected statement. I had to admit with some reluctance that Ribbentrop's methods, which I disliked and criticised so much, seemed to have been successful. The British must have been extraordinarily anxious to achieve an agreement to give in so completely after just a few days. It made me very uncertain in future in my judgement of Hitler's method. I would often recall this scene when translating statements by Hitler or Ribbentrop that made me feel inwardly uneasy and were in complete contrast to how German statesmen advocated matters pre-1933.

After this agreement in principle, it was not very long before full agreement was achieved. Ribbentrop had reason to be proud of the success of his negotiations. His rather awkward manner with the British changed almost to that sociable attitude to which I was accustomed in international discussions. The inferiority complex that he tried to overcome by an assumed brusqueness now disappeared, with only occasional lapses. For instance, towards the end of the negotiations, when he was asked casually by the British how long the agreement should last, he drew himself up and with his most solemn expression said 'Ewig' (for ever). My colleague Kordt grinned at me, amused at my embarrassment. I wondered how I should interpret this without producing a comic effect and decided on 'It is to be a permanent agreement', this being the phrase then incorporated into the text.

On my return home I was often asked why Ribbentrop, who spoke quite good English, should have had everything translated. I had raised this precautionary question with him just before the negotiations, suggesting that if he wanted to speak English he should first have the text or the main points of his remarks written out in English.

'I could quite well negotiate in English myself,' he told me, 'but I want to concentrate my thoughts wholly on the matter in hand, and not be distracted searching for the right English syntax or phrases.' His monstrously suspicious nature struck me especially during these negotiations. At discussions in his room at the Carlton Hotel we delegation members had to huddle round him in the middle of the room talking in whispers just in case the British had put a microphone in the wall to overhear our secrets. It was sometimes difficult not to grin at the sight of the naval delegation grouped around Ribbentrop like a flock of chickens whispering about battleships, destroyers and tonnage displacement.

After the exchange of documents between the incoming British Foreign Minister Sir Samuel Hoare and Ribbentrop defining the naval agreement, we remained in London for a few more days to finish off the technical details and left the Admiralty at four in the morning of 23 June for the airport. Ribbentrop made a triumphant return to the Reich as 'a great statesman'. Hitler especially regarded him as a skilful diplomat after this sensational success while the rest of the world rubbed its eyes at what the German 'Special Ambassador and Commissioner for Armaments Questions' had achieved in London. The French sent the British an unfriendly note. 'A question that affects all the signatories of the Treaty of Versailles has been treated more or less as a private matter between Germany and Great Britain … France reserves her freedom of action in naval matters …' Laval wrote angrily to the British Foreign Minister. Even Italy handed in a critical note. Eden was sent to Paris to calm the French. Hitler seemed to have won all along the line. During this year of Anglo-German rapprochement I had to work for Hitler again on an important occasion. On 15 July he received a British Legion delegation at the Chancellery, conversing for nearly two hours with Major Fetherston-Godley and five British companions. He asked each of them to relate in detail on which sector of the front he had fought, and exchanged war memories with the visitors. It might have been a typical old comrades' meeting but for the difference in language. At the end there was a suggestion of politics in Hitler's short speech. After expressing his heartfelt pleasure at the visit, he emphasised the special value he attached in the interests of peace to collaboration between soldiers of both sides who had fought in the last war.

After a lunch to honour the British visitors just before the reception, Major Fetherston-Godley said that the British had only fought against the Germans once, and that in the opinion of the British Legion this had been a mistake – a mistake that would not be repeated. He now spoke in similar terms to Hitler.

On leaving the Chancellery these visitors undoubtedly felt much impressed by the manner in which Hitler had received them, but now I noticed something that would often strike me in the following years: Hitler's effect on his visitors faded as time went by. During the next few days I accompanied the delegation, showing them round, and I noticed how their attitude to Germany became more critical by the day. Things they saw for themselves in National Socialist Germany seemed to confirm what they had heard at home about the country, rather than what Hitler and his colleagues told them so persuasively.

During the last months of 1935 the conflict between Italy and the League of Nations, and particularly Britain and France, gradually came to the foreground. Mussolini, who had expected to be given a free hand in Abyssinia in return for his support of the western powers against Germany, now suddenly found himself facing unexpected difficulties, largely due to British policy in the League of Nations. Automatically he broke away from the 'unity' of Stresa and was drawn over to Hitler's side.

Altogether 1935 had been a year of triumphs for Hitler in the field of foreign politics. There had been the successful outcome of the Anglo-German conversations of March, the May meeting between Göring and Laval, and the Naval Agreement of June. Most important of all, as far as the majority of Germans were concerned, was the achievement of military equality. As a result of those successes many people completely misjudged Hitler's diplomatic methods. At the time it was not possible to see that he owed his success less to his own statecraft than to the lack of decision and disunity amongst his opponents. It was not until events in the following years revealed this indecision time and again amongst the western powers that those who had a close view of events saw the real explanation for the otherwise inexplicable triumphs of the German dictator.

$$\boxed{\text{TWO}}$$

1936

On 7 March 1936 German troops occupied the demilitarised zone of the Rhineland. On 19 March the Council of the League of Nations was summoned to a special session in London and Ribbentrop, as the representative of Germany, was called to account for the German breach of the Locarno Agreement of 1925 by Hitler's remilitarisation of the Rhineland.

Bright daylight shone through the windows of St James's Palace, where the Council sat in the Queen Anne room. The walls were hung with silken tapestry and impressive old portraits. A huge mirror above a large fireplace added to the friendliness of the warm colours of carpets and hangings. On the mantelpiece stood a magnificent old clock, which together with the room in general vividly recalled the Hall of Clocks at the Quai d'Orsay, and the more hopeful days when Stresemann had signed the Kellogg Pact there. The only symbols of modern times were the horseshoe council table from Geneva and its microphones, at which I sat next to Ribbentrop.

As I took my place at the lower end of the right wing of the horseshoe I felt slightly melancholy. The British had provided me with a fine comfortable chair and I was sitting at the table, but in earlier times I had been much happier, despite the manifold difficulties for interpreting, seated behind Stresemann or Neurath on a stool at the upper end of the table amongst the representatives of the great powers. Then I had always looked with a certain superior demeanour upon those at the lower ends of the horseshoe table, where the representatives of the minor powers presented themselves temporarily for some point to be dealt with that affected their nation. When their business was concluded the president would release the delegates of Liberia, Albania or wherever, who would make a respectful bow and then depart. This was where I was now seated beside Ribbentrop.

All eyes were on the representative of National Socialist Germany, who was the sensation of the day in that old-fashioned diplomatic environment. The Australian delegate Bruce presided; he was a tall, dark man with typical Anglo-Saxon features and an equally typical calm. On his right sat Flandin, who had recently become French Foreign Minister, and whom I remembered from Paris and Geneva, and next to him sat the Italian Foreign Minister Grandi. At the Council table I recognised many other old acquaintances from my Geneva days. Next to Ribbentrop sat Titulescu, who constantly tried to engage him in conversation in German in the most friendly way, but Ribbentrop had put on his frostiest face, and only responded to the Romanian Foreign Minister's overtures with the minimum of courtesy permitted by diplomacy. On the other side of Bruce sat Eden ... and the bespectacled Litvinov, with his mocking sneer. The Soviet Union at the Council of the League! That indeed was sensational, and the most obvious sign of how, with Hitler's help, things had changed in this supreme international body.

It was only natural that I should recognise many old acquaintances, crouching behind their delegates on the notoriously uncomfortable seating provided. When I greeted them before the session I felt that they were as pleased as I at our unexpected meeting. Ribbentrop, however, was somewhat disapproving, remarking, 'Well, you seem to be pretty popular here.' Perhaps he expected that the reason for our presence there – Hitler's denunciation of the Locarno Treaty and the entry of German troops into the Rhineland

– would affect my personal relations with my French and British colleagues and acquaintances.

Following the introduction of conscription the year before, Germany had once again found herself completely isolated from all other countries great and small. On 7 March 1936, shortly after the ratification of the Franco-Soviet Pact of mutual assistance, Hitler had responded by occupying the Rhineland. He justified this action by his statement that the Pact constituted such a grave breach of the Locarno Agreement as to abrogate the latter and that Germany was therefore no longer bound by the provisions of the latter regarding the demilitarised zone of the Rhineland. We were kept so busy translating protest notes and counter-arguments that we felt sure the paper war would almost certainly lead to a shooting war. 'Germany has broken the Locarno Treaty,' wrote the French and the Belgians. 'France broke it first,' replied the Reich, pointing to their pact with Soviet Russia.

On 7 March a Foreign Office friend had expressed an opinion held very widely in our department: 'If France attaches the slightest value to her security,' he said, 'then she must march into the Rhineland now'. More than once, even during the war, I heard Hitler say, 'the forty-eight hours after marching into the Rhineland were the most nerve-racking in my life.' He always added, 'if the French had then invaded the Rhineland, we would have had to withdraw with our tails between our legs, for the military resources at our disposal would have been wholly inadequate even for a moderate resistance.'

For reasons that were still unintelligible to us in the Foreign Office, France had contented herself with calling a meeting of the League Council, which I attended as Ribbentrop's interpreter on the morning of 19 March.

'I have undertaken this mission with real personal satisfaction,' Ribbentrop said, addressing the Council, 'convinced as I am that never has a cause so just, in the highest sense of the word, come before this Council of Nations.' Then, turning immediately to the new Franco-Soviet military alliance, he said with emphasis, 'This pact constitutes the alliance of two states comprising some 275 million people. The two contracting parties are the two strongest military powers in the world. Soviet Russia, so far distant from Germany that she could not possibly be attacked by that country, has advanced indirectly to the German frontier by means of a similar military alliance with Czechoslovakia.' At this point Litvinov was making notes furiously.

'France and Russia,' Ribbentrop continued, 'can, by virtue of their agreement, proceed to war against Germany at their own discretion.' Litvinov shook his head vehemently, and Flandin turned down the corners of his mouth in derision. 'This alliance is directed exclusively against Germany,' I continued with my translation, while all present – delegates, State secretaries, legal advisers and interpreters – followed my words with the closest attention.

After arguing the purely legal aspect, Ribbentrop passed to Hitler's earlier offers regarding disarmament: 'The offer of absolute disarmament: this was turned down. The offer of a standing army of 200,000, applying equally to all: this was turned down. The offer of a standing army of 300,000: this was turned down. The offer of an air force pact: this was turned down ... The offer of a general European settlement made in May 1935: this was simply passed over, except for the proposal that afterwards provided the basis for the Anglo-German Naval Agreement.' Thus he described Hitler's peace efforts in a summary that, so far as I could see, did not fail to have an effect upon some delegates and several press representatives. 'The government of the German Reich must therefore reject as unjust and unwarranted the charge of having unilaterally contravened the Treaty of Locarno,' Ribbentrop concluded, without referring to the real question before the Council – the contravention of the Treaty.

At one of the Council sessions preceding our arrival in London, Flandin had said:

> If the German government was not convinced (by the French counter-arguments in the matter of the Soviet Pact), then it was her duty, by virtue of the Treaty of Arbitration, concluded simultaneously with the Locarno Agreement, to submit the matter to arbitration. This she never attempted to do. Although I myself stated in the Chamber that we would accept the finding of the Hague Court in this matter, the German government ignored the suggestion. Neither did it attempt to discuss the matter through a meeting of the Locarno powers; it simply declared as null and void a treaty whose contracting parties had expressly rejected the right to give notice to withdraw from it, and which could be terminated only by the Council of the League of Nations on their application.'

Hitler had obviously instructed Ribbentrop to follow his own favourite tactic of evading precise questions by giving vague and generalised assurances. 'The German people,' he declaimed:

> who now, after seventeen years, at last see themselves reinstated in freedom and honour ... sincerely desire to live in peace and friendship with their neighbours and henceforth to cooperate to the utmost in the construction

of true European solidarity … They wish to end the long period of Franco-German tension, crises and wars, and to help inaugurate a better understanding and friendship between these two great nations. The German people long for this from the bottom of their hearts. In this spirit the German chancellor has made an historical and indeed a unique and unparalleled offer to the world to unite Europe and ensure peace for the next twenty-five years …'

This speech may not have made much of an impression at the Council table, but it had an unmistakable effect on the press, and set the tone for the diplomatic activity of the next few weeks, which can best be described as the period of bigger and better plans for peace.

After my French colleague Mathieu had translated my English rendering of Ribbentrop's speech into French, the session adjourned for lunch. The German Ambassador in London, von Hoesch, had had to plead hard with Bruce to get this adjournment, for the Council had originally intended to pronounce its verdict of guilty immediately after hearing Ribbentrop and without any further discussion. This would have been the closure by silence that I had often seen at Geneva, the effectiveness of which had first been brought home to me at the preparatory Disarmament Commission. At that time the most telling arguments of our representative, Graf Bernstorff, former German Ambassador to Washington, had been met with complete silence. In fact his case was unanswerable. The efforts of our London Ambassador, and the understanding shown by Bruce and the British, prevented such high-handed action – in its crudest form, at any rate. Judgment was postponed until the afternoon, but there was general agreement that no member of the Council should reply to Ribbentrop's arguments, which, as the press reaction was to show, were not wholly beside the point.

Litvinov was the lone dissenter. While I was giving the speech in English, I had noticed him making feverish notes and shaking his head in emphatic disagreement at many of the points, causing Eden, who sat next to him, to look at him uneasily on several occasions. During the French translation, however, when I had more time to observe the goings-on, I noticed the tall figure of Flandin giving a strong demurrer to the short, portly Litvinov in a corner of the room. It was not difficult to guess what this excited conversation was about. It was obvious (and one of the Britons present confirmed this impression afterwards) that Litvinov, as the Soviet representative, wanted to enjoy the opportunity of attacking National Socialist Germany in public, in much the same way that Vyshinski after 1945 never scorned the chance of doing the same against the United States at the meetings of the Security Council. As I watched Flandin and Litvinov in heated discussion, I looked forward to the Litvinov–Ribbentrop duel that seemed inevitable. Rows are easy to translate, and I would have been glad if the Council's plan of action had failed and I could once again have interpreted a real hell-for-leather debate. Things worked out otherwise however. At the opening of the afternoon session nobody offered to speak. Flandin had evidently won his argument with Litvinov.

'The Council of the League of Nations declares that the German government has committed a breach of Article 43 of the Treaty of Versailles in that, on 7 March 1936, it caused military forces to march into the demilitarised zone as specified in Article 42 and the following Articles of the Treaty and in the Treaty of Locarno.' This was the Franco–Belgian resolution passed by the Council unanimously, thus branding Germany as a treaty-breaker.

Now came a great surprise. Shortly before the vote was taken, the Council President, Bruce, speaking as the Australian representative, said, 'The work of the Council is not completed with the acceptance of this resolution … The powers principally concerned must proceed to find a solution amongst themselves.' Naturally I thought he had in mind the Locarno powers excluding Germany. To my utter astonishment, however, Bruce continued: 'The moderation of the statement by France and Belgium has aroused the greatest admiration in the world. On the other hand Reich Chancellor Hitler has frequently expressed his willingness to cooperate; this morning the German representative has again done so.'

It reminded me of what had happened the year before when the British, after protesting against the German breach of Versailles by the restoration of conscription, went on to ask whether the visit of Simon and Eden to Berlin would still be convenient.

The last thing I expected, after the tremendous excitement caused by the German march into the Rhineland, now came about. 'In these circumstances,' I heard Bruce continue, 'I definitely expect that a solution will be possible.'

I was too intent upon the reaction of France and Belgium to fully appreciate the grotesque contradiction in this last sentence. Nobody objected to the Council President's suggestion that negotiations with us should now be resumed. Ribbentrop made a brief follow-up protest against 'the resolution that the Council has recently passed, which will stand condemned by the verdict of history'. Then Flandin suggested once more that the legal question should be decided by the permanent Court of International Justice. This closed one of the most remarkable sessions of the Council.

Negotiations between Eden and Ribbentrop now began as though nothing had happened. Whereas in the German view the Locarno Agreement no longer existed, the other Locarno powers stated that for them the obligations under that treaty were still valid. They had promised France and Belgium to come to their assistance should they be attacked by Germany. It was under these circumstances that over the next few days the British proceeded to negotiate with Ribbentrop as to how Hitler's offer of twenty-five years' peace, made at the time of his occupation of the Rhineland, could somehow be fitted into this substitute Locarno Treaty. Hitler certainly seemed to have achieved the desired effect upon the British by his offer of peace – namely the softening of their reaction to his unilateral denunciation of the Locarno Treaty.

Eden tried to get from Ribbentrop at least an undertaking that no fortifications would be set up in the Rhineland, at any rate for a period. Ribbentrop countered by objecting to the proposed Anglo-French General Staff conferences which were to decide what action should be taken if France and Belgium actually were attacked. The phrase 'staff talks' was like a red rag to a bull for Ribbentrop at that time. He felt instinctively that concrete military agreements between Britain and France would be a very high price to pay for the militarisation of the Rhineland. He protested against them to Eden and other British personalities in the same vein.

The astonishing change from condemnation to negotiation made me doubt more and more my own ability to judge the international situation. Along with my Foreign Office friends I felt rather foolish when our confident predictions about the consequences of Hitler's action failed to come about. Hitler seemed once more to have been proved right.

We know now that we were nearer to war than we thought. The former French Ambassador to Berlin, François-Poncet, wrote in his memoirs:

The possibility of military intervention was considered very seriously. It was proposed that a force of one army corps should invade the Saar ... The civilian ministers, however, were against it. General Gamelin expressed the view that even a restricted military operation would be a risk and could not therefore be undertaken without general mobilisation ... The government recoiled from such a possibility ... The peace current is still very strong. The idea of war is running up against strong opposition.

We know from Flandin, then French Foreign Minister, what great efforts he made to secure British support. In his war history, Churchill says that

Flandin told him of his intention to propose to the British government a simultaneous mobilisation of the land, sea and air forces of both countries, saying that France already had promises of support from all the nations of the Little Entente. The following diary entry in the biography of Neville Chamberlain throws a striking light on the British position:

> 12 March. Talked to Flandin, emphasising that public opinion here would not support us in sanctions of any kind. His view is that if a firm front is maintained by France and Britain, Germany will yield without war … We cannot accept this as a reliable estimate of a mad dictator's reactions.

'The whole world, especially the small nations, looks today to Britain,' Flandin once said in Churchill's presence at a gathering of prominent British personalities. 'If Britain acts now, she can lead Europe … it is her last chance; if you do not now hold Germany in check, all is lost.'

Churchill, in his war history, has expressed the opinion that 'if the French government had been equal to its task, it would have ordered general mobilisation immediately, thereby compelling all the others to join in.' For France it was a question of to be or not to be. 'Any French government worthy of the name should have acted on its own responsibility and relied on treaty obligations,' he added.

At that time I knew nothing of this. All I remembered was the voice of the French Premier Serraut that I heard on my portable wireless saying with great emotion just after German troops marched into the Rhineland, 'France will never negotiate as long as Strasbourg is within range of German guns.' I had heard the Council of the League pronounce the guilty verdict and yet I was meeting almost daily with Eden and Ribbentrop. The haggling at these negotiations the horse-trading had reached the point where a compromise was being sought on the basis of 'no fortifications, no staff talks', but unsuccessfully, because the 'guilty party' was declining to even delay fortifying the Rhineland.

Throughout March and April we made frequent flights between London and Berlin in Ribbentrop's special plane, the familiar Ju 52 with the registration AMYY – often regarded by well-disposed British people as a very hopeful symbol for a diplomatic mission. Hitler had seen, from the reaction of British statesmen and above all from public opinion, that his tactic of screening the Rhineland adventure with peace proposals had succeeded, and he pursued this method with renewed zeal.

One afternoon at the end of April we took off from Tempelhof in AMYY with a large-scale peace plan Hitler had drawn up. If possible it was to be handed to the British that evening, so I had to translate it in the air. I arranged for our Languages Section to make a rough translation, the last sheets of which were handed to me by special messenger just before the aircraft took off. I set to work in feverish haste. Normally the flight to London took about four hours – not by any means long for the study of such a highly important diplomatic document. Moreover, during the flight a fair copy for transmission to the British government had to be made by Ribbentrop's secretary, who had herself trained as an interpreter at Heidelberg. 'I hope we have a headwind,' she said, 'That will give us a little more time.'

As we were flying over the Wannsee I read the first sentence of the document, which was cleverly attuned to the mood in London as I had found it, to my astonishment, a few days before: 'The German Government concurs sincerely in what it has learnt from Ambassador Ribbentrop to be the desire of the British Government and British people, namely to start as soon as possible with the practical work on a true pacification for Europe.'

It was clear that Hitler thought he had now regained the initiative, and his language was occasionally overbearing. 'Germany,' he wrote a few pages later, 'concluded the Armistice in 1918 on the basis of Wilson's Fourteen Points. The demilitarised zone itself arose only in consequence of the previous breach of an undertaking that was also binding on the Allies. The German government rejects all proposals that unilaterally impose obligations on Germany, and are thus discriminatory.' As I revised the English draft it was passed forward sheet by sheet, and the typewriter, a fixture in the nose of this flying office, was kept busy. We had too much headwind to be comfortable. The papers often slipped off my improvised desk, and it was a good thing that the typewriter was firmly fixed. It is well known that one does not get air sicknesses if one is busy, and our miniature Languages Service did not have a problem of that sort until we reached relative calm over the North Sea.

Meanwhile I had come to the revision of the second part of our document, the actual German peace proposals. These consisted of nineteen points: 'Equality of rights', 'No increase in the strength of the forces in the Rhineland', 'Troops not to be brought nearer to the Belgian and French frontiers for the time being', 'Supervision by British and Italian military attachés', 'twenty-five-year non-aggression or security pact between France, Belgium and Germany', 'Conclusion of an Air Force Pact',

'Inclusion of the Netherlands', 'Instruction of youth in Germany and France', 'Germany prepared to rejoin the League of Nations', … 'Equality of status in colonial matters', … 'Separation of the League from all connection with the Treaty of Versailles', …'Practical measures to be taken against the armaments race.'

I had not finished the translation by the time we landed, but to my relief Eden could not see us until the following morning. This gave me time for revision and to translate Hitler's proposals in the disarmament portion of his peace plan. These were: 'Ban on gas, poison and incendiary bombs', 'Ban on the bombing of undefended inhabited areas', 'Ban on the bombardment of undefended inhabited areas by long-range artillery', 'Abolition of tanks', 'Abolition of heavy artillery'.

The document I had translated between Berlin and London was undoubtedly impressive and contained some interesting proposals. It also seemed to me more concrete and precise than what I was accustomed to from Hitler. However, it contained nothing about the question that the Locarno powers – Britain, France, Italy and Belgium – had raised at the beginning of their own proposals. Eden had spoken to Ribbentrop about it immediately after the verdict at St James's Palace:

> [The four powers] request the German Government to submit to the permanent International Court of Justice at The Hague the question of whether the Pact of Mutual Assistance between France and Russia can be reconciled with the Locarno Treaty, and to undertake to recognise as final the decision of that Court.

Neither was anything said about the Rhineland fortifications, a matter raised by Eden constantly in previous discussions.

The fair copy in English was ready by midnight, and at 10 a.m. the next day Ribbentrop handed it to Eden. 'We shall examine the German proposals very closely,' was Eden's only remark.

The conversations that ensued over the next couple of days between Eden and Ribbentrop were fruitless. Ribbentrop was infuriated at his inability to prevent the hated General Staff conferences between Britain, France and Belgium. 'Contact between the General Staffs of our two countries,' Eden wrote in an official note to the French Ambassador on 1 April, 'will be established and maintained.' It was on the morning of that day that Ribbentrop had handed in the peace plan.

A few days later we flew back to Germany having failed in our mission. A general distrust of Hitler's surprise tactics in foreign affairs had blocked our 'peace offensive' from the outset.

On 7 April the French submitted a counter-proposal, which once more set out all the stock in trade of the Disarmament Conference, such as collective security, etc. On 7 May Sir Eric Phipps, British Ambassador to Berlin, handed in the famous questionnaire, which so enraged Hitler – always averse to any precise statement – that he left it unanswered. Thus Germany's diplomatic initiative finally came to a halt.

The British questionnaire, after expressing regret that the German government had been unable to make any tangible contribution to the restoration of confidence so essential for the comprehensive negotiations that both governments had in view, asked 'whether the German Reich regards itself now as being in a position to conclude genuine treaties ... It is of course clear that negotiations for a treaty would be useless if one of the parties thereafter felt free to deny its obligations on the grounds that that party had not at that time been in a condition to conclude a binding treaty.' The note continued: 'The question is really whether Germany now considers that a point has been reached at which she can declare that she recognises the existing territorial and political order in Europe and intends to respect it.' And so it went on and on, about the relationship with the Soviet Union, not becoming involved in the affairs of other states, and the International Court of Justice in The Hague.

As I read this questionnaire I realised that we had worked so feverishly in AMYY in vain. Hitler's ploy to divert attention from his highly unusual method of treating urgent specific questions by making grandiose general proposals had finally come to grief, or at least as far as the Foreign Offices of the other powers were concerned.

All the same, Hitler's diversionary manoeuvres had been temporarily successful in manipulating world opinion. I noticed this particularly during the August 1936 Olympiad held in Berlin. It would require a whole book to record the hundreds of conversations at which I interpreted for Hitler, Göring, Goebbels and other prominent personalities in conversation with foreign notables during the event: kings, heirs apparent, politicians, academics and men of the people from almost every country in the world.

At the beginning of the year I had worked in the same capacity making similar observations in the more intimate framework of the winter Olympiad at Garmisch-Partenkirchen. By August, the anxiety aroused in all minds by the German reoccupation of the Rhineland had subsided, the threat of war, seemingly imminent in March, had receded, and many eloquent pleas for peace had been spoken by the Germans. Not one of the foreign visitors whose words I translated refrained from expressing his joy at the fortunate turn that events appeared to have taken. Many expressed emphatically their admiration for Hitler and his endeavours for peace, and for the achievements of National Socialist Germany. Those days seemed to me a virtual apotheosis of Hitler and the Third Reich. During the usually rather brief conversations I noticed that almost without exception foreign visitors looked upon Hitler with the greatest interest, and often with real admiration. Only rarely was a certain scepticism apparent, as in Hitler's talk with Lord Vansittart. On this occasion he made a remark to me that I often thought about during the war and that now seems to me especially relevant. 'The next war,' Vansittart said, 'will not be confined within national boundaries. The fronts will go right through individual peoples, for it will be a war not of nations but of ideologies.'

Much has been written about the grandiose setting in which Germany staged those Olympic Games. The production of this fantastic show was first class and those who witnessed it, whether they were friends or foes afterwards, always remembered it. It would certainly have been remembered in 1948, although the greatest pains were taken to avoid ever mentioning it then.

As I have already said, I had to perform an interpreting marathon. At the very start, Göring's adjutant said to Hitler's adjutant: 'Göring declines to welcome the Olympic Committee in the Old Museum on behalf of the government unless he has the services of the Foreign Office's chief interpreter.'

'The Führer needs Schmidt himself, so he cannot work for Göring,' was the reply. 'I'll get you a police car that can get through all barriers,' said Meissner, who always found a way out. 'Then you will be back in the Chancellery in time.'

At 11 a.m. I spoke the closing words of the address to the Olympic Committee into the microphones at the Old Museum. As soon as I was out of sight of that solemn gathering I broke in an undignified trot to the police car, and reached the Chancellery just as the last of the foreign delegations to be received by Hitler was entering his office. Meissner had been right, and I was on the spot on time.

One of the many festivities was a dinner given by Ribbentrop at his Dahlem villa, but the host was in very ill humour, and greeted his guests with a sour smile. He had been appointed London Ambassador that day instead of Foreign Minister, his great ambition. Now the hated Neurath would continue as Foreign Minister in Berlin while he himself would be in London, far away from the Führer, and who knew whether a rival might not steal his place in Hitler's favour. This angered him beyond all measure and it was actually for this reason that he delayed taking up the London appointment for so long, contrary to all rules of international courtesy, and then offended the British by frequent long absences from London. In normal times a prima donna ambassador who neglected his duty in that way because he wanted a different role would have been promptly retired. For some inexplicable reason, on this and subsequent occasions, Hitler overlooked Ribbentrop's gross breach of discipline.

Next day I drove from a picturesque evening entertainment at the Charlottenburg Schloss to an 'Italian Night' on the Pfaueninsel. Goebbels had invited about a thousand people, of whom more than half were foreigners, to an open-air dinner. Over the large meadow in the middle of the island glowed innumerable Chinese lanterns. Dining, dancing ... and interpreting. After-dinner speeches, toasts and individual conversations: 'Oh, Herr Schmidt, do help me, I would like to speak to Lord Londonderry'; 'Monsieur Schmidt, *deux mots seulement avec le docteur Goebbels*'; 'Do you know where Göring is?' One after another. Fortunately there was enough of the 'right stuff' to prevent my throat going hoarse, but I slept for two days after the Olympic fires were extinguished.

I had the impression of having taken part in a great event uniting the peoples, and to an interpreter that is always a very pleasant feeling. I had seen the masterly talent for stage production of the National Socialist leaders, and how powerful had been the effect of this truly superb spectacle on the international public, on the parquet, in the boxes and the gallery. Only later, together with those enthralled spectators, did I realise that stagecraft and statecraft are wholly different.

It was not only on these festive occasions that I noticed the keen interest in Hitler and Göring shown by the foreign visitors for whom I interpreted. It was exactly the same in personal, man-to-man discussions. Lord Londonderry, the former British Air Minister, was a fairly frequent guest of Göring, then German Air Minister, who often invited him to go hunting. He usually came to Berlin with his wife and daughter in his private plane, and spent a few days in the capital. The first time I interpreted for him was in February 1936, and it was for that reason that I first visited the famous Karinhall, Göring's country estate in the middle of Schorfheide, 40 miles north of Berlin.

In those days Karinhall was just a long log house in the Scandinavian style, with only a few rooms. It was nothing more than a very comfortable hunting lodge, built of crude logs but provided with all the most modern devices for lighting, heating and water supply: a cosy home away from the noisy capital, in the huge Schorfheide forest on the banks of a lake. The centre of the lodge was a long room with a rough wooden table and massive wooden chairs for a number people. Seated at this table, Londonderry and Göring discussed the political situation. It was of course not the kind of diplomatic or political discussion with which I usually dealt, but more in the nature of a pleasant chat. General questions and personal views were talked about rather than concrete problems. Much of the conversation was actually about hunting, for which I had to learn a new vocabulary to cover their talk about aurochs, elk and deer. The second great theme was naturally the Luftwaffe, on which they talked technical shop, so that my experience on the Air Committee at the Disarmament Conference (the square root of hp x wing surface) as well as my experience as an enthusiastic passenger stood me in good stead. Göring was often surprisingly frank when proudly recounting the latest achievements of the Luftwaffe. Lord Londonderry often referred to the talks between Hitler and Simon, asking whether Germany had really achieved air parity with Britain at that time. According to the British Air Ministry's very careful investigations, he said this could not possibly have been the case. From his insistence on the point it was evident that as Air Minister at the time the parity claimed by Hitler must have caused him much embarrassment.

When Anglo-German relations were discussed Göring conveyed with remarkable skill the impression that Germany desired nothing more ardently than to be on friendly terms with Great Britain. 'If Germany and Britain stand together,' Göring emphasised more than once, 'there is no combination of powers in the whole world that can oppose us.' Lord Londonderry spoke with more reserve. 'Above all we must build up world confidence,' he was apt to reply somewhat evasively, though being himself a devotee of Anglo-German friendship. More than once he emphasised the close kinship of the two peoples, the many characteristics they had in common and the favourable conditions these advantages provided for common political action. Listening to the tall, spare British nobleman, who faintly resembled the King of Sweden, as he sought somewhat hesitatingly for the right words in his deep, sonorous voice, one knew at once that this man did sincerely desire an understanding with Germany. Göring must also have had this impression, for I have seldom heard him speak with less reserve than in his conversations with Lord Londonderry. There was a kind of mutual confidence between the two of them that the country atmosphere of Karinhall, the family meals and their long walks together naturally fostered.

The German Air Minister, Prime Minister of Prussia, would stride across the heathland clad in a white-sleeved leather jerkin wearing a huge hunting hat and wielding a sort of spear the ancient *Germanen* used. In this rig he would be accompanied by the British lord and lady, and sometimes their daughter. At the bison enclosure he would blow his horn. At the sound all the huge beasts came up, giving the impression that they knew Göring personally, but their little eyes gleamed angrily as they approached and butted their horns against the fence stakes, almost breaking them. The Lord of the Schorfheide would laugh noisily as he turned proudly to face his guests who gazed upon this curious spectacle with smiling interest. They had obviously not seen anything of the kind in British noble circles and were clearly amused at the behaviour of their host and his dress. There was no condescension or contempt in their laughter: they obviously liked the man in the jerkin with his strange spear and childish delight, which he made no attempt to conceal. They regarded him with the sympathetic understanding that the British feel for anyone who is original or eccentric.

No doubt the Londonderrys realised that there was another Göring besides their cheery Karinhall host – a man who could act with ruthless energy and brutality. This was apparent from various remarks dropped by mother and daughter during meals. 'To live in the upper levels of National Socialist Germany may be quite pleasant,' Lady Londonderry once said to me, 'but woe betide the poor folk who do not belong in the upper orders.' Nor did she hesitate to make such critical remarks to Göring, who did not take them amiss as Hitler would certainly have done, but usually answered with some humorous observation. On the whole he seemed to understand such criticism quite well.

Emmy Göring administered her office of housewife quietly and modestly, creating an atmosphere of hospitality in the best sense of the word. Occasionally she would give a soothing or apologetic smile when her Hermann got carried away and used coarse language. She said very little herself, contributing unobtrusively to the pleasant family atmosphere of those Anglo-German conversations at Schorfheide.

During this February visit, the first of a whole series of meetings between Göring and Londonderry, the latter was received by Hitler at the Reich Chancellery. Hitler spoke about the political situation and Anglo-German relations exactly as Göring had done, except that Göring had been more emphatic and forthright and therefore more convincing. No doubt he had been instructed by Hitler. At that time the policy was to concentrate on an understanding with Great Britain, almost as if Hitler were wooing coy Britannia. This was most noticeable during the talk with Londonderry. 'How often during the war,' Hitler said, 'when I was opposite British troops, did I say to myself that it was absolute madness to be fighting against these men who might well have belonged to our own people! That must never happen again.'

Londonderry listened with friendly and sympathetic interest, and sought the right phrases to express similar hopes as convincingly as possible. Hitler's eloquence on Anglo-German relations had impressed him visibly. Once again I noticed how strongly foreign visitors came under Hitler's spell at such interviews.

I interpreted for a whole series of foreign personalities who came to see Hitler during 1936, including Labeyrie, Governor of the Bank of France, and Bastide, Minister of Commerce. They were not very important conversations, but they confirmed my impression that foreign countries, at any rate so far as their visitors to Germany were representative of them, regarded Hitler at that time with an extraordinarily close and by no means unfriendly interest:

> Hitler has impressed Europe as an exceptional personality. He arouses not only fear and aversion, he inspires curiosity and also wins sympathy. His reputation is growing. The power of the attraction that he exercises extends beyond the German frontiers. Kings, princes and celebrities of all kinds come to the capital to meet this man of destiny, who seems to hold the fate of the continent in his hands, also to see this Germany that he has changed and invigorated with irresistible compulsion.

This was how French Ambassador François-Poncet described in his memoirs what I experienced at all these meetings.

One of the most noteworthy of such meetings was that between Lloyd George and Hitler at the Berghof early in September. As he went forward to meet the former British Prime Minister with outstretched hand, Hitler said, 'I am exceptionally pleased to be able to welcome to my house the man whom we in Germany have always regarded as the actual victor of the World War.' With a smile and a wave of the hand Lloyd George disclaimed this, but I thought I detected a certain satisfaction at this compliment from the former German lance corporal. 'And I deem myself lucky,' Lloyd George answered readily, 'to meet the man who, after defeat, has united the whole German people behind him and led them to recovery.' Looking out of the big window over the sunny mountainous landscape of Obersalzberg he said, 'What a splendid place you have found here.' The great reception room at the Berghof was dominated by this gigantic window, which filled almost the whole wall. The Untersberg with its dark woods and bright green meadows seemed like a landscape painting in a huge frame.

We sat at a table a little back from the window, Hitler, Lloyd George, Ribbentrop and I. Ribbentrop was like a shadow; during the whole talk he scarcely uttered a word. Lloyd George's flowing white hair contrasted vividly with his youthful expressive face and merry, penetrating eyes. His movements too showed an almost youthful elasticity as he punctuated his talk with vivacious gestures from his small, shapely hands. The victor of the First World War! And facing him was the man who, as it then seemed, was set fair to bring Lloyd George's work to naught.

It was one of Hitler's best days. Refreshed by his stay in the mountains, slightly bronzed by the sun, obviously delighted by the recognition implied in this visit from the world-famous statesman, he began to speak excitedly of his experiences as a humble soldier at the front. 'I often faced the British,' he said, enumerating many well-known places on the Western Front. He praised British soldiers, and went into details about British equipment and military tactics. Lloyd George was astonishingly well informed about all these matters. He was able to tell Hitler exactly why any particular offensive had been launched on any particular day.

'The Americans had no artillery at all,' he remarked when Hitler spoke about the firepower and accuracy of the enemy artillery, 'They were using only British guns.' By the questions he interpolated, Lloyd George showed how much Hitler's front experiences interested him, and from there he returned the conversation repeatedly to military decisions taken at the higher level.

After more of this they began to discuss politics. 'Alliances are always dangerous,' Lloyd George said. 'In the last war they extended the hostilities like a prairie fire. If it were not for them the conflict might have been localised.' Whether or not consciously he had exactly expressed Hitler's opinion on collective security. One of Hitler's favourite mottoes was: 'No multilateral undertakings, but only mutual non-aggression pacts between neighbours.' Hitler elaborated this theme as though he had only been waiting for a cue, expounding in all its details the peace plan that I had translated in the aircraft to London in March and that had since sunk into oblivion. Lloyd George took this opportunity of expressing himself very definitely, if in quite general terms, about the German peace efforts, 'which have unfortunately been frustrated by the General Staff talks.' Intentionally or not, he had again touched upon a favourite theme of Hitler's. What efforts Ribbentrop had made in London to prevent these, and how annoyed he had been when finally they came about!

Somewhat abruptly Lloyd George then turned the conversation from politics to the social measures 'by which Germany has always distinguished herself'. National Socialism had embarked on experiments in this field that were of especial interest to Britain. 'They are not experiments, but well worked-out plans,' Hitler interjected, thinking that the word 'experiment' implied some criticism. That was far from Lloyd George's intention. With eloquent enthusiasm he spoke of the German measures for abolishing unemployment, of health insurance, social welfare and holidays, saying he had already investigated much of what was being done on the labour front and seemed to be deeply impressed by what he had seen.

Hitler was quite enchanted by his visitor, not only on that afternoon but long afterwards whenever he referred to his talk 'with the great British statesman, Lloyd George'. He invited him most warmly to attend the forthcoming rally at Nuremberg but Lloyd George firmly declined. 'I did not come to Germany for politics,' he said, 'but only to study your social measures and above all your solution of the unemployment problem, which is such a menace in Britain too.' If he went to Nuremberg, it would be taken very amiss in Britain. That was Hitler's first disappointment of the whole conversation, and it was some time before it recovered from the chill caused by this remark.

The sun was setting when after almost three hours this memorable conversation ended towards 7 p.m. The old victor of the Great War took his warm leave of the young dictator of the Third Reich. They arranged that Lloyd George should come to tea next day bringing his daughter Megan and son Gwilym who were with him on this visit. 'The whole Liberal Party has accompanied him to Germany,' spiteful newspapers in Britain reported.

Ribbentrop remained with Hitler at the Berghof while I went back to Berchtesgaden with Lloyd George. He was at his most genial, asking where exactly I had been during the war. I was able to tell him of my experiences as a machine gunner near Reims and of the first great turn of events when Foch started the counter-offensive in July 1918. He asked from what positions we had then retired and what had been the moral effect of the Allied counter attack, cross-examining me closely.

In due course I was emboldened enough to put some questions to him, and I asked if he would confirm the following story. Briand had once told Stresemann in my presence that Lloyd George had congratulated him on the particularly brave conduct of a Breton regiment from his home province. 'Well, you know, Monsieur Lloyd George,' Briand had replied, 'we Bretons do not adjust ourselves easily to new relationships. The troops were therefore told before the action that they would be attacking the British, and that is why they fought so bravely.' Lloyd George laughed heartily and said, 'I remember that very well. Old Briand was always an incorrigible joker.'

I also asked him to confirm a second story and he said, 'By all means, if it is as amusing.' In Clemenceau's memoirs I had read that at a dinner on Armistice Day 1918, Lloyd George and he had discussed Germany's future, their opinions being materially different. 'What has come over you?' Clemenceau had asked rather bluntly, 'you seem to have changed completely.' Lloyd George replied, 'Yes, hadn't you heard that I had become pro-German?' Lloyd George confirmed this story too.

As our car stopped at his hotel, his daughter greeted him jokingly with the Nazi salute and '*Heil* Hitler!' Thereupon the aged Lloyd George became quite serious and answered with quiet decision: 'Certainly, *Heil* Hitler! I say it too, for he is really a great man.'

In the first volume of his war history, Churchill wrote:

No one was more completely misled by Hitler than Mr Lloyd George, whose rapturous accounts of his conversations with him make odd reading today. There is no doubt that Hitler exercised a fascinating effect on people, and that the impression of strength and authority forced its way into the foreground excessively with his visitors.

THREE

1937

'The period of surprises is over. Peace is now our highest priority,' our Languages Service translated from a speech made on 30 January 1937. I hoped rather than believed that he meant this statement seriously. During his conversations with foreign statesmen and other visitors I had observed how he represented things differently to what they were. 'In Germany we have true democracy, I am the elected representative of the people,' he had often said, but I knew from everyday life only too well how different the reality was in practice.

At elections there was no choice, for there was only ever one candidate and one manifesto. Opposition was not tolerated: those who spoke out were gagged in all ways imaginable. 'What is it really like to live in Germany nowadays under the dictatorship?' my British friends asked me occasionally. 'You get this strange feeling,' I would reply, 'of being a foreigner in your own country.'

I had this sensation more than once. The old pre-1933 Germany, which had won for itself the ever increasing sympathy and above all esteem of the European world, had been 'dismantled' with iron resolve piece by piece until finally nothing remained of it but one of those outwardly uniform totalitarian structures in whose framework a whole people marches in step behind a dictator. Not until later did I become aware that I was not living as a foreigner in Germany, but that the old Germany that I had known and loved continued to exist. It became ever clearer to me that the 'flimsy layer' to which Goebbels in particular referred when speaking of the opponents of the National Socialist regime in fact embraced large circles of the population, and during the war it was truer to speak of a 'flimsy layer' of real National Socialists.

All these contradictions intruded into my consciousness most clearly when Hitler spoke to his visitors of the 'unanimity' of the German people for his decisions and their rejection of the views of the Western democracies. For this reason therefore I doubted that the period of surprises was really over.

In his talks with foreigners, which were still frequent in 1937, I noted that Hitler was becoming stiffer in his attitude towards the rest of the world. This may have been partly because he had achieved such wide recognition, but without doubt he became more uncompromising as the anti-Nazi coalition weakened. Whereas at Stresa Mussolini had stood on the other side together with France and Britain, the result of the Abyssinian conflict had been to force him into the arms of Germany.

From a distance I had followed with lively interest the conflict over Abyssinia as enacted at Geneva. From my experience of Geneva I would not have thought it possible that the whole League of Nations would unite in a common front, and seek by means of economic sanctions to hinder Italy from carrying out its plan of aggression. I hoped profoundly that the League would succeed, for I believed that nothing would have a more salutary effect upon Hitler than Mussolini's failure. In 1938, on the eve of the Munich Conference, Mussolini admitted that the League of Nations had very nearly succeeded in countering aggression by means of collective security. 'If the League of Nations had followed Eden's advice in the Abyssinian dispute,' he told Hitler, 'and had extended economic sanctions to oil, I would have had to withdraw from Abyssinia within eight days. That would have been an incalculable disaster for me.'

Oddly enough it was owing to the opposition of the French government, the protagonist of collective security, that oil sanctions were not applied. Laval did not want an open breach with Italy. When during the war he complained to me repeatedly about the difficulties being caused to France by Italy, I was able to retort on one occasion with some justification: 'How ungrateful of Mussolini, Prime Minister, for you saved his life in the Abyssinian dispute. He admitted as much at Munich in my presence.' Quick though he was, Laval had no answer. How different history might have been had the League been successful in bringing Mussolini to heel!

As Hitler announced in his speech in January 1937, there were no more surprises – that year. Looking back on it now, one could almost call it a year of calm before the storm. I was nevertheless kept busy with a great variety of assignments. The coronation celebrations in London, the International Exhibition in Paris, the Nuremberg rally and Mussolini's state visit to Germany – these were the highlights. My varied programme also included the following, however: the meeting between Hitler and Lansbury, former leader of the British Labour Party, in March; Göring's talks with Mussolini in Rome in April; the visit by the Duke of Windsor, formerly King Edward VIII, to Obersalzberg; the negotiations between Hitler and Lord Halifax at Berchtesgaden, and between Göring and Lord Halifax in Berlin; the visits of the Aga Khan, of the British fascist leader Sir Oswald Mosley, and of a descendant of Confucius, the Finance Minister Kung, brother-in-law of Chiang Kai-shek.

The day before Hitler's birthday on 20 April, in the study at the Reich Chancellery, I interpreted the conversation he had with Lansbury. The world-famous pacifist, 'the patriarch of decent feelings' as a German newspaper called him, laid a plan before Hitler for a peace conference that should be called for by US President Roosevelt. This was purely a private undertaking of Lansbury's and of well-meaning pacifist circles in Britain, and the plan was discussed only in broad outline and very superficially. One could tell from his eloquent exposition how enthusiastic Lansbury was, but most of the time I noticed that Hitler's thoughts were elsewhere. This was the first time that I saw the other Hitler, pale from sleeplessness, a man of almost grey complexion with somewhat puffy features, whose distracted expression showed clearly that he was brooding over other things.

Only occasionally did Hitler attend to what Lansbury was saying through me, and make some vague non-committal remark about Germany's participation in a peace conference, or about the peace policy that he wanted to pursue himself. I almost felt sorry for the old gentleman from Britain. Repeatedly he put forward his pacifist plans with great enthusiasm and persistence. He seemed wholly unaware of Hitler's lack of interest, being obviously delighted with his replies, vague though they might have been. It was plain that Hitler had assessed the man sat there lost in dreams as one of the pacifist idealists whom he had met so often at international gatherings. The longer the conversation went on, the more monosyllabic Hitler became, and the more Lansbury warmed to his theme. After all, not once had Hitler contradicted him; he had agreed that Germany would attend the peace conference; he had pronounced the word freedom with appropriate emphasis!

Hitler terminated the conversation somewhat abruptly. It had begun to bore him. It was hardly to be expected that a practising pacifist would have any effect on him. What seemed to me extraordinary was that Lansbury left the Chancellery highly satisfied, and that his statements to the press and on the wireless were very confident. 'I return to England,' he said, 'with the conviction that the catastrophe of war will be avoided.'

A few days later I was surprised to receive instructions to go to Rome for the talks between Göring and Mussolini. I had to leave Berlin so hurriedly that I was forced to take the Lufthansa Sunday flight. It was my medium-haul flight. The morning after our arrival I went with Göring to the Palazzo Chigi, the Italian Foreign Office, for a short call on Count Ciano. Our main topic was the Spanish Civil War, then fully under way, in which Italy and Germany were giving Franco military assistance.

In the afternoon, together with Göring, I entered the famous Palazzo Venezia, the Italian Chancellery, for the first time. A small lift with accommodation for only two people took Göring and the Italian *chef de protocole* to the first floor. This meant that I had to run up the antiquated staircase two steps at a time, meeting Göring at the lift door, breathless. This was a performance that I later had to repeat often. We were taken through various smaller rooms decorated with medieval armour and other trophies to the hall of the Fascist High Council, a medium-sized, sombre room. The long tables and Mussolini's raised dais, and also the seats, were all covered with dark blue velvet. We went on to Mussolini's anteroom, where Ciano greeted us. Then came the door to the Italian dictator's study. My impression was of a vast, sober, bare room. In the far distance, on the side facing us, there were a few solitary pieces of furniture and a globe. With its cold marble floor and grey walls, the room struck me as forbidding, unfriendly and un-Italian.

As we entered a figure rose up at the far end where, looking closely, I saw a long, smooth table and some simple chairs in Venetian style. It was Mussolini, and he walked the whole length of the room to meet us. Raising his arm in the Fascist salute, he shook hands with Göring and gave me a friendly nod. Bareness was the outstanding feature of this office. There were a few books, but no files anywhere.

We sat down – Mussolini at his desk, Göring and I opposite him on visitors' chairs. Ciano, to whom his father-in-law paid little attention, found himself a seat next to us. The situation in Spain was the first subject for discussion. Various technical details about the military were exchanged somewhat guardedly, both parties keeping up the pretence, even between each other, that the Germans and Italians fighting for Franco were volunteers having no official connection with their governments. In the course of the conversation Göring became more frank, providing with obvious satisfaction all the details of how French Moroccan troops were flown to Spain by Ju 52 transport aircraft at the beginning of the civil war in 1936. 'Franco has much to thank us for,' Göring said, but added at once, as if assailed by a certain presentiment, 'I hope he'll remember it later.'

Both criticised violently the Spanish strategy and tactics of both sides although the bravery of both the Falangists and the reds was fully recognised by Mussolini and Göring. Both spoke disparagingly of the war materials supplied to the republicans by the Soviet Union, especially the aircraft, and both were completely confident of their own superiority over the Red Army.

They passed on to discuss the general political situation in Europe, Mussolini using strong language in condemning the League of Nations and the sanctions policy of Britain and France. Listening to him one would never have thought that only two years ago at Stresa, in concert with Britain and France, he had condemned the introduction of conscription in Germany, and the year before that he had sent Italian divisions to the Brenner frontier when Dollfuss was assassinated during a National Socialist *putsch* in Austria. Times had changed, and the discussion of the Austrian question itself showed how fundamental was the change in Mussolini's outlook. Göring was very outspoken on this matter, telling Mussolini frankly that the annexation would and must come, and without much delay.

Mussolini spoke good German and listened attentively to Göring but evidently he could not have understood this passage, for it was only in the course of my translating it into French that he shook his head vehemently. It was the only sign of opposition he showed that day, almost a year before the annexation occurred. His silence was a clear indication that although he continued to regard the idea of the annexation of Austria with mixed feelings, he realised that it 'would and must come', as Göring put it. Naturally I did not know what instructions Hitler had given Göring for Rome, but from the talk with Mussolini I formed the impression that the main purpose of the visit was to sound out the Italians on the idea of the annexation.

I was more interested than surprised to see how far Mussolini had already put distance between himself and the western powers, and how he now shared Germany's views on fundamental questions of European policy. Sitting there very upright with expressive looks and few gestures, he gave his opinions with concise Latin clarity. As he eyed Göring or me, I felt that here was a man with little of the vague visionary about him; he was a clear-sighted Roman with both feet on the ground who knew exactly what he wanted. In conversations he held later with Hitler, I was constantly struck by Mussolini's clear, concise and realistic phraseology, in contrast to Hitler's vague and imprecise generalities. This was the great difference between the two dictators – so long, at any rate, as Italy and Mussolini were able to make more or less independent decisions. As he gradually declined to the status of Hitler's vassal, being more or less told what he had to do, he fell more silent. When now I look back at the gradual change in his demeanour during their many conversations, I am inclined to think that Mussolini realised before many others did just where the journey was taking them and that he certainly foresaw the looming catastrophe long before Hitler did. But by that time he had lost his freedom to act independently.

Another sudden change of scene for me. From Mussolini's bare office in the Palazzo Venezia, I flew home a few days later on the Rome–Berlin air axis, to restart immediately on the much more familiar and shorter air route to London for the coronation of King George VI. I was to be available in London to interpret at political discussions for War Minister General von Blomberg, the leader of the German delegation. The Third Reich was still hoping for a Berlin–London agreement, although all the time the gap between the two capitals was widening in the same proportion as that between Rome and Berlin was narrowing.

The morning after my arrival in London, I was awakened at 7 a.m. by a military band passing the German Embassy. My room was at the rear, overlooking The Mall, along which the coronation procession was to pass. From 8 a.m. onwards this room, with the terraces in front of it, was no longer my own. The Ambassador, von Ribbentrop, had provided accommodation for the entire German colony in the rooms of the embassy at No. 9 Carlton House Terrace, and I had a large share of the guests. Even so, I had an excellent view of the procession.

First the Lord Mayor of London passed in a glass coach. This traditional vehicle seemed to come straight from Grimm's fairy tales. The members of the royal family, each with their splendidly uniformed escorts, brought up the rear of the great procession. Already in the distance one could see approaching the golden state coach, drawn by eight greys, in which were seated the royal couple. Surrounded by the pageantry of this centuries-old tradition, Their Majesties, symbols of the greatest empire in the world, made an unforgettable impression on me. I could not but envy the way in which the ordinary British person took this manifestation of the might of the British Empire for granted. There was nothing extravagant or overdone about it. The applause was not hysterical but came naturally and spontaneously from the heart of the common man. Here the ceremonial uniforms did not seem out of place. They clearly derived from an unbroken line of ancient tradition.

Ribbentrop had invited some leading NSDAP members to come to London for the coronation. I was interested to see their reaction. It did not win their approval, mainly because it was too 'historical'. 'We National Socialists do this kind of thing much better,' one of the party men told me. 'We dispense with all this traditional mumbo-jumbo. You don't see so many old, greying figures with us. We give youth and the modern uniform of the brown shirt precedence over age and historical tradition.'

On this memorable occasion, Britain seemed to me like a weathered oak – gnarled but still vital. Compared with this, our National Socialist displays in Germany were more like brilliant hothouse plants, prize blooms forced by every conceivable device of modern horticulture and about whose staying power one might well feel doubtful.

The day after the coronation I accompanied our War Minister, von Blomberg, to see the Prime Minister, Mr Stanley Baldwin, at No. 10 Downing Street, whose threshold I had first crossed with Stresemann in 1924. Nothing seemed to have changed and Baldwin himself gave the impression that he was part of the house. Short and heavily built, he sat smoking a pipe at his desk. From all he said I got the impression that he was conveying carefully considered opinions that he had held for some time. His every movement expressed unshakeable calm and self-confidence.

We knew already that soon he was to be succeeded by the Chancellor of the Exchequer, Neville Chamberlain, and we also knew that Baldwin had never been much interested in questions of foreign policy. He was the great leader of the Conservatives in British internal politics. In these circumstances, hardly anything was said of the relations between Germany and Britain. Both parties confined themselves to expressing the wish that existing difficulties might be eliminated. Blomberg pointed out that the attitude of the British press caused great displeasure to National Socialist circles in Germany without actually saying what he wanted done about it. Baldwin contented himself with the answer, made often enough later to Hitler and other Germans when they complained about the British press, that 'Britain is the land of a free press, and the British government cannot possibly influence newspapers.'

That same afternoon I went to see Neville Chamberlain who was to play such an important role in the Munich crisis in 1938. The difference between Baldwin and Chamberlain was striking. The former was phlegmatic while the other seemed – for London – almost lively. He did not have fixed, immutable opinions, was obviously interested in the most recent developments in Germany and enquired about various details of the administrative organisation of the Third Reich. His wishes for friendly relations between Germany and Britain were far more convincing than those of Baldwin, although he expressed them with a certain caution. Probably Chamberlain was by nature somewhat reserved, but the fact that he was still only Chancellor of the Exchequer understandably made him more so on this occasion. This was little more than a courtesy visit.

I also accompanied Blomberg to pay a brief call on Eden at the Foreign Office. Eden was extraordinarily reticent, which I attributed to the fact that the British would have liked Foreign Minister von Neurath to have represented Germany at the coronation. I was told that certain feelers had been extended to this effect, but that Ribbentrop was determined not to have his role as Germany's political representative questioned, and had therefore intrigued successfully to prevent the Foreign Minister being sent over for the occasion.

After my return home I was kept extremely busy in Germany. Von Neurath, just like Stresemann and Curtius in earlier days, made me available to other prominent personalities including Cabinet members and other leading figures of the Third Reich.

I did much interpreting for Goebbels at official press functions and in private conversations. On these occasions he was the wolf in exceptionally well-tailored sheep's clothing. Before his suicide in 1945 when the Third

Reich lay in ruins all around him, according to an eyewitness he tore off the mask and said to his most faithful colleagues: 'Now you see what you get for having worked for us. Now your number's up and the whole German people too deserve nothing better than this defeat.' In those earlier days when I interpreted for Goebbels and his foreign visitors, however, he was invariably the cultivated intellectual – affable, well-groomed and smiling – the very antithesis of the raging demagogue that he often showed himself to be in his radio speeches and election meetings. This contrast might have been too great for the impression on his foreign visitors to be lasting. The future French premier Paul Reynaud was not taken in by him. I once interpreted for them in Berlin and it was clear that Goebbels, for all his skill, had met his match in the shrewd Frenchman.

One of the many assignments that followed in quick succession was that of attending the Nuremberg Party Congress to interpret for the many distinguished foreign visitors. It was not the first time that I had had this job, and it was stressful work, for the Grand Hotel in which I was lodged in 1935 was full of British and French guests who could hardly contain themselves in their enthusiasm for Hitler. I never shared in any such emotion, for not only did I know only too well the other side of the coin, but my Foreign Office training had taught me to be strictly neutral as an interpreter. In 1937 I was spared such complications, for now I was lodged at the Deutscher Hof, which was Hitler's headquarters and as such was cordoned off to Germans and foreigners alike. During the week of the rally I did have a number of interpreting duties to perform but spent the rest of my time in my room, for the situation on the streets was oppressive.

It was one of my duties on the day of Hitler's triumphal procession through Nuremberg to drive in an open car a few yards behind Hitler with the most prominent British and French guests. Triumphal it undoubtedly was. A vast crowd applauding Hitler ecstatically created an overwhelming impression. It was as though at the sight of him mass intoxication had seized the countless thousands all along the way. They greeted him deliriously with outstretched arms and shouts of 'Heil!' To drive through the midst of this frenzied applause was physically exhausting.

I had the feeling that I really needed to keep a grip on myself so as not to be carried away by all the jubilation. Fortunately my attention was diverted constantly by the need to interpret, but I saw British and French people almost moved to tears by these passionate scenes, and even some hard-boiled journalists were groggy when we reached our destination.

When the procession was over, Hitler would throw a banquet for a few party leaders and foreigners. After the gruelling experience of the morning, scarcely any of the visitors would be capable of sensible conversation.

In 1937 the diplomatic corps was fully represented for the first time at a Nuremberg Rally. This year the ambassadors of France and Britain, and the US Chargé D'affaires were present. The ambassadors of Argentina, Brazil, Chile, China, France, Great Britain, Italy, Japan, Poland, Spain and Turkey were conveyed to Nuremberg in two long trains of wagons-lits, and in another train there followed the ministers of the smaller countries as well as the Chargés D'affaires of the United States, South Africa, Czechoslovakia, Lithuania, Afghanistan and Iran.

On one of the days during Nuremberg week, Hitler was in the habit of holding a tea reception for all these diplomats at the Deutscher Hof at which I would translate his speech into French. François-Poncet, who spoke excellent German, would reply as Senior Ambassador, and seldom failed to introduce one of the witty remarks for which he was famous in diplomatic circles in Berlin.

'You speak so well,' Hitler once said to him, 'that I would very much like to have you as Reich spokesman.' François-Poncet replied immediately, 'I would gladly accept the office, but only as Reich spokesman-zbV,' a dig at the prevalent mania for creating ad hoc posts 'for special purposes'. On these occasions François-Poncet could also introduce a serious note. 'The finest laurel wreath,' he said with slow emphasis a year later, when the Sudeten crisis was threatening war, 'will always be the one that can be made without a single mother having to shed her tears.'

Scarcely had the Nuremberg Rally terminated than I had to travel from Berlin for my next big political assignment to Kufstein on the Austrian border. Here I waited with the German escort service at the small border village of Kiefersfelden to receive Mussolini and Ciano, arriving by special train for a state visit to German soil on 25 September, an elaborately staged demonstration of the increasing solidarity between the two countries. This was the first time that I had boarded one of the famous special trains that Hitler and Mussolini used on their political journeys. The Italian train had more than ten large saloon, dining and wagon-lit coaches, and two Mitropa sleeping cars were coupled up to it for our use. Mussolini and Ciano greeted me heartily, being as I was one of the few in the German party whom they already knew. I was also conspicuous as the only person in the whole train dressed in civilian clothes. The Germans and Italians were all wearing uniforms resplendent with gold and silver trim. Conversation between the Italian guests and the German reception committee, which included the Reich ministers Hess and Frank, was very low key. In Mussolini's swaying saloon the two sides contented themselves with embarrassed smiles at each other, while the escort service was at pains to point out even the smallest and least significant features of the landscape to encourage some show of conversation. The ordeal came to an end at Munich.

At Munich Central station, transformed by all its banners and garlands, Hitler was surrounded by a vast entourage, all in uniform. He held out both hands to Mussolini, who was standing at the carriage window. The music of bands, drum rolls, shouts of 'Heil!' and 'Duce!' echoed back from the station roof, and the tumult continued as we made our way to the exit along a carpet of red cloth that stretched right through the main booking hall. I had no interpreting to do not only because Mussolini spoke German very well but also because I could not possibly have made myself heard above the din.

In our drive through the cordoned-off streets to the Prinz-Karl Palace, I noticed at once a marked difference from the drive through Nuremberg a few days before. The public applause was very cool; no one would have been moved to tears here. 'Munich people can't stand a rabble-rouser,' one of the Bavarians seated next to me in the car told me softly, so that our Italian guests could not overhear.

'The chief of police is responsible for all this!' I heard Hitler shout to his adjutants later, 'He placed the barriers like a lunatic would!'

The arrival of the guests at the Munich block of flats was greeted by subdued shouts of 'Heil!' and 'Duce!' The talks that followed in Hitler's five-roomed apartment were the first between the two dictators since they had met in Venice some years before. Mussolini was in good humour as he entered Hitler's study, since he had not found the reception too frosty. As they spoke in German, I had ample opportunity to observe and compare them.

Hitler did not sit upright at the table but leaned forward. When he became worked up the much caricatured lock of long black hair fell over his receding forehead, giving him an untidy, Bohemian appearance. I noticed his coarse nose and undistinguished mouth with its little moustache. When I recall the impression he made on me that day, I see now how he might have had some Czech blood as his genealogy suggests. His voice was rough and often hoarse as he flung out sentences full of rolling Rs either at me or Mussolini. Sometimes his eyes blazed suddenly, and then equally suddenly became dull as if in a fit of absent-mindedness. I never had the feeling that here was a typical German. He always seemed to me like a product of miscegenation from the Austro-Hungarian Empire, striking examples of which are to be seen in many districts of Vienna.

Mussolini was of a wholly different type. He stood firmly erect, swaying from the hips as he talked. His Caesarian head, with its powerful forehead and broad, square chin thrust forward under a wide mouth, might easily have been modelled from the Romans of old. His face bore a much more animated expression than Hitler's when his turn came to thunder against the Bolshevists or the League of Nations. Indignation, contempt, determination and cunning alternately lit up his highly mobile face, and he had the histrionic sense native to Latins. At particularly eloquent passages his dark brown eyes would gleam. He never said a word too many, and everything he uttered could have been sent straight to the printers. The differences in the way they laughed was also interesting. Hitler's laugh always had a flavour of derision and sarcasm. It showed traces of past disappointments and suppressed ambitions, whereas Mussolini's laugh was free and whole-hearted, a liberating laugh that betrayed his sense of humour. The conversation began with what was for me an amusing ceremony – Hitler being appointed by Mussolini an honorary corporal in the Fascist militia. Mussolini had even brought along a certificate, dagger and badge to mark the occasion.

The discussion itself lasted only about an hour, and was general rather than particular, as indeed were all the subsequent conversations they had. Hitler discoursed vaguely and at great length while Mussolini spoke briefly and clearly, yet without giving anything away. All that could be gleaned from what they said was that both had decided on a friendly attitude towards Japan, that they would give Franco the maximum possible assistance and that they both heartily despised Britain and France. This was actually the only political talk between Hitler and Mussolini during the whole visit. The 'festival programme' left scarcely a quiet moment for serious discussion. Parades in Munich, manouevres in Mecklenburg, inspection of the Krupp works at Essen and other such activities followed one another without respite.

I travelled all over Germany with Mussolini in his special train. Hitler always accompanied him to the station and then followed in his own brand-new special train, passing us on the way so as to be able to receive his guest again at our destination, like the fable of the hare and the tortoise.

Undoubtedly the most splendid ceremony of Mussolini's German visit was his triumphal entry into Berlin. Hitler's train drew alongside Mussolini's at Spandau West station unexpectedly on the adjacent track and from there kept exactly level with us – a masterpiece of locomotive driving. The two heavy trains each had two locomotives, and I was told later that the engine drivers had rehearsed the operation for days beforehand. Thus for a quarter of an hour the trains ran along side by side, and we could carry on a conversation comfortably with occupants of the other train. Just before Heerstrasse station Hitler's train began to gain almost imperceptibly so that it reached the terminus platform a few seconds before the Italian train. This had also been carefully timed by the Reichsbahn so that Hitler could walk the few paces along the platform and hold out his hand to Mussolini the moment the latter's train stopped.

Later as we drove through Berlin, my car, twenty-fifth in the column, got a special ovation because I was the only passenger in civilian clothes and my top hat attracted special attention. Berliners like a joke – they had come there to shout and were glad of the opportunity I had given them unintentionally.

On the following day there were parades, banquets, a visit to Karinhall and, in the evening, a great public meeting at the Olympia Stadium. 'Italy, and particularly Fascist Italy, has no part in the humiliation of our people,' Hitler told the masses. The speech was broadcast to the '115 million citizens of our two nations who are sharing in this historic event with deep emotion'. He spoke of 'community, not only of opinion, but also of action. Germany is once again a world power. The strength of our two nations constitutes … the strongest guarantee for the preservation of a civilised Europe, true to her cultural mission, and armed against disruptive forces.'

A sudden cloudburst drenched the '1 million people' who were in and around the stadium as Mussolini's turn came at the microphone. 'The Berlin–Rome Axis was formed in the summer of 1935, and during the last two years it has worked splendidly for the ever closer association of our two peoples and for peace in Europe,' he said. 'My visit must not be judged by the same standards as ordinary diplomatic or political visits are judged … Tomorrow I am not going on to somewhere else' (an obvious allusion to Eden's journey from Hitler to Stalin). 'The greatest and most genuine democracies that the world knows today are Germany and Italy.' Despite the pouring rain, thunder and lightning, the return journey was made with the cars still open – special orders were given to this effect.

When it was all over, a storm of another kind broke over my innocent head at the Chancellery. My 'plutocratic' top hat and morning coat had attracted Hitler's very unfavourable attention as the only civilian amongst the uniformed Axis officials. The fact was brought to his notice again when he saw the press photographs from Munich that evening. I was not at all displeased with my suit, and had long since become inured to taunts by party men such as: 'You look like the President of the Weimar Republic', or the sarcastic observations of Staff Officers at manouevres such as: 'If you look straight past the gentleman in mufti, you will see the advancing panzers'; or 'You look like the owner of a battlefield assessing damage to his land.' Now at last I was informed that my outfit was 'not possible' and that henceforth I must be in uniform when interpreting for Hitler in public. Hitler gave me an SS uniform, and Göring loaned me a Luftwaffe uniform, and in due course the entire Foreign Office staff got uniforms too.

Some time afterwards, the bewildered director of personnel at the Air Ministry asked me, 'What on earth was the *Feldmarschall* thinking of when he gave you a Luftwaffe uniform? Officially that is not permitted.' After 1945 the Americans questioned me about my SS uniform with similar surprise. Especially the former Germans amongst them were still bound by tradition to the pre-1933 era and it was some time before they finally understood that in the Third Reich a uniform was often nothing more than the costume of a stage extra. In the next great show, however, which was Hitler's return visit to Italy, I wore neither of the two military uniforms but the new dark blue uniform of the Foreign Office, specially created for the occasion. So much did it resemble a naval officer's uniform to the Italians that I heard cries of 'Here come the *Amiranti*!'

As I had expected, the programme of Mussolini's visit to Germany allowed no time for serious political discussion. Not even a final communiqué was issued, and it was only in the toasts exchanged between Hitler and Mussolini at a Chancellery banquet that serious matters were touched upon. Hitler spoke of Italy and Germany having been drawn together in sincere friendship by a common political purpose, saying that they would 'strive to secure peace and a general international understanding.' Mussolini replied: 'German-Italian solidarity is a living and active solidarity … Italy and Germany are ready to work together with all other peoples … They are immune against any attempt to separate them.'

On the afternoon of 29 September I left the Berlin-Lehrter station in Mussolini's train. Hitler saw the Duce off. The strenuous days of this first 'Axis conversation' were ended. Next morning at Munich station I was loaned to Dr Todt, builder of the German autobahns, for a tour of inspection by a British delegation under Lord Wolmer. It came as a blessed relief from the foregoing eight days of 'imprisonment' in special trains, cavalcades of automobiles and life in cordoned-off streets. I had worked for Dr Todt once previously when we flew all over Germany in a Zeppelin airship to view the autobahn network from above.

I had only just got back to Berlin when at the beginning of October I was called upon to interpret for the Duke and Duchess of Windsor on the occasion of their visit to Göring at Karinhall. At that time they were studying our social system.

Karinhall had been greatly enlarged since Lord Londonderry's visit. With childish pride Göring showed the guests over the whole house including his gymnasium with its elaborate massage apparatus ('given to me by Elizabeth Arden') in the basement. All his decorations tinkled on his uniform as he forced his generous body between one of the pairs of rollers to show the smiling Duchess how they worked. The spacious attic was entirely taken up with an elaborate model railway for the benefit of one of Göring's nephews. Göring switched the current on and the two men were soon quite absorbed with the fascinating train set. Finally Göring sent a toy aeroplane attached to an overhead wire flying across the room. As it flew over the railway it actually dropped some small wooden bombs on the station installation.

At tea afterwards I did not have to translate for the Duke, who spoke fairly good German, but I kept up a running commentary for the Duchess.

Two days later the Windsors were received by Hitler at the Berghof. The Duke expressed his admiration for the industrial welfare arrangements he had seen, especially at the Krupp works in Essen. Social progress in Germany was the principal subject of conversation between Hitler and the Windsors during the afternoon. Hitler was evidently making the effort to be as amiable as possible towards the Duke whom he regarded as a friend of Germany having especially in mind a speech the Duke had made several years before, extending the hand of friendship to German ex-servicemen's associations.

In these conversations there was, so far as I could see, nothing whatever to indicate whether the Duke of Windsor really sympathised with the ideology and practices of the Third Reich as Hitler seemed to assume. Apart from some appreciative words for the measures taken in Germany in the field of social welfare the Duke did not discuss political matters. He was frank and friendly with Hitler and displayed the social charm for which he was known throughout the world. The Duchess joined in the conversation only occasionally and then with great reserve when any social question of special interest to women arose. She was dressed simply and appropriate to the occasion and made a lasting impression on Hitler. 'She would certainly have made a good Queen,' he said when they were gone.

My next assignment was as interpreter for the visit of Lord Halifax which received so much publicity. The pretence was made that the visit was purely private, and that Lord Halifax had come to see the international hunting exhibition elaborately staged by Göring. The Berliners immediately gave him the nickname 'Lord Halalifax' (*Halali* is the German equivalent of Tally Ho!). In reality, Halifax's trip formed part of the effort then being made by Chamberlain to establish good, or at least tolerable, relations with Germany. Halifax was briefed to sound out Hitler and Göring on this subject. After staying a few days in Berlin, on the evening of 18 November he left for the Berghof with von Neurath and myself on the night sleeper and had a fairly long conversation with Hitler the following morning.

Hitler met him on the steps with a friendly smile and showed him over the house after which we sat down at the inconveniently low round table in his study on the first floor. 'I have brought no new proposals from London,' was Halifax's opening remark. 'I have come chiefly to ascertain the German government's views on the existing political situation and to see what possibilities of a solution there may be.'

This was dangerously reminiscent of Eden's questionnaire that had so provoked Hitler, who reacted accordingly. As I translated Halifax's words he frowned angrily, and I thought he would sulk and refuse to speak. But Hitler found it hard to remain silent for long and so, in spite of his annoyance, he embarked on a lengthy dissertation, presenting Germany's wishes in the form of highly categorical demands. This angry Hitler was very different from the quiet, friendly Chancellor who had spoken with Simon and Eden two years before. He was no longer cautiously feeling his way as in 1935, but obviously confident of his own strength and of the other's weakness.

He began with a bitter complaint against the British press, which, he said, had tried to torpedo the visit of Halifax by publishing alleged German demands. To Hitler's further annoyance, Halifax produced in reply a stereotyped paper justifying the freedom of the British press. The Führer went on to speak about Germany's relations with south-east Europe. A close union between Austria and the Reich was absolutely imperative and had been urgently desired by the Austrian people ever since 1919. Nor could the Czechs be allowed to suppress the Sudeten Germans any longer. Finally, Germany must be freely able to extend her economic relations with south-eastern and Eastern Europe, for those areas provided the natural complement to the German economy. Germany was the principal European importer of the products of all those countries. 'Obstacles are being put in my way repeatedly in south-east Europe by the western powers,' he shouted, 'and political ambitions that I have never entertained are being attributed to me.'

Halifax observed that Britain was ready to consider any solution provided it was not based on force. 'That also applies to Austria,' he added emphatically.

This excited Hitler again. There was no question of using force in the case of Austria: the wishes of the people were clearly evident. Then he turned to Danzig and the Polish Corridor. Here again Halifax said that he was prepared to discuss any solution not brought about by force. Hitler stressed at great length Germany's desire for peace and I felt that Halifax was impressed by the way he based this on Germany's need of peace for her internal development programme. On the whole, however, the meeting was not auspicious. One could scarcely have conceived a greater contrast between two men: Halifax, the deeply religious Yorkshire nobleman, the enthusiastic protagonist of peace, and Hitler, wilful and uncompromising by nature, and now rendered even more so by his recent successes and the manifest weakness of his opponents.

When the conversation turned to fundamental ideas the two were completely at cross purposes. Hitler's racial theories were just as foreign to Halifax as the latter's conception of neighbourly love and peace was to Hitler. Later on, he sometimes spoke of him slightingly as 'the English parson'. When the conversation came to an end, I felt that a battle for peace had been lost. Neurath also looked pensive.

The conversation over dinner brought nothing new although Hitler had got over his bad temper and was once more the amiable and attentive host I knew so well. Halifax gave no sign of emotion or disappointment. The whole time he remained the typical, quiet, phlegmatic Englishman and said goodbye to Hitler apparently without rancour.

We returned to Berlin by the night train and next morning I drove to Karinhall with Göring, on Hitler's instructions providing Göring with an account of the Berghof conversation before Halifax's arrival. I did not conceal how badly things had gone and expressed the fear that Halifax would return to London with a very poor opinion of the chances of reaching an agreement with Germany. Göring listened very attentively but made no comment.

I realised from his conversation with Halifax that afternoon that Göring must have received precise instructions from Hitler. He dealt with exactly the same questions as Hitler had done, only with infinitely more diplomacy. He remained quite calm, even about Austria, and treated matters as though the solutions sought by Germany were inevitable and unquestionable. 'Under no circumstances shall we use force,' he said reassuringly. On this matter too he seemed to have received a hint either from Hitler or von Neurath and added, 'That would be completely unnecessary.'

Everything could be settled quite well by negotiation. Later conversations showed me that this was in fact Göring's innermost conviction and it came out constantly in his conversation with Halifax. We know from Chamberlain's diary that Halifax went back with a favourable report, which in my opinion was due mainly to his talk with Göring at Karinhall.

Hitler had kept his word in 1937, for there were no surprises. But he had been preparing both militarily and politically for coming events. That year of peace was followed by a year in which Germany came within a hair's breadth of world war.

FOUR

1938

Right from the beginning of 1938 it was clear, despite what Hitler had said in 1937, that the period of surprises was by no means over. First came the internal crisis of February, in the course of which von Neurath was sacked and succeeded by Ribbentrop as Foreign Minister. Then came the entry of German troops into Austria, and the Czech crisis of September, when for many days Europe hovered on the brink of war.

Hitler's state visit to Mussolini in the first half of May amidst all these storms was like an Indian summer interlude, reminding me of the festivals of 1936 and 1937. Mussolini had suggested this visit in my presence under the influence of the magnificently organised reception accorded to him in Germany. Whether the invitation would have been so hearty if the annexation of Austria had already been an accomplished fact seems to me somewhat doubtful in view of the emphatic way Mussolini shook his head when Göring sounded him out on the matter in April 1937. Since then the subject of the annexation had not been mentioned to Mussolini again in my presence.

It was only just before German troops marched into Austria that Hitler sent Prince Philip of Hesse, son-in-law of the King of Italy, with a letter to the Duce setting out the reasons for his action. 'Pale but resolute, the Prince of Hesse left by aeroplane early this morning to see Mussolini,' became an almost routine Foreign Office joke later on whenever Hitler sent a messenger to inform Mussolini at the last moment of some startling new move he had decided upon. Once I was recalled from leave because the Languages Section could not finish a translation for Mussolini into Italian fast enough. Eventually for such emergencies I had to find an airworthy Italian-language translator to work on Hitler's letters during a flight in the same way as I had translated his peace plan between Berlin and London.

Despite Göring's hint Mussolini was somewhat surprised, but he swallowed the *fait accompli* of the annexation with good grace and assured Hitler that he understood the necessity for his action. 'Duce, I shall never forget this,' Hitler telegraphed in reply, and he kept his word until 1945. If anybody in his entourage so much as hinted anything against Mussolini personally, Hitler always mentioned his conduct over the annexation. I concluded from this that Hitler regarded Austria's 'return home' to the Reich as a considerable risk in his foreign policy. Only his relief that it had brought no change in Italy's attitude to Germany can, in my opinion, explain his undying gratitude. The closer relations between Italy and Britain after the annexation showed that Hitler was justified in his fears that Italy might turn away from Germany towards the European anti-Nazi front. This rapprochement was fostered by Chamberlain to such an extent that Eden resigned in protest, to be succeeded by Halifax. On 16 April it led to a whole series of agreements between the two nations, the most important of which was Britain's recognition of the annexation of Abyssinia. We now know that very soon after Hitler's stormy meeting with Austrian Chancellor Schuschnigg, Italian Foreign Minister Ciano told Lord Perth (British Ambassador to Rome) that he had instructed Grandi (Italian Ambassador to London) to press for an early start of conversations in view of 'possible future happenings'. Such was the background to the German State visit to Italy, concealed completely from the general public.

That this visit was to be a major show was clear to me from the long preparations for it on our side. All the Foreign Office members of the delegation spent much time at the tailor's fitting their 'Admiral's' uniforms based on sketches by the stage designer Benno von Arent and approved by Frau von Ribbentrop. It was dark blue with gold buttons, and gold rings on the sleeves, and for special occasions could be fitted with silver-coloured aiguillettes. Actually this uniform was no more ornate than the traditional uniform worn by French or British diplomats on formal occasions but in republican Germany we Foreign Office officials along with the Americans were the only ones accustomed to wearing simple frock coats. So we had little enthusiasm for the new costume. One of its drawbacks was the diplomatic dagger, so mounted that it could not be removed even for banquets: when one sat down it often gave the wearer a jab in the ribs and thus contributed to the comical aspects of its design.

I set off on 2 May in this uniform for Italy with Hitler and Ribbentrop. Our delegation, consisting of about 500 persons, travelled in three special trains. Half the members of the government, most of the party leaders, prominent journalists and ministers' wives including Frau von Ribbentrop took part in this 'invasion of Italy' as some of us called it. Each of us had a sleeping compartment in which our whole array of uniforms was hung up ready for use. Besides my 'Admiral's' outfit I had the Luftwaffe one as well in case I should have to work for Göring alone. In the eight days of the visit I never needed it.

The Foreign Office head of protocol had prescribed our dress for each hour of the day. During the journey from one Italian city to another we had to constantly change from uniform to civilian clothes, then into tails, then into another uniform, with sword or dagger as the case might be, so that our compartments looked like actors' dressing rooms. Putting on and pulling off heavy riding boots was most exhausting.

'I never expected to travel to Italy in a wardrobe,' a colleague of mine commented.

'You've got your belt on the wrong way round,' I was reprimanded by one of Hitler's adjutants on a railway platform. The only touch of reality on the journey was provided by the familiar faces of friends grinning from their strange costumes.

The train rolled down through Germany; every station was decorated and crowds had turned out at each to shout '*Heil!*' until we reached Leipzig at nightfall. Flowers and banners greeted us at Brenner station while the platform was covered with carpet. Along its edge formations of the Italian army and Fascist Party were lined up. As our train drew in the national anthems were played, and the Duke of Pistoia, representing the King of Italy, stepped up to the train in welcome surrounded by a large delegation in splendid uniforms. As we travelled on through South Tyrol, crowds came to look at us at the stations, but they remained noticeably quiet. There were no Fascist salutes and scarcely a single handkerchief was waved, nor any other greeting accorded. These splendid Germans of the South Tyrol looked thoughtful and serious. I seemed to read on their faces the anxious question: 'Are you going to betray us in Rome?' When we reached Bozen the atmosphere of resigned melancholy suddenly changed, and the rest of the way to Rome we received unrestrained enthusiasm.

We reached the capital in the evening. King Victor Emmanuel and Mussolini, with the heads of state, party members and their entourages, met us at a railway station specially constructed for the occasion. We drove into the city in carriages drawn by four horses, and as we passed the Cestius Pyramid and were met by Prince Colonna, Governor of Rome, at the city's ancient gateway I thought to myself, 'Now I am myself sitting in a fairy-tale coach such as I admired last year at the coronation in London.' Passing huge illuminated fountains, we drove along the old triumphal way of the Romans. This had been widened by Mussolini to form a real Via Triumphalis along the foot of the Palatine, lit as bright as day by countless candelabras, up to the Arch of Constantine. Continuing through it we passed the Colosseum, whose red floodlighting made it seem as though it were on fire, and on either side of the street great metal pans of flame, floodlit pylons, banners and cheering crowds. Hitler was to stay in the Royal Palace. We juniors were fortunately able to step down from the stage and stay at the Grand Hotel, where Italian hospitality had gone to the lengths of putting magnificent baskets of fruit and bottles of grappa in every room.

We were not disappointed in our programme, which was a rare combination of good taste and magnificence. At Naples there was a naval review. I was aboard the battleship *Julio Cesare* from which I saw 100 submarines submerge simultaneously, surface after a few minutes with clockwork precision and fire a round. I was free to enjoy myself since Hitler, Mussolini, the King and the leading personalities were all on the battleship *Cavour*.

The gala performance of *Aida* at the San Carlo Theatre that evening seemed almost dull and commonplace, and Verdi's music grey and subdued compared to the fantastic scenes and exuberant sounds and colours of the preceding days.

One man who did not enjoy that evening was the hapless chief of protocol, von Bülow-Schwante. The unfortunate man had allowed Hitler to go bareheaded in evening dress to inspect the guard of honour after leaving the opera, while the King of Italy was resplendent in full uniform. Hitler was beside himself with rage, and Bülow-Schwante lost his job.

This week of palace receptions, state banquets and other ceremonial occasions in uninterrupted succession left me with relatively little interpreting to do. Quite apart from the fact that we had brought along two Italian-language specialists, the festival programme left practically no time for real discussions or negotiations. I had already noted this during Mussolini's visit to Germany and I got the impression later that it was characteristic of all the meetings between dictators. The chief strain, both for myself and all the others, was the constant quick change of uniform. It was also very exhausting to have to maintain, for anything up to twelve hours per day, an appropriately solemn, dignified or delighted expression. As the great processions passed through the populous Italian cities we were under the eyes of a watchful public, and indoors the elite looked critically at the barbarians from the north.

The conclusion and artistic highlight of the Italian visit was the brief stopover in Florence. In marked contrast to the Fascist and Royal Italy of Rome and Naples, here was the historical and artistic Italy. Party banners gave way to the Florentine flag of a crimson lily on a white background, while on the Ponte Vecchio were flown the flags of the old corporations and dynasties, and the insignia of the Florentine republic. Hitler's quarters were located in the Palazzo Pitti, totally bereft of any adornment. During the war a few years later it would house a meeting of grave consequence between Hitler and Mussolini.

The main reason why I had an easy time as interpreter was that Mussolini and Ciano were obviously trying to avoid any serious political discussion, whereas Hitler, and even more so Ribbentrop, were constantly seeking it. The programme had been deliberately planned so that there was no time for serious talk, but even during the various social meetings, at which Hitler and Ribbentrop were always ready for discussions, Mussolini and Ciano showed quite clearly that they were not. This impression was confirmed beyond all doubt when we handed Ciano a draft treaty for an Italo-German alliance. Despite all the beautiful speeches, we were still not formally allies. Hitler no doubt regarded it as vital to his future plans to take this opportunity to bind Italy to him irrevocably. A few days later Ciano handed us an 'amended draft' of the treaty. It proved to be a completely meaningless paper, whose emptiness amounted to a plain refusal. In a brief interview Ribbentrop had a very violent argument about it with Ciano, a grotesque contrast to what was being presented to the world on the public stage. Ribbentrop's chief characteristic was the persistence and obstinacy with which he would try to get his own way. Later I often saw him keep at it so long, without the least regard for tact or politeness, that the other side gave in through sheer exhaustion. He tried this tactic on Ciano but without success. 'The solidarity existing between our two governments,' Ciano said with what seemed to me a sarcastic smile, 'has been so clearly evinced during these days that a formal treaty of alliance is superfluous.' At the time I inferred from these words that the Italians had by no means got over their shock at the annexation of Austria, and especially at Hitler's method of carrying it out, and that their eyes were still turned westwards, as Chamberlain's diary entries substantiate. Outwardly, however, nothing of this could be seen at the time.

'It is my unshakeable will and testament to the German people that the frontier of the Alps, erected by nature, providence and history between us and Italy, shall be regarded as eternally inviolate,' Hitler said, turning to Mussolini as he drank a toast at a state banquet at the Palazzo Venezia. He had also no doubt noticed that the Austrian affair was still sensitive and wished this frontier guarantee to allay Italian anxieties. Austria had been annexed to Germany since March, making Italy's immediate neighbour not Austria but the German Reich. This was the only political result to emerge from the whirl of festivities. As I listened to Hitler's words that evening my thoughts went back to the German population of Tyrol, south of the Brenner, now finally become a part of Italy, but I could not see their reactions as our train steamed towards the Brenner because it had grown dark.

On 21 May I interpreted at a stormy meeting between Ribbentrop and Sir Neville Henderson at which Czechoslovakia was discussed face to face in Bismarck's historic office at Wilhelmstrasse 76. 'You have gone behind my back, Ambassador, and asked General Keitel about alleged German troop movements on the Czechoslovak frontier,' Ribbentrop accused Henderson in a fury. 'I shall see to it that in future you are given no information on military matters.'

'I shall have to report that to my government,' Henderson replied with an unusual degree of emotion. 'I can only conclude from your remarks that Keitel's statement to me was incorrect.'

The cause for this excitement lay in the growing tension in the Sudetenland, for whose inhabitants the Germans were claiming autonomy within the

Czech state. Conditions within the Sudeten territory were worsening from day to day; incidents were increasing and then being duly exploited and exaggerated by the German press. There were many rumours abroad that German troops were massing on the Czech border ready to march into the Sudeten territory just as they had done into Austria in March. These rumours were actually either pure invention or were circulated by the Czechs for political reasons. Henderson had asked Keitel about this and received a categorical denial.

There had long been a strong personal antagonism between Keitel and Ribbentrop, which naturally contributed to Ribbentrop's annoyance with Henderson. In addition, Ribbentrop had disliked the British in general since his time as ambassador in London where his arrogance had brought him many rebuffs. Now he unleashed his resentment on Henderson, a distinguished Englishman of the old school who, being in the diplomatic service, had no training in responding tit for tat to the kind of rudeness Ribbentrop exhibited.

Ribbentrop raged away about the Czechs. Mentioning the death of two Sudeten Germans, which Henderson tried to play down by saying that it was not as bad as losing hundreds of thousands of men in a war, Ribbentrop replied that every German was ready to die for his country. These remarks in the conversation by both sides show more eloquently than any long description the atmosphere of tension and irritation that prevailed. Henderson even went so far as to utter a fairly plain warning. He reminded Ribbentrop that France had definite obligations towards Czechoslovakia. 'The British government cannot guarantee that it may not be drawn inevitably into any conflict that might break out,' he said. To this Ribbentrop replied: 'If a general war should result, it would be a war of aggression provoked by France, and Germany would fight, just as she did in 1914.'

Henderson saw Ribbentrop twice on that 21 May, and on both occasions he spoke with equal emphasis, almost threateningly. On the Sunday following, he communicated a special personal warning from Halifax that drew attention to the danger of any rash action that might easily lead to a general war and bring about the destruction of European civilisation.

As one can see, the British were bringing up very heavy artillery. At that time it was totally unnecessary. I knew from a reliable source that all the accusations then being made against Germany were fabricated. When I heard the British Ambassador addressing Ribbentrop so heatedly I thought he was convinced that Hitler was preparing to invade Czechoslovakia, which accounted for Ribbentrop's excitement. We know now from Henderson's memoirs that the British military attaché and his assistant, after an intensive tour of investigation through Saxony and Silesia (the regions bordering Czechoslovakia), had reported that there were no signs of any unusual troop movements, and that other military attachés had also arrived at the same conclusion. I still do not quite understand why, in these circumstances, he took such a strong line. From countless other instances I know that he was not a person who liked to stir up trouble and indeed always endeavoured to do his best to clear up differences and to preserve peace. I can only assume therefore that it was Ribbentrop's attack at the beginning of the conversation that disconcerted him. Moreover, I noted both before and later that Henderson's way of communicating the ideas of his government, in the typical manner of Western diplomats, and his general bearing, which was that of the perfect English gentleman, always somehow irritated Ribbentrop, and also Hitler, who could not endure 'people of refinement'. As far as I can recollect, Hitler was only open and friendly to Henderson on one occasion. That was at the 1937 party rally when Hitler assumed that the presence of the diplomatic corps in full strength, and especially the representatives of the great powers, was due to the influence of the British Ambassador. On every other occasion the sight of Henderson seemed to arouse Hitler's antagonism.

This antagonism had struck me particularly during a conversation at the Chancellery early in March 1938, in the course of which Henderson made a very remarkable proposal on his government's behalf regarding the colonial question. If it had been put into effect, Germany would have received colonial territory in Central Africa. This proposal was to pool European possessions in Central Africa and then to distribute them anew, with Germany receiving a share. Here again, it was the manner in which Henderson put forward the project that irritated Hitler intensely. Instead of launching the matter with a sensational announcement that he was offering territory in Africa to Germany as colonies for the first time, Henderson began his statement with a series of reservations. He said that the British government had not yet discussed its proposal in any detail with any of the other governments concerned or arrived at any definite agreements on the plan, so this was an entirely unofficial step. He wanted to sound out the German government as British Ambassador. He made it worse by implying that there would be conditions affecting the transfer of these colonial territories. For instance, he asked whether the German government would abide by the provisions of the Congo Act regarding the prohibition of giving military training to the indigenous populations and building of fortifications, and observe certain humanitarian principles in the treatment of the indigenous populations.

When Henderson concluded his rather lengthy exposition, Hitler showed not the slightest interest, saying there was no hurry at all about the colonial question, but his annoyance was evident from his excited answer to other observations Henderson made. The Austrian and Czech questions were acute at that time – only a few days later German troops marched into Austria – and the Sudeten question was being zealously canvassed in the German press. Henderson expressed the attitude of the British government as Halifax did later, saying that with regard to both matters it considered changes to be possible but only if they were undertaken in a peaceful way.

Hitler then gave free rein to his anger, but without raging at Henderson personally as Ribbentrop had done in the discussion of 21 May. Hitler stated that only a small percentage of Austrians supported Schuschnigg. If Britain opposed a just settlement, and interfered in 'German family matters' that were no concern of the British, then Germany would fight. Hitler enlarged on this theme of 'British interference in matters that are no concern of theirs' at length and with great indignation. He had especially hard words to say against the press and against religious circles in Britain for involving themselves in the German Church dispute. As he spoke he became more and more agitated, as though his long-restrained resentment against Britain had suddenly burst the floodgates. With reference to the Sudeten question, he had demanded autonomy for it within the Czech borders and he was particularly violent about the Czech–Soviet Treaty, saying that it was a crime for European countries to let Russia into Central Europe.

With all this in mind, I could well imagine with what rage Hitler would receive Ribbentrop's report on his conversation with the British Ambassador of 21 May containing the British warnings. After that meeting Ribbentrop had flown at once to Munich. The following day, Sunday 22 May, Halifax's personal warning was received. The barometer pointed clearly to storm.

Furthermore, on account of the alleged German troop concentrations, the Czechs had carried out a partial mobilisation on 20 May, and when Germany did nothing the world press announced jubilantly that Hitler had yielded. One only had to stand up to him, as the Czechs had done, they said, to make him see reason. Anyone planning deliberately to infuriate Hitler could have thought of no better method. To openly accuse a dictator of weakness is the thing least likely to make him see reason, all the more so when, as in this case, the whole affair was pure invention. The consequences were not long delayed.

During the summer of 1938 my interpreting activity slowed ominously. The tone of the German press on Czechoslovakia became more and more strident. I worked twice for Göring, wearing the Luftwaffe uniform because purely Luftwaffe matters were being dealt with. The first occasion was the visit of the Italian Air Minister, Balbo; the second that of General Vuillemin, head of the French Air Force, who had come to Germany with a group of French airmen at Göring's invitation. The Italians always addressed me as 'Colonello' on account of my uniform. The French officers made a very good impression on all the Germans they met, and I also realised the profound effect made on them by the state of German air armaments. The French visited Göring at Karinhall. 'What will France do if war breaks out between Germany and Czechoslovakia?' Göring asked.

Vuillemin replied promptly, 'Keep her word.' On the drive back from Karinhall, according to François-Poncet's memoirs, Vuillemin told the French Ambassador, 'If war does break out at the end of September as you believe, there won't be a French aircraft left in a fortnight.'

At the beginning of September I was again on duty at the Nuremberg Rally. Foreign countries were represented even more strongly than in 1937. The British Ambassador, who had only spent two days at Nuremberg at the last rally, remained almost until the end. Amongst the British guests were the lords Stamp, Clive, Hollenden, Brocket and McGowan, and Norman Hulbert MP who not only participated in the event but also dined with Hitler at a special reception later. France and other nations were no less strongly represented. From the conversations I translated, I sensed the daily increasing tension that prevailed throughout Europe in September 1938. Rarely had I translated so much about war and the danger of war as in those days. It was noteworthy that one of those who considered the situation with the greatest anxiety was the Spanish Ambassador, who openly expressed his fear that in the event of war the French government, supported by the Spanish leftist circles, would bring about the fall of the Franco regime.

The news that reached Nuremberg from abroad was also alarming. I can still see the anxious faces of some of my colleagues when they handed to me for translation and forwarding to Hitler a statement by the British government that German aggression against Czechoslovakia would be grounds for intervention by the western powers. Almost concurrently I translated for Hitler a report stating that Britain might be prepared to give military support to Czechoslovakia. That was on 11 September:

'I can only tell the representatives of these democracies that if these tormented creatures (i.e. the Sudeten Germans) cannot themselves obtain justice and help, they will receive both from us,' Hitler ranted in a speech full of threats against the Czechs on 12 September, the last day of the party rally. 'The Germans in Czechoslovakia are neither defenceless nor abandoned!' I heard through the loudspeakers at the airport as I left Nuremberg.

With Hitler's threats still ringing in my ears I arrived back in Berlin to find, not only at the Foreign Office but amongst friends and acquaintances generally, profound depression at what was generally felt to be the imminence of war. I heard many hard words against Hitler, and also learnt of the plan of the opposition to have him summarily arrested by the army as soon as he ordered general mobilisation. On 13 September the tension had become almost unbearable.

On the morning of 14 September events took a dramatic and sensational turn. I translated for Hitler a seven-line message: 'Having regard to the increasingly critical situation, I propose to visit you immediately in order to make an attempt to find a peaceful solution. I could come to you by air and am ready to leave tomorrow. Please inform me of the earliest time you can receive me, and tell me the place of meeting. I should be grateful for a very early reply. Neville Chamberlain.'

That same evening, in civilian clothes, I left for Munich in a special train, feeling that this time I was not going to act as an extra in an international show but to play a modest but not unimportant part in a real historical drama. In the train von Weizsäcker, State Secretary at the Foreign Office told me, 'Keep your mind quite clear. Tomorrow at Berchtesgaden it will be a matter of war or peace.'

Next day at noon, together with Ribbentrop, sent by Hitler for the purpose, I met Chamberlain at Munich airport. As he disembarked, Chamberlain told Ribbentrop, 'I stood the passage very well, although we had bad weather part of the way. I had never been in an aeroplane before.'

Accompanying Chamberlain were Sir Horace Wilson, the Prime Minister's most confidential adviser on all political questions, and Sir William Strang, head of the Central European Section of the British Foreign Office. As we drove through Munich to the railway station in open cars, the people greeted Chamberlain very warmly – considerably more so, it seemed to me, than they had Mussolini the year before.

We lunched in the dining car of Hitler's special train on the way to Berchtesgaden. A small longitudinal banqueting table had been set up.

The British sat one side, the Germans on the other. The scene is still very clear in my memory. During almost the whole of the three-hour journey, troop transports rolled past, providing a dramatic background with their new uniforms and gun barrels pointing skywards. 'Peace envoy Chamberlain', as he was then called in Germany, came in curious contrast to this warlike picture.

Shortly before we reached Berchtesgaden it began to rain, and as we drove up to the Berghof with Chamberlain the sky darkened and cloud hid the mountains. Hitler received his guests at the foot of the steps leading up to the house. After greetings, the shaking of hands and introductions, we all seated ourselves around the tea table in the large room with the view towards the Untersberg in which Hitler had received Lloyd George and the Duke of Windsor. Not only was the weather threatening but indoors too the tension was noticeable. It was clear that the protagonists were sizing each other up for the coming discussion at which the issue was war or peace.

After conventional remarks about the weather, the size of the room, the possibility of Hitler visiting Britain and Chamberlain's journey, Chamberlain asked rather abruptly if Hitler would speak to him alone or whether he wanted the support of his advisers. 'Of course, Herr Schmidt must be there as interpreter, but as an interpreter he is neutral and forms part of neither group,' Hitler said. I knew in advance that Chamberlain would be expressing the wish to speak to Hitler alone. This had been arranged with Hitler's knowledge between the British and Germans beforehand and behind Ribbentrop's back. Both sides felt that our Foreign Minister would prove a disturbing element in any endeavour to achieve a friendly settlement between Britain and Germany. Hitler himself had noticed the feelings of wounded vanity that the presence of the British aroused in his former London Ambassador, and for that reason he had agreed to a plan excluding him. This had the approval of Henderson and Weizsäcker and the warm support of Göring.

Therefore the angered Ribbentrop remained in the background while I accompanied Hitler and Chamberlain to the study on the first floor. It was the same simple, almost bare room in which Hitler and Halifax had got on so badly in 1937. This conversation, on which the issue of peace or war rested, was not conducted in an exactly serene atmosphere and became occasionally stormy. It lasted nearly three hours. The Nuremberg Rally being just over, Hitler was apparently still attuned to long speeches and from time to time got so carried away by his rage against Czech Prime Minister Benes and Czechoslovakia that his harangues went on interminably.

Hitler had begun fairly quietly by presenting in full the list of complaints against Germany's neighbours that he always brought up: the Versailles treaty, the League of Nations and disarmament were discussed in detail as well as economic difficulties, unemployment and National Socialist reconstruction. Chamberlain was reproached in a rising tone for the attitude of the British press, for Britain's interference in Reich affairs generally and in its relationship with south-east Europe including Austria.

Chamberlain listened attentively, looking at Hitler frankly. Nothing in his clear-cut, typically English features – bushy eyebrows, pointed nose and strong mouth – betrayed what was going on behind his high forehead. His brother Sir Austen Chamberlain, sitting opposite Stresemann at Locarno, had always looked like that. But Neville Chamberlain had nothing of his brother's aloof frigidity; on the contrary, he dealt in lively manner with individual points brought up by Hitler, giving the stock answer about the press with a friendly and almost conciliatory smile. Then, looking Hitler full in the face, he emphasised that he was prepared to discuss every possibility of righting German grievances, but that in all circumstances the use of force must be excluded.

'Force!' Hitler exclaimed. 'Who speaks of force? Herr Benes applies force against my countrymen in the Sudetenland, Herr Benes mobilised in May, not I.' Outside it was pouring with rain and the wind was howling. 'I shall not put up with this any longer. I shall settle this question one way or another. I shall take matters into my own hands.' This was the first time, in a discussion with a foreign statesman, that the phrase 'so oder so' – 'one way or another' – had been used. It was a phrase that I observed then and later to be an extreme danger signal. I translated it rightly 'one way or another', but its meaning now and on later occasions amounted to 'either the other side gives in or a solution will be found by the means of the application of force, invasion or war.'

At this Chamberlain, who until then had listened to everything with serious calm, also became excited. 'If I have understood you aright,' he said, 'you are determined in any case to proceed against Czechoslovakia.' After pausing for a second he added, 'If that is so, why have you had me come to Berchtesgaden? Under the circumstances it is best for me to return at once. Anything else now seems pointless.'

Hitler hesitated. If he really wants it to come to war, I thought, now is the moment; and I looked at him in agonised suspense. At that moment the question of war or peace really was poised on a razor's edge. But the astonishing happened: Hitler recoiled.

'If, in considering the Sudeten question you are prepared to recognise the principle of the right of peoples to self-determination,' he said, in one of those sudden changes from rage to complete calm and collectedness, 'then we can continue the discussion in order to see how that principle can be applied in practice.'

I thought that Chamberlain would assent immediately. The principle of self-determination had always played an important part in British political thinking and its relevance to the Sudeten question had been generally admitted by the British press and prominent British visitors to Germany. At once Chamberlain raised an objection. Whether this was because he had been angered by Hitler's aggressive manner, or because as a practical administrator he recognised the complications in applying this principle to Czechoslovakia it is difficult to say.

'If, in the application of the right of self-determination in Czechoslovakia, a plebiscite were held among the Sudeten Germans, the practical difficulties would be enormous,' he replied. Even so Hitler did not become indignant. Had Chamberlain's threat to return home frightened him? Was he really recoiling from the prospect of war? 'If I am to give you an answer on the question of self-determination, I must first consult my colleagues,' Chamberlain said. 'I suggest therefore that we break off our conversation at this point and that I return to London immediately for consultations, and then meet you again.'

When I translated these words about breaking off the discussion, Hitler looked up uneasily, but when he understood that Chamberlain would meet him again, he agreed with obvious relief. The atmosphere had suddenly become friendly again, and Chamberlain at once availed himself of this change to secure a promise from Hitler that in the interval no aggressive action would be taken against Czechoslovakia. Hitler gave this assurance without hesitation, but added that it was subject to no particularly atrocious incident occurring.

Thus the discussion terminated. After Hitler's change of direction, the prospects for the maintenance of peace seemed to me more than hopeful. I drove with the British to their Berchtesgaden hotel where we dined and spent the night.

As always after such a discussion, I dictated a report the same evening. Henderson kept coming into my room asking impatiently how I was getting on with it because Chamberlain wanted my note that night if possible in order to offer the Cabinet a detailed report next day. On similar occasions as a matter of course I had always handed the other party to a discussion a copy of my report if he requested it. The first time I did so was at The Hague Conference of 1929, when I gave Arthur Henderson the English-language version of my report on the discussions between the Foreign Ministers of Germany, France, Britain and Belgium. I was always interested in any amendments they might wish to make. These were always minor matters, sometimes purely questions of style. Nobody had ever raised an objection on matters of substance. Corrections by Hitler and Ribbentrop were usually the deletion of certain passages in their statements, but their alterations never made any essential change. Hitler's corrections were usually of style, often complementing the text with interjections to soften his assertions.

That evening, however, Ribbentrop suddenly arrived in a stormy mood beside Henderson in my room. 'You think you're still in Geneva,' he told me once Henderson had gone, 'where all secret papers were distributed freely to everybody. We don't have that sort of thing in National Socialist Germany. This report is intended for the Führer alone. Please note that!'

I now had the highly unpleasant task of informing Henderson and Chamberlain that I could not give them my report. I recalled that at other conversations Hitler had already suggested to those taking part that a written record would militate against its character as a man–to–man talk. In itself this was plausible, but as nothing of the kind had been said before the conversation it was in this case quite unconvincing to Chamberlain. Indeed, he complained emphatically that if these were the circumstances then at the next conversation he must have his own interpreter, or at any rate bring somebody with him who could make him his report. I appreciated for the first time what a mark of confidence it had been that none of the foreigners for whom I had interpreted, from Herriot and Briand to Henderson, MacDonald and Laval, had ever in all these years brought their own interpreter, but had always relied on my services. I regretted this contretemps all the more because I realised that it was a pure act of spite by Ribbentrop, who wanted his revenge for being excluded from the conversation with Chamberlain.

Later I had constant difficulties with Ribbentrop about handing my reports of such conversations to foreigners. Later on, even Mussolini had to ask for my report on each occasion. The Duce never found fault with my work, and as a matter of fact he often congratulated me on the accuracy with which I reported his words.

Next morning we drove with Chamberlain to Munich, where he took the flight to London from Oberwiesenfeld exactly twenty-four hours after his arrival. That same evening I returned to Berlin. The more I reflected on the vital discussions at Berchtesgaden and recalled how Hitler had shrunk from taking the fatal step, the more hopeful I felt. Profound pessimism still prevailed in Berlin, however, as a result of the press reports of clashes between Germans and Czechs in the Sudeten territory. Goebbels stepped up the tone of the German press day by day. He had almost reached the limit of indignant abuse when five days later I left for Cologne by the night train. Chamberlain arrived at noon on 22 September. We escorted him to his hotel on the banks of the Rhine opposite Godesberg and the same afternoon he held his first conversation with Hitler at Hotel Dreesen in the town.

Hitler met Chamberlain at the hotel with very friendly enquiries about his journey and accommodation at the Hotel Petersberg. The first-floor conference room had a glorious view over the Rhine and the Siebengebirge. But the statesmen had no eyes for natural scenery and with barely a glance out of the window they sat down at the end of the long conference table. Owing to the earlier incident about my report, Chamberlain had brought with him as interpreter Sir Ivone Kirkpatrick from the British Embassy in Berlin, who spoke excellent German.

Chamberlain opened the session with an account of his talks in London, recalling that he had agreed to get the Cabinet's views on the recognition of the Sudetenland's right to self-determination. The Cabinet had agreed to this and so had the French ministers who had come to London at his invitation. Even the Czechoslovak government had expressed its agreement. Together with the French, he had drawn up a plan in London whereby the territories inhabited by Sudeten Germans were to be transferred to Germany. Even the details of a new frontier were provided for. Chamberlain then outlined a comprehensive and complicated system of agreements involving relatively protracted handing-over periods. He concluded by announcing the guarantee that France and Britain were prepared to give to the new Germany–Czechoslovakia frontier. Germany, for her part, was to conclude a non-aggression pact with Czechoslovakia.

Chamberlain leant back after this exposition with an expression of satisfaction, as much as to say, 'Haven't I worked splendidly these five days?' That was what I felt too, for the agreement of the French, and still more of the Czechoslovaks, to a definite cession of territory seemed to me an extraordinary concession. I was all the more surprised therefore to hear Hitler say quietly, almost regretfully, but firmly, 'I am exceedingly sorry, Mr Chamberlain, but I can no longer discuss these matters. This solution, after the developments of the last few days, is no longer practicable.'

Chamberlain sat up with a start. He flushed with anger at Hitler's attitude, at the ingratitude for his pains. I noticed that his kindly eyes could gleam very angrily under their bushy brows. Chamberlain was extremely surprised and indignant; he said he could not understand why Hitler should now suddenly say that the solution was no longer practicable when the demands he had made at Berchtesgaden had been met and after very considerable effort.

At first Hitler evaded a direct reply, saying that he could not conclude a non-aggression pact with Czechoslovakia while the claims of Poland and Hungary on that country remained outstanding. Then, speaking relatively calmly, he criticised the individual points of the plan elaborated by Chamberlain. Above all, the period of transfer contemplated was far too long. 'The occupation of the Sudeten territories to be ceded must take place forthwith,' he stated.

Chamberlain pointed out rightly that this constituted a completely new demand going far beyond the request put forward at Berchtesgaden; but Hitler continued to demand immediate Reich occupation of the Sudeten territories. As the conversation proceeded he became more and more excited, more and more violent in his abuse of Benes and Czechoslovakia; Chamberlain became more reserved and withdrawn.

'The oppression of the Sudeten Germans and the terror exercised by Benes admit of no delay,' Hitler declared hoarsely, and propounded the settlement he himself envisaged. This amounted to almost unconditional capitulation by Czechoslovakia.

Thus that first meeting in the ill-starred Godesberg conference room ended with complete discord. Chamberlain returned angrily to his hotel on the other side of the Rhine. The only ray of hope was that another meeting had been agreed upon for the following morning and Hitler, at Chamberlain's express request, had renewed his Berchtesgaden promise not to take any action against Czechoslovakia during the course of the negotiations.

We received a letter from Chamberlain next morning, however, which amounted more or less to a rejection of Hitler's ideas. 'I do not think,' he wrote, 'you have realised the impossibility of my agreeing to put forward any plan unless I have reason to suppose that it will be considered by public opinion in my country, in France and indeed in the world generally as carrying out the principles already agreed in an orderly fashion, and free from the threat of force … In the event of German troops moving into the areas you propose, there is no doubt that the Czech government would have no option but to order their forces to resist.'

Although the letter was couched in quite a friendly form, beginning 'My dear *Reichskanzler'*, its impact was explosive. The negotiations seemed to have reached a deadlock on the first day. There were feverish discussions between Hitler, Ribbentrop and their advisers. Finally Hitler dictated a reply that amounted to a long and far from friendly repetition of what he had said the previous day. 'When Your Excellency informs me that the cession to the Reich of the Sudeten territories has been recognised in principle, I must regretfully point out that theoretical recognition of principle was already accorded to Germany long ago.' He reminded Chamberlain of President Woodrow Wilson's Fourteen Points of 1918, whose promises had been 'most shamefully broken'.

'I am interested, Excellency,' he wrote, 'not in the recognition of the principle, but solely in its realisation, and in such a way that in the shortest possible time the sufferings of the unhappy victims of Czech tyranny will be ended and at the same time the dignity of a great power will receive its due.' He continued in the same vein for four or five typed sheets and, there being no time for a written translation, Hitler instructed me to hand the letter to Chamberlain personally and to translate it verbally.

The eyes of the world were on Godesberg. Tension over the hitch in the negotiations was increasing hourly. The representatives of the world press continued to receive ever more pressing enquiries from their editors in Europe and America. Were negotiations broken off? Would there be war over Czechoslovakia? These were the newspaper headlines and the anxious speculations of broadcasters. The press representatives at the Hotel Petersberg, and probably also the British delegation with Chamberlain at its head, gazed across the Rhine at the Hotel Dreesen with a disquiet growing hourly. Over there nothing stirred. The ferry exclusively reserved for conveying delegations cars across the Rhine remained moored at the riverbank.

I was well aware of all this as I left Hotel Dreesen at about 3 p.m. with a large brown envelope under my arm. I realised that all the binoculars at the Hotel Petersberg would be trained on my car, to drop again in disappointment when it was seen that I was alone with the driver. We took the ferry across and then headed for the Hotel Petersberg. As I approached the hotel I knew they would have spotted the brown envelope; from afar I saw the journalists thronging around the hotel entrance. I pressed through the lounge with a non-committal expression, saying in reply to all questions that I must get to Chamberlain.

'Do you bring peace or war?' an American whom I knew very well from the Café Bavaria in Geneva shouted to me. I did not even venture to shrug my shoulders, since the smallest gesture might have been misinterpreted. I was thankful when a member of the British delegation met me on the stairs and took me at once to Chamberlain. He was standing on his balcony. No doubt he too had been looking anxiously across the Rhine, but he did not seem to me in the least excited, greeting me as he might any acquaintance encountered casually. He took me into his office, where I translated the letter in the presence of Sir Horace Wilson, Henderson and Kirkpatrick. It took some time, and I had to add some verbal explanations, so that it was an hour before I left Chamberlain's room. In order to escape the questions of the journalists besieging the lounge, I called on our head of protocol, Freiherr von Dörnberg, fortified myself with several swigs of the right stuff to strengthen me for running the gauntlet and then made a run for it. I had so many friends amongst the journalists that I could only escape their questions by taking to my heels.

'What did he say?' How did he take my letter?' Hitler asked me eagerly on my return. I reported my impressions, and he seemed to feel somewhat easier when I told him that Chamberlain had showed no excitement, merely stating that he would reply in writing today. An hour after my return the reply was handed to Ribbentrop by Henderson and Wilson, and a somewhat confused discussion ensued as to what was to be done next.

In his letter Chamberlain again proved conciliatory, saying that he was ready 'as a mediator' to transmit to the Czechoslovak government the proposals 'on which Your Excellency absolutely insists as you did yesterday evening'. He therefore asked Hitler to let him have these proposals in the form of a memorandum, announcing that he proposed to return to London to make the necessary preparations for passing them on.

During the discussion with Ribbentrop it was agreed that Chamberlain should be asked to come again that evening to receive the memorandum and hear Hitler's explanatory remarks on it.

This discussion with Chamberlain, which began just before eleven that night of 23 September, was one of the most dramatic in the whole of the Sudeten crisis. As there was to be a larger number of people present, it took place in a small dining room of the hotel. 'All the best people are invited,' a colleague said on hearing that Ribbentrop had managed to avoid exclusion this time. Also present were Sir Horace Wilson, Henderson, Weizsäcker and the head of our Foreign Office Legal Department. They sat informally in a semi-circle before Hitler and Chamberlain. I opened the session by translating the memorandum contained in a couple of typed pages.

'The news of hourly increasing incidents in the Sudetenland proves that the condition of the Sudeten Germans is quite intolerable and has therefore become a danger to European peace,' I read out. The main demand was 'Withdrawal of all Czech armed forces from an area shown on the accompanying map, evacuation of which will start on 26 September, and which will be ceded to Germany on 28 September ... The evacuated territory to be handed over in its present condition ... The Czech government to release all prisoners of German origin arrested for political offences ... Voting (in certain areas) under the supervision of an International Commission' – some of the many points in the brief document.

The effect on Chamberlain and the other British was devastating. 'But that's an ultimatum,' Chamberlain exclaimed, raising his hands in protest. '*Ein Diktat*,' interjected Henderson, who always liked to introduce German words into a discussion. Speaking forcibly, Chamberlain declared that it was quite out of the question for him to transmit such an ultimatum to the Czechoslovak government. Not only the content, but also the tone of the document upon its becoming known would arouse violent indignation in neutral countries. 'With the most profound regret and disappointment, *Herr Reichskanzler*, I have to state that you have made no effort to assist my attempts to secure peace.'

Hitler seemed surprised by the violence of the reaction and went on the defensive, attempting clumsily to ward off the accusation that he had handed over an ultimatum by pointing out that it was headed 'memorandum' and not 'ultimatum'. Chamberlain, Wilson and Henderson returned to the attack, asserting that his proposals would certainly fail if only because of his suggested timetable for implementation. It would allow the Czechoslovak government scarcely forty-eight hours to give the necessary orders, and its troops had to evacuate themselves from the whole territory within four days. The danger that such circumstances would lead to shooting incidents was enormously increased. The consequences of hostilities between Germany and Czechoslovakia were unpredictable. A European war would certainly result.

Negotiation had therefore reached absolute deadlock. At that moment the door opened and an adjutant handed a note to Hitler. After reading it he passed it to me saying, 'Read this to Mr Chamberlain.'

I translated: 'Benes has just announced on the wireless general mobilisation of the Czechoslovak forces.' A deathly hush fell over the room. 'Now war is inevitable,' I thought, and all present probably thought the same. Although Hitler had promised Chamberlain he would make no move against

Czechoslovakia, he had always added the rider 'unless any exceptional action by the Czechs forces me to act.' Was this such an action?

Afterwards when telling friends of this dramatic scene I often used the analogy of the kettledrum beat in a symphony. After the drumbeat of 'Czech mobilisation' there was silence for a few bars before the violins took up the melody again. In a scarcely audible voice, Hitler said to Chamberlain, who looked thunderstruck: 'Despite this unparalleled provocation, I shall of course keep my promise not to proceed against Czechoslovakia during the course of negotiations, or at any rate, Mr Chamberlain, so long as you remain on German soil.'

The tension began to relax. Discussion was resumed in a more subdued, quieter tone. There was general relief that the catastrophe had been postponed. Negotiations were continuing, that was the main thing.

Suddenly Hitler was prepared to discuss the question of evacuation dates, which Chamberlain had cited as the chief difficulty. 'To please you, Mr Chamberlain,' he said, 'I will make a concession over the matter of the timetable. You are one of the few men for whom I have ever done such a thing. I will agree to 1 October as the date for evacuation.' He corrected the date in his memorandum, made a few other moderating alterations, which as far so far I can recollect affected the form rather than the content of the document, and it was then sent out for a fair copy to be made.

In the course of further conversation Hitler pointed out that he had supported Chamberlain's endeavours for peace inasmuch as the boundaries of the areas to be ceded were quite different in his proposal from those he would seize should he have to use force against Czechoslovakia. Finally Chamberlain said that he was prepared to transmit the German memorandum to the Czech government. The crisis had cleared the air like a thunderstorm, and at two in the morning Hitler and Chamberlain parted in a thoroughly amiable atmosphere after talking alone together for a brief while with my assistance. In this talk, Hitler thanked Chamberlain in words that seemed sincere for his work on behalf of peace, and said that as far as he was concerned the Sudeten question was the last great problem that required solution. He also spoke about closer relations between Germany and Britain and about their cooperation. It was evident how much store he set on good relations with the British. He returned to his old theme. 'There need be no differences between us: we shall not get in the way of the exercise of your extra-European interests, while you can leave us a free hand in central and south-east Europe without harm.' At some time the colonial question would also have to be settled, but there was no hurry about it and it was not something over which they needed to go to war. Chamberlain returned to London later that morning.

Two days later, on 26 September, Sir Horace Wilson arrived in Berlin with a personal letter from Chamberlain to Hitler. In company with Henderson and Kirkpatrick he was received by Hitler at the Chancellery that afternoon. At this session for the first and only time in my presence Hitler lost his nerve completely. I do not recollect whether the British brought a German translation of Chamberlain's letter or whether I had to translate it. Whatever the case it produced one of the stormiest meetings I have ever experienced.

'I have just been informed by the government of Czechoslovakia,' Chamberlain wrote, 'that it regards the proposals contained in your Memorandum as wholly unacceptable.' In the course of the letter Chamberlain said more or less 'I told you so at Godesberg' and appeared to support the Czech position. Hitler had listened with growing restlessness and then jumped up suddenly, shouting, 'There's no point at all in going on with the negotiations,' and rushed to the door. It was an exceptionally embarrassing scene, especially as Hitler, upon reaching the door, seemed to realise how childish was his behaviour, abandoning his study to his guests, and returned to his seat like a defiant boy. He now had himself sufficiently under control for me to continue reading out the letter. When I had ended, however, he raged more loudly than I ever heard him do during a diplomatic interview, although it in no way resembled the legendary fits of rage so frequently described abroad: in the course of my duties I never saw anything that suggested them.

A very confused discussion followed during which everybody talked at once except Kirkpatrick and myself. It was one of the rare occasions when I was unable to get myself heard as interpreter in Hitler's presence. At other stormy meetings, especially during the conference of the Big Four held at Munich a few days later, I succeeded in restoring order by calling the attention of Hitler, or of some other speaker who had interrupted heatedly, to the fact that I had not finished my translation. Sir Horace Wilson's quiet and sober efforts to persuade Hitler to be reasonable only increased his fury; nearby, Henderson and Ribbentrop conducted their own excited special conversation on the subject of Benes the terrorist and the Czechs as warmongers.

It was in this mood that Hitler made his famous speech at the Sports Palace a few hours later. 'The question that has stirred us most deeply these last few weeks is known to you all,' he said. 'It is called not so much Czechoslovakia as

Herr Benes. In this name is summed up all the emotion of millions of people today, that makes them despair or fills them with fanatical determination! … He is now driving the Germans out! But that is where his little game must stop … The decision now rests with him. Peace or war! Either he accepts this offer, and at last gives freedom to the Germans, or we shall come and fetch that freedom for ourselves!'

All the same, there were other tones in his speech. Hitler spoke in a friendly way about Chamberlain and added the much quoted, significant sentence: 'I have assured Mr Chamberlain that as soon as the Czechs have settled with their minorities … I shall have no further interest in the Czech state. I will guarantee him that. We want no Czechs.'

The next day I was summoned to the Reich Chancellery again to meet Wilson who had received a new message during the night from Chamberlain for forwarding to Hitler. In this the British Prime Minister acknowledged the friendly words contained in Hitler's speech, linking this to an offer of guarantee to monitor that the Czech evacuation was carried out if Germany, for her part, would abstain from using force.

Hitler refused to discuss this proposal, even when Wilson asked what he was to report back to Chamberlain. Hitler kept saying that there were now only two possibilities open to the Czech government – either acceptance or refusal of the German proposal – 'and if they refuse I shall smash Czechoslovakia!' he raged. 'If the Czechs have not accepted my demands by two of the afternoon on Wednesday 28 September I shall march into the Sudeten territory on 1 October with the German army.' That morning it was quite impossible to talk to Hitler reasonably. Abuse of the Czechs and dark threats were all he would utter. Wilson and his escort sat there helpless: they were not equal to such violence.

Suddenly Sir Horace Wilson rose to his feet. In a firm voice, weighing each word, he said: 'In these circumstances there is a further commission from the Prime Minister that I must carry out. I must request you, *Herr Reichskanzler*, to take note of the following communication.' At that he read out a short but pregnant message, which I translated to Hitler as slowly and emphatically as possible so that he could appreciate its significance. 'If France, in fulfilment of her treaty obligations, should become actively involved in hostilities against Germany, the United Kingdom would deem itself obliged to support France.'

Hitler replied furiously that he took note of the communication. 'It means that if France chooses to attack Germany, Britain also feels it her duty to attack Germany,' he added, and raising his voice continued, 'If France and

Britain want to unleash war they can do so. It is all the same to me. I am prepared for all eventualities. I can only take note of the position. So, next week we shall all find ourselves at war with each other.' That was his last word to Wilson, and his answer to Chamberlain.

That same evening, I translated a letter to Chamberlain that Hitler phrased in a rather more conciliatory manner. This was the second time in these critical days that I had the impression that Hitler shrank back from the extreme step. Had Wilson's final statement caused him to change course? In this letter, as I still remember particularly, the German dictator said that he was preparing to participate in an international guarantee for the remaining part of Czechoslovakia as soon as the minorities question had been settled.

Hitler's change of tone between promising war next week and the writing of the conciliatory letter was perhaps due to something significant he saw late that afternoon. In dull autumn weather a motorised division passed along the Wilhelmstrasse. The completely apathetic and melancholy behaviour of the Berlin populace observed by Hitler from a window of the Chancellery made a deep impression on him. I was told at the time by his adjutants, with whom I had a lot to do in those days, that he found the scene most disappointing.

I had to be constantly at hand in the Chancellery to translate incoming reports and documents or to act as interpreter at the numerous ambassadorial sessions. The next day, 28 September, there was an almost uninterrupted coming and going of ambassadors. François-Poncet, Henderson and the Italian Ambassador Attolico passed each other at the door to Hitler's office, and in the neighbouring rooms and passages the usual high-pressure activity of a time of crisis reigned. Ministers and generals with their retinue of party members, adjutants, personal advisers, officers and heads of departments who had hurried round to consult Hitler were sitting or standing everywhere. None of these discussions were held as part of formal meetings.

Hitler strolled the rooms, speaking now to one, now another. Whoever happened to be near could get at him, but nobody could actually get a word in. Irrespective of whether one wanted to listen or not, Hitler would deliver a long harangue about his view of the situation. This came out as the Sports Palace speech shortened. Now and again Hitler would withdraw to his office for a longer discussion with Ribbentrop, Göring or one of the generals, Keitel in particular. At that time the Reichs Chancellery reminded me more of an army camp than a well-ordered centre of government.

The first ambassador to appear that morning of 28 September was François-Poncet. He spoke excellent German, but I had to be there 'just in case'. Having nothing to do I was able to listen quietly to a conversation that I often recalled in later years for the statesmanlike wisdom and the extraordinary diplomatic ability with which François-Poncet conducted it. In the truest sense of the word the French Ambassador *wrestled* for peace. 'You deceive yourself, Chancellor, if you believe that you can confine the conflict to Czechoslovakia,' he said. 'If you attack that country you will set all Europe ablaze.' He chose his words well and with characteristic thoughtfulness. He spoke a grammatically perfect German with a slight French accent, which somehow contributed to the impressiveness of what he was saying. 'You are naturally confident of winning such a war,' he went on, 'just as we believe that we can defeat you, but why should you take this risk when your essential demands can be met without war?'

Hitler gave no sign of agreement as he abused Benes once again, stressed his own endeavours for peace and stated emphatically that he could wait no longer. François-Poncet was not to be sidetracked; with great diplomatic skill he continued to demonstrate the senselessness of the action Hitler was proposing to take.

From my corner of the room I watched the actors in this tense battle for peace closely. From Hitler's reactions I observed how very gradually the balance tilted in favour of peace. He no longer flared up and it was only with the greatest difficulty that he could find anything to counter the arguments advanced by François-Poncet with devastating French logic. There is a Berliner expression, 'He talked to him as if he were a sick white horse', and if ever that was fitting it was here. Hitler became visibly pensive. Ribbentrop tried to intervene once or twice, and not on the side of peace. With suppressed irritation François-Poncet, who fully realised the danger of even one false word in such a situation, called him sharply to order. Obviously this did not displease Hitler; he was always impressed when somebody stood up to anyone other than himself.

Another successful stroke of diplomacy on the part of the French Ambassador was the production of a clearly drawn map showing the separation phases of the evacuation. When speaking of the Sudeten crisis later, Hitler said, 'François-Poncet was the only one to make a sensible proposal. One could see at once from his map that it was the work of military men who understood their job.'

A door opened and an adjutant entered. I wondered whether this was to be another startling announcement. Had the Czechs perhaps decided to strike first? I caught the name Attolico and was at once relieved, for I knew that the Italian Ambassador was one of the friends of peace. He had attached himself to the group that included Göring, von Neurath and Weizsäcker doing all they could to divert Hitler from his war plans. Attolico wanted to speak to Hitler at once 'on an urgent matter'. I left the room with Hitler since Attolico spoke little German and I had to serve as his interpreter at all his conversations with Hitler and Ribbentrop.

Breathlessly, his face flushed with excitement, without protocol ceremony he shouted from a distance, 'I have an urgent message to you from the Duce, Führer!' I translated his message: 'The British government has just let it be known through its ambassador in Rome that it will accept the mediation of the Duce in the Sudeten question. It regards the area of disagreement as relatively narrow.' He made the interesting addition: 'The Duce informs you that whatever you decide, Führer, Fascist Italy stands behind you,' but then went on, 'The *Duce* is of the opinion, however, that it would be wise to accept the British proposal, and begs you to refrain from mobilisation.' Hitler, already reflective after his talk with François-Poncet, was clearly impressed by Mussolini's message. Attolico watched him intently.

It was at this moment that the decision was made in favour of peace. It was just before noon on 28 September, two hours before Hitler's ultimatum expired. Hitler replied, 'Tell the *Duce* that I accept his proposal.'

At that time Mussolini's advice still carried great weight with Hitler; in addition, I had seen him shrink back from the extreme brink on two occasions. After that, his acceptance of Mussolini's proposal convinced me that he had turned away from war.

We went back to his office where François-Poncet was still waiting with Ribbentrop. 'Mussolini has just asked if I will accept his mediation,' Hitler said briefly. He continued his conversation with François-Poncet, but his mind was no longer on it. He was more concerned about Mussolini's message than with anything the French Ambassador still had to say, and so the interview was terminated somewhat abruptly shortly afterwards.

François-Poncet had scarcely left when Henderson appeared. He had another message from Chamberlain for me to translate. 'After reading your letter,' Chamberlain had written, 'I feel certain that you can get all that is essential without war and without delay. I am ready to come to Berlin myself with you and representatives of the Czech government, together with representatives of France and Italy if you so desire ... I cannot believe that you will take the responsibility of starting a world war which may end civilisation for the sake of a few days' delay in settling this long-standing problem.'

Hitler replied that he must contact Mussolini about this proposal. 'I have postponed German mobilisation for twenty-four hours to meet the wishes of my great Italian ally,' Hitler told Henderson. The latter took his leave after a perfectly friendly interview.

The same afternoon Hitler telephoned Mussolini, and the conversation resulted in the greatest sensation of the interwar period – the decision that Hitler should invite Chamberlain, Daladier and Mussolini to a conference at Munich. That night I headed south from Berlin by special train.

The Munich Conference was regarded at the time as the decisive turning point in the Sudeten crisis, although this had actually occurred the day before in Hitler's talk with Attolico after the vital preparatory work by François-Poncet. Indeed it had been foreshadowed at Berchtesgaden when Hitler first gave ground to Chamberlain, and at Godesberg where he did so the second time after the shock of the Czech mobilisation.

The course of the Munich Conference held in the new Führer building on the Königsplatz was described in such detail at the time that it would be superfluous for me to write at length about it. It was not in any case the peak of the crisis.

Soon after my arrival at Munich I drove with Hitler to Kufstein where he boarded the Italian special train and talked with Mussolini during the journey, a conversation that confirmed my assumption that peace was assured. Mussolini, in words similar to those used by François-Poncet, emphatically advocated a peaceful solution.

Shortly before 2 p.m. that day I took my seat at a round table with the Big Four – Hitler, Chamberlain, Mussolini and Daladier – in the Führer Building (now the Amerikahaus) at Munich. Ribbentrop, Ciano, Wilson and Alexis Leger, head of the French Foreign Office, were also there. The historic Munich Conference had begun. Its course was far less sensational than was then universally assumed, for the actual decision had already been taken.

First the four principals briefly expounded the attitude of their respective countries. They all spoke against a solution by force, even Hitler emphasising that he was all for a peaceful settlement of the matter. An atmosphere of general goodwill prevailed, broken only once or twice when Hitler raged against Benes and Czechoslovakia and Daladier made a highly temperamental response.

Daladier was still an unknown figure in that circle. A short man, he sat silent most of the time. He was clearly perturbed by the fact that decisions were being taken about the cession of territory by Czechoslovakia, an ally of France, without Czechoslovakia being represented at the conference. I noticed Alexis Leger speaking to him several times, apparently urging him to oppose some point or other. Daladier did not react, however, except on the occasions already mentioned, when he adopted a fairly stiff attitude towards Hitler. Surprisingly enough, Hitler was not put out by this. He seemed to like Daladier, and they exchanged war experiences in the breaks. I heard Hitler tell Mussolini, 'I can get on very well with Daladier; he's been at the front like we have, and so one can talk sense with him.'

There was also a slight clash with Chamberlain at Munich after he raised a question of very minor significance in the scheme of things. It concerned the transfer of Czech public property to Germany in the ceded territory. Chamberlain kept on asking who would compensate the Czechoslovak government for the buildings and installations that would pass to Germany with the Sudeten territory. It was obvious here that not the Prime Minister and politician was speaking but the former Chancellor of the Exchequer and businessman. Hitler became ever more restive. 'These installations and buildings result from taxes paid by the Sudeten Germans,' he kept saying with growing impatience, 'and so there can be no question of indemnification.' This failed to satisfy Chamberlain's sense of tidiness in matters affecting property. Finally Hitler exploded. 'Our time is too valuable to be wasted on such trivialities,' he shouted. This was when Chamberlain, for full measure, also raised the question of whether cattle were to remain in Sudeten territory or perhaps some of the livestock might be driven into what remained of Czechoslovakia.

During these arguments between Hitler, Chamberlain and Daladier I would often be interrupted by the person addressed as I translated the statement made to him into one of the three conference languages – German, French and English. 'I must say something about that at once,' one of them would interrupt – but on each occasion I asked to be allowed to continue my translation to the end so that the other participants were kept in the picture. From my long experience of conferences I knew that it produces great confusion if as the result of interrupted translations some of the delegates can no longer follow the argument. Friends who were watching the Big Four session through glass doors told me that when I demanded that my translations should be heard, I looked like a schoolmaster trying to keep an unruly class in order. After that we always used to give Big Four conferences the code name 'classroom', especially during the crisis year 1939. Even my 'clientele', Göring for example, took it up.

After Mussolini had submitted a written proposal for the solution of the Sudeten question, the conference adjourned for a short lunch interval at about 3 p.m. Mussolini's proposal was in Italian, but its translation was easy as I had already translated it once from German into French in Berlin. On that critical morning of the day before, 28 September, State Secretary von Weizsäcker had handed it to me requesting the French translation as soon as possible so that Attolico would have it for Mussolini before Ribbentrop had the chance to alter it. I was delighted to renew my acquaintance with the proposal again here at Munich. Although it was presented to the conference as Mussolini's proposal, it had in fact originated with Göring, von Neurath and von Weizsäcker.

Negotiations continued somewhat disjointedly after lunch. The meeting was no longer confined to the Big Four with their Foreign Ministers or diplomatic advisers; gradually Göring, François-Poncet, Henderson, Attolico, von Weizsäcker, legal advisers, secretaries and adjutants came into the room and formed a tense audience encircling the four heads of governments. In the meantime, Mussolini's draft agreement had been translated into the three conference languages and from it, with a few minor alterations, emerged the famous Munich Agreement, signed between 2 and 3 a.m. on 30 September.

In the course of the afternoon and evening the talks tended to break down into a number of separate conversations while the legal experts argued at length about the final phrasing. In these pauses Hitler had several lively conversations with Daladier. He spoke to Chamberlain too, but perceptibly more coolly than to Daladier. When Chamberlain suggested that he should call on Hitler next day for a tête-à-tête, the latter assented with pleasure. I also saw Mussolini and Chamberlain having a lengthy conversation and remembered the Anglo–Italian agreement and Chamberlain's efforts to come to terms with Italy.

At about nine Hitler had invited everyone to dine with him in the banqueting hall at the Führer building. Chamberlain and Daladier were obviously in no mood for a banquet and said they had to telephone their governments. They had secured peace, but at the cost of a serious loss in prestige. Under pressure from Hitler they had arranged for an ally of France to cede part of its sovereign territory to Germany. As we now know, considerable pressure had been brought to bear on Czechoslovakia by both France and Britain; it was therefore understandable that Chamberlain and Daladier seemed decidedly depressed that evening.

Therefore it was an exclusively Italo-German company that accompanied Hitler at a banqueting table that was much too long. It was on this occasion that Mussolini made his statement about the catastrophic consequences that would have ensued for Italy at the time of the Abyssinian War if the League of Nations had extended its sanctions to oil for even so short a time as one week.

As far as I was concerned, the Munich Conference lasted without respite for nearly thirteen hours, for I also had to interpret during lunch and dinner. I had to translate everything that was said continuously into three languages, and so spoke literally twice as many words as the Big Four put together.

There was only a brief rest after the signing of the agreement, for next morning I sat in Hitler's private apartment interpreting his conversation with Chamberlain. Hitler looked quite different as he sat beside me, pale and moody. He listened distractedly to Chamberlain's remarks about Anglo-German relations, disarmament and economic questions, contributing comparatively little to the conversation. Towards its end Chamberlain drew the famous Anglo-German Declaration from his pocket:

> We regard the agreement signed last night and the Anglo-German Naval Agreement as symbolic of the desire of our two peoples never to go to war with each other again. We are resolved that the method of consultation shall be the method adopted to deal with any other questions that may concern our two countries, and we are determined to continue our efforts to remove possible sources of differences, and thus to contribute to assuring the peace of Europe.

Slowly, with emphasis, I translated this statement to Hitler. I did not share Chamberlain's impression, as expressed in a private letter of his since published, that Hitler assented eagerly to this declaration. My own feeling was that he agreed to the wording with a certain reluctance, and I believe he appended his signature only to please Chamberlain, without promising any too much from the effects of the declaration himself.

Next I drove through Munich in an open car and experienced at close quarters the enthusiasm with which the people greeted the British Prime Minister. On our slow drive he was recognised immediately everywhere. People shouted their greetings and pressed around our car, many trying to shake his hand. I looked at their faces closely just as I always did during Hitler's triumphal progress through Nuremberg. In moments of excitement people's expressions speak very plainly. Here in Munich the sight of the elderly Englishman sitting next to me did not excite the ecstatic fanaticism of Nuremberg, but every face beamed happily. 'Thank you, dear old

Chamberlain, for having preserved peace for us' was what these thousands of joyous faces were clearly saying.

For me, these obviously spontaneous and unorganised ovations for Chamberlain implied a certain criticism of Hitler. When a crowd in an authoritarian state so demonstratively applauds not its godlike dictator but also a foreign statesman from the democratic West, this constitutes a very definite expression of public opinion – more significant, perhaps, than any number of hostile articles in the free press of a democratic country.

That I was not alone in these thoughts was confirmed to me that afternoon by several prominent National Socialists of Hitler's entourage. I knew that they always, almost without thinking, echoed their master's voice as they heard it in the course of their constant association with Hitler. The latter was profoundly disappointed that the German people, confronted by war, reacted so differently from the manner expected. Instead of showing delight at the prospect of taking up arms against the enemy, the populations of Berlin and Munich had demonstrated unmistakably their aversion to war, and their joy at the maintenance of peace. A certain tribute of routine applause had indeed been paid to Hitler, the man of war, but at least in Munich it lagged far behind the spontaneous manifestations of sympathy that I had seen accorded to Chamberlain, and such as he and Daladier received outside their hotels. I also heard that when the conclusion of the Munich Agreement became known in the city that night there had been much alcoholic celebration. Part of Hitler's world must have fallen about this ears when he learned of all this the following day, and it suddenly dawned on me why he had been so completely changed and distracted when Chamberlain visited him.

Scarcely a fortnight later, in his Saarbrücken speech, Hitler said, 'There are weaklings amongst us who possibly did not realise what a stern decision had to be taken.' This was public confirmation of my impression. This speech of 9 October at Saarbrücken was for many Germans a rude awakening from the dream that the Munich Agreement had settled everything, and that a permanent peace had been secured. 'I know, what apparently the rest of the world and also some individuals in Germany do not know, that the people of 1938 are not the people of 1918.' Once again, here is clear confirmation of his disappointment of the bearing of the Germans. 'It needs only for Mr Duff Cooper, or Mr Eden or Mr Churchill to come to power in Britain instead of Chamberlain; we know well that the first aim of these men would be to start a new world war ... This makes it our duty to be on guard and to take heed for the safety of the Reich.'

Personally I had been of cheerful hope with the settlement of the 'last territorial problem in Europe' that peace would reign for many a day. With infinite regret I saw that the spirit of suspicion and resentment had once again gained the upper hand in Hitler.

At that time I heard much in the Reich Chancellery of Hitler's indignation at the severe criticism of the Munich Agreement in Britain and France, and at the British drive to increase her armaments. Hitler did not seem to understand what a severe reverse he had inflicted on Britain and France.'I am now going to a dying man to give him supreme unction, but I have not even got oil with me to pour on his wounds,' François-Poncet said very aptly as he went in the small hours of 30 September to inform the Czechs, the allies of France, of the verdict passed on them in their absence.

The British Prime Minister had flown three times to Germany; step by step he had allowed Hitler to push him into a solution that contributed very little to the prestige of the western powers. Hitler was astonished and indignant that Britain and France, after their transitory relief at the maintenance of peace, were not congratulating themselves on the price they had had to pay for it and that they were naturally determined to do everything possible to see that they were never again in such a helpless position.

In that period of 1938 it became startlingly clear to me once again how little Hitler understood the mentality of Western Europe. Despite these unpleasant impressions, my colleagues at the Foreign Office and I retained up to the end of that eventful year the feeling of relief that the great slaughter had been prevented. Yet those of us who had been closest to the events in those days of crisis found Chamberlain's description of them in a published private letter of 2 October 1938 very disquieting. In his words, the Munich Agreement had been 'a last desperate grab for the last haulm of grass at the edge of the abyss'.

FIVE

JANUARY <u>TO</u> 3 SEPTEMBER
1939

Although Germany had not plunged into war in 1938, I realised from the words I had to translate for Hitler and Ribbentrop in the first months of the fateful year 1939 that Germany was again approaching the abyss, slowly at first and then at an ever increasing speed.

There can have been no period in my career when I took part in such a plethora of separate talks as between the Munich Conference and the disastrous 3 September 1939. Part of my duties was to make reports on all these conversations, many of which have since been published. I was aware when I wrote them that, together with other documents, they would be the raw material from which historians would form an impartial judgment of the events with which the reports were concerned. At the same time I bore in mind that my fellow Germans might see for themselves from these reports how Hitler was conducting his foreign policy. Soon after the Munich Conference my fear intensified that catastrophe was inevitable although I had as yet no concept of its extent.

All I can do is indicate the theme running through all these discussions and events. After the fateful German march into Prague, which my friends and I regarded with horror as the prelude to disaster, there followed the shrill, jarring symphony of August 1939 that culminated in the final agreement between Britain and France to declare war on Germany.

During this period there was a significant absence of the brilliant festivals that had dazzled the world in 1937 and at the beginning of 1938. In retrospect, the main feature of those last months before the outbreak of the Second World War seems to me to have been the wide contrast between the continued protestations of peace to the outside world and the busy preparations for war at home. From the position where I saw it, this was the vital feature of the last years before the outbreak of the Second World War.

An Italo-German tribunal met in October 1938 in the magnificent setting of Schloss Belvedere in Vienna, once the summer residence of Prinz Eugen of Savoy, to settle Hungary's territorial claims on the remnants of Czechoslovakia. A map of the disputed territories was spread out on a large table, around which stood Ribbentrop and Ciano with their advisers. Each of the Foreign Ministers had a thick pencil, and as they spoke they corrected the frontier line that had been drawn up by experts as the basis for arbitration.

'If you go on defending Czech interests like that,' Ciano exclaimed to Ribbentrop with a malicious smile, 'Hacha will give you a decoration.' He altered the line with thick pencil strokes in Hungary's favour.

A Foreign Office expert whispered to Ribbentrop who then protested, 'That's definitely too far,' and he redrew part of the line. The Foreign Ministers went on arguing in this way for quite a while, rubbing out and drawing in new lines, the pencils getting blunter and the frontiers thicker. 'The boundary commission will find it hard to determine the line,' a colleague whispered to me, 'those thick pencil marks are each a few kilometres broad.'

Seldom have I been made so acutely aware of the contrast between the light-hearted decisions on frontiers taken by statesmen in the splendid apartments of historic castles and the consequences of their decisions in terms of everyday life in the territories affected.

I was aware of a similar conflict between outward form and inner significance in the 'friendly visits' on which I accompanied Ribbentrop to Paris and Warsaw in December 1938 and January 1939. 'The German and French governments share the conviction that peaceful and good-neighbourly relations between Germany and France constitute one of the most essential elements for stabilising conditions in Europe and maintaining peace', ran the statement solemnly signed by Ribbentrop and Bonnet on 6 December 1938 in the Salle de l'Horloge at the Quai d'Orsay. It was in the same room that ten years earlier I had seen Stresemann, Briand and Kellogg put their signatures to the pact outlawing war.

'Both governments … solemnly recognise as final the frontier between their countries as it runs at present,' the text continued. I read out the German version while photographers cluttered the room with their apparatus, robbing the occasion of much of its dignity. 'Both governments are resolved,' I read on, 'subject to their special relations with third powers, in all questions affecting their two countries … to enter into consultation if the future development of such questions should lead to international difficulties.'

This was the deceptive facade behind which a rather disjointed discussion of the general situation took place in another room of the French Foreign Office between Bonnet and Ribbentrop a short time after the statement was signed. Ribbentrop sometimes spoke in French, and sometimes I translated into French from German for him. Nothing was translated into German, and this perhaps is how the misunderstanding arose that marked this conversation.

At one point Bonnet, who had previously expressed the intention of France to vigorously develop her colonial empire, had stated that at the Munich Conference France had shown herself to be disinterested in Eastern Europe. These words were in fact spoken during that earlier discussion, although they were later disputed by the French. Bonnet had probably meant them to refer only to past events in Czechoslovakia. Ribbentrop on the other hand applied them also and primarily to the future attitude of France towards Poland, the more so as Bonnet referred to the desirability of a German–Polish agreement about the Corridor and Danzig.

Ribbentrop had some grounds for this interpretation in the tension that had then existed for some time between Paris and Warsaw. This had found expression in severe attacks against Poland in the French and British press because of the way the Polish government, taking advantage of the Czechoslovak weakness following the Sudeten crisis, had occupied the Olsa area. 'If Hitler now invades Poland, I will shout, *Sieg Heil*!' the well-known British author and broadcaster Stephen King-Hall wrote.

Another feature of this conversation was Ribbentrop's violent outburst against Britain. In the harsh words he uttered against the British government, press and individual MP's such as Duff Cooper and Eden, I recognised immediately the angry voice of his master.

Hitler at that time was wont to shout 'Britain is to blame for everything!' with the same tenacity in foreign affairs as that with which his declaration 'The Jews are to blame for everything!' occurred in internal matters. Ribbentrop made such a point in Paris of this 'Britain is to blame for everything' that even the gentle Bonner replied rather emphatically that in no circumstances would there be any change in Anglo-French cooperation, which must provide the basis for detente between France and Germany.

I saw at once that Ribbentrop was merely echoing Hitler's dislike of Britain and was not trying to drive a wedge between Britain and France when, after Bonnet's emphatic reply, he changed his tune at once and said he approved of close Anglo-French cooperation. This was the counterpart to Italo-German understanding. Thus the atmosphere during this 'friendship visit' was anything but one of friendly understanding between France and Germany.

The French could not have taken more pains on the material side, even having sent to Berlin for our journey to Paris a special train with Pullman coach built recently for the visit of King George VI, but during Ribbentrop's talks we kept coming up against French distrust, particularly from the permanent officials such as Alexis Leger.

In due course, we in our Foreign Office 'admiral's' uniforms laid a large wreath on the Tomb of the Unknown Soldier at the Arc de Triomphe. The swastika ribbon for it had to be flown by special courier from Berlin because our protocol department had forgotten to include it in the hurry of our departure. We all had the feeling that it was only a theatrical gesture, however.

Such also was probably the feeling of the people of Paris with regard to the whole visit. In so far as the rigorous police precautions enabled us to get a sight of the Parisians, they showed themselves to be completely apathetic and uninterested. At the time the attention of the world was fixed on Paris in some suspense suspecting that much more lay behind the three hours' conversation at the Quai d'Orsay than in fact there was in that very superficial exchange of views.

I had a most interesting personal experience during this visit when I had the good fortune to have a long talk at a German Embassy reception with the famous French writer Jules Romains. I esteemed him highly as the author of the monumental *Les Hommes de Bonne Volonté*. He was clearly agreeably surprised that someone who had come to Paris with Ribbentrop should speak with so much enthusiasm of his work and even be able to quote from it. I had met enough men *de bonne volonté*, of goodwill, in politics to realise that the salvation of the world, then as now, depends upon these men and that fanatics, of whatever nationality or race, are the real enemies of mankind.

At the end of January 1939 I accompanied Ribbentrop to Warsaw on another 'goodwill' visit. Here the difference between the outward show and the inner reality was greater even than in Paris.

The station of the Polish capital, when we arrived there on the afternoon of 26 January 1939, was decorated with swastika banners, there was a guard of honour and military bands played the national anthems. Beck, the Polish Foreign Minister, received us. He was accompanied by a numerous entourage as well as by his wife, who presented Frau von Ribbentrop with a bouquet. Here also we laid a wreath on the tomb of Poland's unknown soldier. Although protestations of friendship were expressed only moderately in the toasts proposed at a banquet, none of the dangerous outward difficulties between the two countries, which had surfaced fairly sharply during a visit made by Beck to Obersalzberg early in the year, were mentioned, although they did become the theme afterwards in discussions between Ribbentrop and Beck.

During the course of Beck's earlier visit to Hitler, I had been able to plainly foresee the impending Polish–German trouble that was to culminate in the British Ambassador handing me, on 3 September 1939, the ultimatum that plunged the world into war.

At the Obersalzberg talk in January, Hitler had spoken again of a proposal that had just emerged after the Munich Agreement. Incidentally, the meeting had been arranged at a time when Polish objections were being made known regarding the declaration of independence by the Carpathian Ukraine, which had previously been part of Czechoslovakia. It was the stated Polish view that the Carpathian Ukraine should be annexed by Hungary, and Poland opposed the undertaking given by Hitler at Munich in connection with his guarantee to the remaining part of Czechoslovakia.

German demands were concerned principally with the return of Danzig, although Poland's economic interests in that city were to be safeguarded. Hitler also demanded the construction of an extraterritorial highway and railway track through the Corridor to secure communications between Reich territory and East Prussia, and in return offered a guarantee of the

German–Polish frontier and a renewal of their non-aggression pact. The conclusion of this pact on 26 January 1934 had been Hitler's first major act of foreign policy.

The day before Beck saw Hitler at the Obersalzberg, Ribbentrop had hammered away at him for hours with that peculiar insistence that observers and victims have rather aptly called 'insistent penetration' in order to get him to accept the German requirements at least in principle. With equal obstinacy Beck had refused persistently, being especially resolute over Danzig. If he had had his way, he would have offered a precisely opposite arrangement, offering Germany safeguards for her economic interests in the city but refusing to consider any political reincorporation. 'I cannot ask public opinion in Poland to agree to that,' was his stock answer.

This argument had been repeated standing by the large window in Hitler's study at the Berghof, although Beck had then put his refusal more mildly. He had gone so far to agree to an examination of the question as a whole, but with the clear implication that the Polish attitude would be negative.

These differences were naturally very fresh in my mind during the outwardly friendly meetings at Warsaw at the end of January. Ribbentrop tried again, with even greater persistence than before, to get Beck to agree to the German proposals. He was again met with a refusal that was no less definite for the polite and tortuous form in which the Polish Foreign Minister knew how to deliver it. This was the last major attempt to reach agreement with Poland by peaceful negotiation.

In the early hours of the fateful 15 March 1939, a date that I personally regard as the beginning of the end, Hitler received the Czech President Dr Hacha and his Foreign Minister, Chvalkovsky, in a huge room at the newly completed Reich Chancellery for the mysterious discussion that resulted in the sensational creation of a German protectorate over Bohemia and Moravia. The detailed circumstances of this move caused much speculation both at the time and later. The dark panelling of the room, lit only by a few bronze lamps, produced a sinister atmosphere, so gloomy that the portraits on the walls and the statue of Frederick the Great could hardly be made out – a fitting framework for the tragic scene of that night.

President Hacha was the successor to Benes. A short, elderly man with dark eyes set in a face flushed with agitation, he was shown into this room shortly after 1 a.m. He had done his best to give no occasion for criticism to his giant neighbour Germany, which bordered the diminished Czechoslovakia on three sides. I had often been present at discussions in Berlin when

Chvalkovsky had tried to divine Ribbentrop's wishes from his expression, as it were, lest by some mischance he should give Ribbentrop the least offence. In the commercial field he had expressed his readiness for a customs union and for granting Germany preferential treatment in general, and in political matters he had acquiesced in every way conceivable. The short, dark Foreign Minister expressed his pathetic anxiety to please in a sentence that could not have summed up the situation better: 'And in foreign matters we would like to depend on you, *Herr Reichsminister*, if we may.'

All this had been to no avail, however, for the Czechs were like a red rag to Hitler. At the time I ascribed this to his Austrian past, whereas I now connect his irrational rage against the Czechs to the theory that he himself had Czech blood. I had already heard it being said in the Chancellery in early January that Hitler had decided to liquidate the Czech State. I was appalled by this report for several times during the Sudeten crisis in 1938 I had translated Hitler's assurance to Chamberlain that the Sudeten problem constituted his last territorial demand. The phrase 'We want no Czechs' from his Sports Palace speech still resounded in my ears. Hitler and Chamberlain had assured each other that they were 'resolved to deal with other matters also … by the method of consultation.' The day of reckoning could not be long delayed if Chamberlain, the exponent of a friendly policy towards the Reich, were to be so blatantly repudiated; if this man, highly esteemed throughout the world (including in Germany as I had seen for myself) were made to look ridiculous by having all promises, written or verbal, torn up and flung defiantly at his feet.

My awareness of Hitler's true intentions showed me the motives behind the press campaign against the remnant of Czechoslovakia, and against the declarations of independence by Slovakia and Carpathian Ukraine. Accordingly a few days before 13 March I was not surprised to learn that German troops would march into Czech territory in the early hours of 15 March.

Hacha and Chvalkovsky had also seen disaster approaching and this was their last-minute desperate effort to save their country. They sought an interview with Hitler, who agreed to receive them in Berlin. They were met at the Berlin-Anhalter station with all the honours due a head of state, and when they reached the Chancellery they were welcomed in the courtyard by the watch company of the SS Leibstandarte Panzer Division, whose band played the regimental march and who, as a final touch of grotesque irony, were then inspected by Hacha.

In Hitler's gloomy office the realities of the situation emerged by contrast even more starkly. Here was no intimate discussion man to man, for there was a relatively large number of people present, but Hacha, Chvalkovsky and the rest, even Göring and Ribbentrop, were the audience, Hitler the speaker.

I had worked for Hitler at longer sessions than this talk lasting scarcely three quarters of an hour, and I had seen him much more excited than at this encounter with the Czechs, but I have never reported a more fateful discussion. Indeed, it could hardly be called a discussion at all; rather it consisted of one long accusation by Hitler against the Czechs, to whom he now repeated the same calendar of crimes that he had already enumerated exhaustively to the British and French. No new matter was raised. Hitler asserted that as, compared with the Benes regime, nothing had changed: under the surface the Benes spirit lived on in the new Czechoslovakia. He said that he did not mean to imply any distrust of Hacha, for in Germany they were convinced of his loyalty. For the security of the Reich, however, it was necessary for Germany to install its own protectorate over the remnant of Czechoslovakia.

Hitler said this with considerable fervour, and in fact he never could speak normally about the Czechs and Benes. There were, however, none of those turbulent scenes that night between him and Hacha that were described in the foreign press. As I have said, I had already seen Hitler a good deal more excited on other occasions, for instance at the discussion with Sir Horace Wilson at the end of September 1938.

Hacha and Chvalkovsky sat as though turned to stone while Hitler spoke. Only their eyes showed that they were alive. It must have been an extraordinarily heavy blow to learn from Hitler himself that the end of their country had come. They had set out from Prague in the hope that they would be able to meet with Hitler but already, just before Hacha inspected the guard of honour at Berlin-Anhalter station in a sudden snowstorm, they had been told by the Czech Minister in Berlin, Mastny, that German troops had crossed their frontier at Ostrau. Then Hacha had had to sit and wait for hours at the Adlon Hotel for a telephone call from the Chancellery, Hitler finally receiving him at 1 a.m.

It was astonishing how the old gentleman kept his composure with Hitler after all this strain. 'The entry of German troops cannot be stopped,' Hitler said. 'If you want to avoid bloodshed you had better telephone to Prague at once and instruct your Minister of War to order Czech forces to offer no resistance.' With these words Hitler brought the interview to an end.

Unfortunately the telephone line to Prague was out of order. A nervy Ribbentrop told me to find out 'who's let us down'. I moved heaven and earth with the Reichspost but could only obtain the assurance that the German line was in order and that Prague did not answer.

'Call the Reichspost Minister at once for me personally,' Ribbentrop shouted, scarlet with rage. I redoubled my efforts, knowing that failure to get through might cost many lives if a clash occurred between German and Czech troops.

Meanwhile, Göring was talking to Hacha in another room. Prague got through suddenly, and I rushed into the room to accept the call there. They were sitting quietly at the table, talking without any sign of excitement. Hacha took the telephone immediately and I stayed a moment to make sure that he really got through. This was just as well, for a moment later the connection was broken off again. I left the room, and Ribbentrop told me to 'get the Reichspost Minister out of his bed' with an angry allusion to 'ministers who sleep during such a situation while we're hard at work here!'

I had only just started dialling again when I heard Göring shouting for Professor Morell, Hitler's personal physician. 'Hacha has fainted!' Göring said with great agitation, 'I hope nothing happens to him.' He added thoughtfully, 'It has been a very strenuous day for such an old man.'

'If Hacha dies now,' I thought, 'the whole world will say tomorrow that he was murdered at the Reich Chancellery.' I was recalled abruptly from these grim reflections by the Foreign Office central telephone exchange advising me that Prague was now at long last on the line (they had been told by Ribbentrop that they and their superintendent would be sacked at once if they didn't get the connection within an hour).

I went back to the room to find Hacha and Göring still there and talking in low tones. Outwardly, at any rate, Hacha had got over his fainting attack. Morell's injection had apparently done the trick. Hacha and Chvalkovsky spoke to Prague. Göring and I left the room while they conversed in Czech. The connection did not seem very good, for Chvalkovsky who spoke first had to raise his voice and speak very slowly.

I was now busy preparing a fair copy of the communiqué, only a few lines long:

At the meeting [of Hitler and Hacha] the serious situation arising from the events of recent weeks in what was formerly Czechoslovak territory was considered frankly. The conviction was expressed on both sides that all endeavours must be directed to securing calm, order and peace in that part of Central Europe. The president of the Czechoslovak state has declared that in order to serve this aim and final pacification, he confidently lays the fate of the Czech people and country in the hands of the Führer of the German Reich. The Führer has accepted this declaration, and has announced his decision to take the Czech people under the protection of the German Reich, and to accord it the autonomous development of its national life in accordance with its special characteristics.

This text, which had been prepared beforehand by Hitler, was signed at 3.55 a.m. on 15 March 1939 by him and Hacha as well as by Ribbentrop and Chvalkovsky. Very few of us who left that grey building on Wilhelmsplatz shortly afterwards, tired and exhausted, guessed that the end of Czechoslovakia also heralded *Finis Germaniae*.

A few days later I translated Chamberlain's speech made at Birmingham on 17 March:

Public opinion in the world has received a sharper shock than has ever yet been administered to it … Speaking with great earnestness at Godesberg, Herr Hitler repeated to me what he had already said at Berchtesgaden, namely that this was the last of his territorial ambitions in Europe, and that he had no wish to include in the Reich people of other than German race.

I could clearly remember these words of Hitler's, having myself translated them to Chamberlain.

Chamberlain continued:

Herr Hitler himself confirmed this account of the conversation in the speech which he made at the Sports Palace in Berlin. 'I have no further interest in the Czech state; this I can guarantee. We do not want any Czechs.'

The Prime Minister proceeded in his indictment of Hitler to call attention to the Munich Agreement signed by Hitler, of which paragraph six provided that the *final* determination of the boundaries of Czechoslovakia should be fixed by an International Committee; he put special emphasis on the word 'final'. In conclusion, he pointed out that in the Anglo–German Declaration, signed by himself and Hitler:

We declared that any other question which might concern our two countries should be dealt with by the method of consultation ... Does not the question inevitably arise in our minds, if it is so easy to discover good reasons for ignoring assurances so solemnly and so repeatedly given, what reliance can be placed upon any other assurances coming from the same source?

I do not know whether Hitler ever saw my translation of the speech – such things were withheld from the German people – but even without reading Chamberlain's words he must have been aware of the breach of faith he had committed.

'Hitler has gone behind my back, he has made me look ridiculous,' Daladier said to the German Ambassador in Paris. In the Chamber he declared, 'The time for words is past.' He was granted extraordinary powers for the strengthening of the French armed forces. France and Britain entered upon immediate negotiations with regard to the protection of Poland and Romania. Europe was on the move.

Dismissing out of hand the proposals for the settlement of the Polish question, including the extraterritorial *Autobahn*, on 26 March 1939 Polish Ambassador Lipski informed Ribbentrop that 'any further progress with the plan regarding Danzig means war with Poland.' Ribbentrop replied in kind, 'If Poland should infringe upon the territorial sovereignty of (the Free State of) Danzig, we shall consider that to be an attack on the German borders.'

Shortly afterwards the German Ambassador to Warsaw, von Moltke, reported a conversation with the Polish Foreign Minister Beck in which the latter had warned that 'if Ribbentrop considers the use of force against Danzig to be an act of war, then any attempt by Germany to impose a unilateral change in the status of Danzig will be seen by Poland as an act of war.'

At the end of March I translated a statement by Chamberlain. This time I knew for sure that Hitler would read it. It said:

I have to advise the House that in the case of a move which clearly threatens Polish independence and of which the Polish government takes the view that it is of vital importance to resist such a move using its armed forces, H.M. Government will feel itself duty-bound to provide the Polish government with all assistance in its power. The British government has given the Polish government a corresponding guarantee in this respect. I would add that I am authorised by the French government to say that in this matter it adopts the same stance as the British government … The British dominions have been fully and completely advised.

Therefore fourteen days after Hitler's 'triumphant' entry into the Hradschin at Prague, the stage had already been set upon which the German drama was to be played out at the end of August.

In the course of the following weeks my work mirrored the realignment of forces that was taking place. Friend and foe began to be recognisable as such: between them was the hesitant and uncertain group, making visits to Berlin and the Western democracies.

On the evening of 14 April I met Göring in Rome, and on the following day he explained to a worried-looking Duce the necessity for the German action against Czechoslovakia and the advantages it brought, particularly the acquisition of the Skoda Works for armaments.

Strong words were spoken against Britain and worse against Poland. Mussolini looked thoughtful while hiding his obvious disquiet at the ever more reckless statements made by Göring. Ciano, who always kept silent in the presence of Mussolini, gave cautious expression to his own concerns in a private conversation with Göring in my presence while dining at the Armed Forces Club. 'What unsettled me most,' he noted in his diary on 16 April 1939, 'was the tone that Göring used when speaking of the relationship with Poland: it reminded me only too well of the manner of expression used some time previously in respect of Austria and Czechoslovakia. The Germans are deceiving themselves if they think they can go about Poland in the same way … the Poles will only lay down their weapons after a bitter fight.'

Whilst I was in Rome, an Albanian delegation in native costume was evidence of Mussolini's recent coup against that country on 7 April 1939, of which the Italian Ambassador had given Hitler a hint just before the march into Prague. After the achievements of his fellow dictator against Austria and Czechoslovakia, I gathered that Mussolini felt a pressing need to be able to report some success of his own for the sake of prestige. In his talks with the Italian Ambassador, Hitler was more reserved than Mussolini had been here in Rome with Göring. At first Hitler had thought that Mussolini's plans were directed against France and had warned him against hasty action. I inferred that he was anxious about the reactions of the western powers to his Prague venture and did not want any further complications at that moment.

Another important event occurred at the time of our visit to Rome. Alarmed by the march into Prague, the United States intervened in the

European scene. Roosevelt sent a personal message to Hitler and Mussolini in which he referred to the fact that 'three nations in Europe and one in Africa have lost their independence.' It was quite clear even at the time that he was speaking of Austria, Czechoslovakia and Abyssinia, as Cordell Hull confirmed explicitly in his memoirs later. Roosevelt also stated that a large area of another independent nation in the Far East had been occupied by a neighbouring state and continued, 'Reports, which we trust are not true, indicate further acts of planned aggression against other independent nations.' This was a clear reference to Poland, or at least it immediately appeared to be so to Göring, to whom I translated Roosevelt's appeal.

'Are you prepared,' Roosevelt asked Hitler and Mussolini, 'to give an assurance that your forces will neither attack nor invade the territory or the possessions of the following independent nations ...' and there then followed a list of thirty named countries, European and otherwise. Roosevelt proposed that this promise of non-aggression should be valid for ten to twenty-five years, and that it should be agreed mutually with the countries concerned. He also offered American mediation for the settlement of European difficulties at the conference table.

In addressing the Reichstag on 28 April, Hitler replied, 'I have taken the trouble to ascertain from the states mentioned ... if they feel themselves to be threatened, and if Mr Roosevelt made this enquiry at their suggestion, or at least with their assent. The reply was in the negative and, in some cases, an emphatic repudiation.'

In his angry speech the Führer expressed his annoyance at the reaction abroad to his Prague adventure: 'Since Britain now voices the opinion, officially and in its press, that action must be taken against Germany, and applies this by the familiar policy of encirclement, then the conditions for the Naval Agreement are no longer valid. I have decided to inform the British government of this today.' Ribbentrop's diplomatic laurels of 1935 thus sank withered in the dust.

'I regard the agreement concluded between myself and Marshal Pilsudski as having been unilaterally broken by Poland, and therefore as no longer valid. I have communicated this to the Polish government.' Such was Hitler's wrathful response to the Anglo-French guarantee to Poland. This speech was translated that same night at the Foreign Office and sent to the American Embassy with the observation that it was the answer to Roosevelt's enquiry.

Among the waverers who had not yet declared for either side was Romania's Foreign Minister Gafencu, who visited Berlin on 19 April. He was severely reproached by Ribbentrop for having accepted a British guarantee in a moment of fright following the march into Prague and the occupation of Albania. From Berlin he went on to London and Paris.

Another waverer was Paul, Prince Regent of Yugoslavia, who was staying in Berlin at the beginning of June. This highly cultured man, interested in the arts, often said in my presence that he 'very much regretted' being called upon to succeed the murdered King Alexander. Hitler made a particular effort to impress him with a display of German military power. Preparing for the celebrations of his 50th birthday, Hitler had said to Ribbentrop, 'As many cowardly civilians and democrats as possible must be invited to see a parade of the most modern of all armies', and in June he subjected Prince Paul to this treatment, though without any better success than that he had had in the case of Gafencu. His conversations with Kiosseivanov, the Bulgarian Prime Minister, whom I had met in Sofia in 1938, had a similar outcome.

There was also complete failure with the Secretary-General of the Turkish Foreign Office, Numan Menemencoglu, who in July had a protracted discussion with Ribbentrop at his Sonnenburg country house near Bad Freienwalde. With stupefying persistence Ribbentrop kept on pressing him to clear the way for Turkey's accession to the Axis and to include Germany in the Montreux Convention on the Dardanelles, but with admirable adroitness Numan always evaded the issue and after hours of talk even the obstinate Ribbentrop gave up the struggle and sulked.

At the end of May and early in June I also took part in brief negotiations in Berlin between Ribbentrop and the Foreign Ministers of Denmark and the Baltic states of Estonia and Latvia, at which non-aggression pacts were concluded between these countries and Germany. These were an indirect consequence of Roosevelt's appeal.

In the face of so many 'undecided' states and in view of the counter-measures taken by the western democracies, there was now a substantial consolidation of the German association with Italy. On 4 May I went with Ribbentrop and a small delegation to Milan, where he met Ciano. The two Foreign Ministers, after a long discussion, agreed on a formal alliance. By Article I the contracting parties were bound 'to remain in constant contact with each other in order to agree upon those questions of common interest or which affect the overall European situation.' Article III provided: 'If one of the contracting parties should become involved in hostilities with another power, the other contracting party shall immediately come to its assistance as an ally, and support it with all its military forces by land, sea and air'. By the terms of Article V both countries undertook '... in the event of war conducted jointly, to conclude an armistice and peace only by mutual agreement.'

It was not until 22 May that this so-called 'Pact of Steel' was signed with great ceremony by Ribbentrop and Ciano in Hitler's presence in the New Chancellery in Berlin. It represented Hitler's aggressive reply to the defensive measures taken by Britain and France – closer Anglo-French cooperation, Anglo-French guarantees to Poland and Romania, plenary powers given to Daladier by the French parliament for the development of national defence and the introduction of conscription in Great Britain on 27 April 1939.

The future alignment of forces was becoming more clearly marked. Italy had now finally tied herself to Germany. Just as during Göring's conversations in Rome, so now in Berlin I noticed a certain reserve in Ciano as though he were alarmed at his own boldness. In his talks with Hitler and Ribbentrop, the Italian Foreign Minister made a point of emphasising the common need of both Axis partners for a fair period of peaceful development that he estimated should last for three years.

Throughout the summer tension in Europe increased daily. Preparations for war were put in hand more or less openly in every country; menaces, warnings and challenges filled the ether and the columns of the press.

After the series of visits that ended in July with the fruitless conversations between Ribbentrop and Menemencoglu, I went on leave to Norderney in the Frisian Islands with an uneasy presentiment that I might be extremely busy the following month. I had just managed to find myself a lodging at the overcrowded summer resort when I was called to the telephone to be told by a friend at the Foreign Office that I had to interrupt my leave. 'The Foreign Office special plane has already left for you, please be at the aerodrome in two hours.'

The old Ju 52 AMYY arrived punctually. The pilot, my namesake, did not know our next destination. 'I'm getting my instructions just after taking off,' he remarked mysteriously. We flew to the other end of the Reich – to Salzburg, where I was needed for a surprise visit by Ciano. He arrived there on 11 August.

At the Hotel Oesterreicher Hof I found the Italian delegation in a state of great excitement. 'You can take my word for it,' Attolico told me. 'Britain and France are resolved to let it come to war if Germany proceeds against Poland as she did against Czechoslovakia.'

I agreed without hesitation, 'I need no convincing of that. If your Foreign Minister expresses this opinion in his conversation with Hitler, you may rely on me to translate what he says with full conviction and great emphasis.'

'You are going to be very busy,' Attolico replied. 'In fact you will have to translate to the Reich Chancellor exactly what I have been telling you. That is the reason why Mussolini has sent Ciano to Hitler.'

We drove out to Schloss Fuschl, one of Ribbentrop's country estates by a lake of the same name a few kilometres outside of Salzburg. Ciano, though he spoke with the tongue of an angel, warning, pleading for calm and underlining Italy's weakness, made no impression on Ribbentrop, completely intractable, straining like a hound at the leash, raging against Britain, France and Poland and boasting grotesquely about the military might of Germany. After the discussion at Fuschl, we made an excursion with Ciano to St Wolfgang, where a jolly folk festival was being held, and dined at the Weissl Rossl amongst the unsuspecting summer visitors. In the same way, at the conclusion of the military alliance in Milan a few weeks before, the Italians had entertained us at the Villa d'Este on Lake Como. These colourful and attractive occasions were in striking contrast to the storm clouds massing over Europe.

At the meeting the next day, Hitler was set on war, although he was not so tense as his Foreign Minister had been the day before. That Ribbentrop had been his master's voice again was obvious by the similarity of his arguments to Hitler's. 'It is all Britain's fault,' was Hitler's main theme. 'The Poles need a severe lesson. The democracies are not as powerful as Germany and will not fight,' was the refrain. The military and technological supremacy of the Reich, to which he referred often, underpinned everything.

On this first day Ciano stood up to Hitler very energetically. As he revealed in his diary, he had received detailed instructions from the Duce to instruct Hitler in the 'madness' of embarking on war. With all the eloquence at his command, more than once he pointed out that a war against Poland would not be confined to that country. This time the Western democracies would certainly declare war. Obviously acting on the Duce's orders, Ciano kept returning to the theme of Italy's weakness and unpreparedness, telling Hitler bluntly that Italy could not sustain a war for more than a few months at the most; the situation regarding war materiel alone made it impossible to fight for longer. He could not have been more explicit. In conclusion he submitted the draft of a communiqué that suggested international negotiations for the problems threatening the peace of Europe. Ribbentrop had already discarded it, and he put forward instead a draft confining itself to talk of 'an impressively close alliance of the two nations'.

During the meeting with Ciano at the Berghof next day Hitler spoke a sentence that still echoes in my mind: 'I am convinced unshakeably that neither Britain nor France will embark upon a general war.' On this second day Ciano made no further effort to force Mussolini's advice on Hitler. He said no more on Italy's incapacity for involvement in hostilities. Quite inexplicably, he folded up like a jackknife; 'You have been proved right so often before when we others held the opposite view,' he told Hitler, 'that I think it very possible that this time too you see things more clearly than we do.'

I was profoundly disappointed. When I told Attolico how Ciano had shifted his ground, he expressed to the other Italians his deep concern at the results that might flow from their Foreign Minister's new attitude. Naturally, in these circumstances the question of the press communiqué was dropped. Ciano did not make the point that by virtue of the Pact of Steel, Italy was entitled to insist upon a common decision on the attitude to be adopted in the matter of Poland. He left Salzburg the same afternoon of 13 August, noting in his diary, 'I return to Rome full of disgust for Germany, its leaders and their conduct.'

I was not allotted an aircraft to return me to the North Sea and was only too thankful that Ribbentrop let me continue my leave. I arrived back at Norderney the following afternoon.

A few days later the Foreign Office rang me once more: 'Unfortunately you must interrupt your leave again,' I was told. I received no reply to my angry question about what was up this time. 'You will probably be able to bathe in the North Sea again in a few days,' was all that I could get out of my contact. Flight-Captain Schmidt landed on the island two hours later but had no idea of my ultimate destination. 'I am only to take you to Berlin. Beyond that I know nothing,' he told me, as we flew over the Frisian islands.

When I reached Berlin, a sensation awaited me in the shape of a sealed envelope on my desk at the Foreign Office. I had instructions to fly to Moscow with Ribbentrop in order to be present at discussions with Stalin. In this case I was not going as an interpreter because I spoke no Russian. I was to exercise my alternative function and report on the course the negotiations took, recording any agreements arising. It was the very last thing I had expected. An interpreter, by the nature of his calling, is unlikely to find himself speechless, but on this occasion words would have failed me had I tried to give expression to my surprise. In fact I might have overheard remarks by my colleagues that Hitler had been flirting with the idea of an approach to the Soviet Union for some time. Ribbentrop's liaison man with Hitler, later Ambassador Hewel, had also told me how admiringly, almost enthusiastically, Hitler had spoken about Stalin when a Russian newsreel was being shown at the Chancellery in which the Russian dictator was seen giving friendly waves of the hand to his troops on parade. I had not attached any particular significance to these things, however, with the result that the new turn was almost as sensational to me as to Germany and the world. 'The sinister news broke upon the world like an explosion,' Churchill wrote in *The Gathering Storm*.

The impression made by this news on friends and acquaintances in Berlin, who naturally envied me my journey to 'the distant planet', was, after the first shock of surprise, by no means a sinister one. On the contrary, the prevailing feeling in Berlin, and no doubt throughout Germany, was a sense of relief – as far as the general public was concerned, at any rate.

It was felt that a German–Soviet agreement such as this visit seemed to portend would remove the threat of war. The opinion was commonly held that the encirclement of Germany would thus be broken, and that in the circumstances Britain and France would not go to war on Poland's account; after all, in the preceding year when the groupings were far more favourable, they had not taken up arms for Czechoslovakia.

Accordingly, on 22 August I set out by air in a four-engined FW 200 Condor for Moscow with Ribbentrop and a large delegation. We landed at midnight at Königsberg, but there was no question of rest, for all night long Ribbentrop prepared the material for his discussions with Stalin, filling many sheets with notes in handwriting that grew larger in size as the night wore on, telephoning to Berlin and Berchtesgaden, asking for papers from the most remote archives, and keeping the whole delegation on the run.

We younger members used the pauses in this statesmanlike activity to drink a farewell toast to peace in the bar of the Park Hotel, where we were lodged. Unlike the general public in Germany, we were far from soothed by the prospect of an understanding with the Russians. I now knew Hitler well enough personally to realise that with Stalin protecting his back he would become still more rash and irresponsible in his foreign policy.

At 7 a.m. the next day we proceeded to Moscow, flying over the endless Russian plain, with its vast forests, widely scattered villages and lonely farmsteads with their dark thatched roofs. One realised immediately after crossing the frontier that one was no longer over Germany, where the red tiled roofs had looked bright amongst the cultivated fields. After four hours flying we reached Moscow, whose sea of houses looked just like Berlin or London from the air. The whole delegation, including Ribbentrop, stared fascinated through the windows. The great moment of landing 'on the distant planet' had arrived.

What first struck me on leaving the plane was the sight of a shield with the word 'Moscou' in French and at its side the Swastika banner in friendly contact with the Soviet hammer-and-sickle flag. Before them stood Potemkin, deputy people's commissioner for foreign affairs, whose name seemed to me symbolic of the unreality of the whole scene. He was head of a delegation of high Russian officials who had come to welcome us. With him were the Italian Ambassador Rosso, whom I had known at Geneva, and the German Ambassador Graf von der Schulenburg with his embassy staff. We drove to Moscow in Russian automobiles, which were very comfortable and looked like American Buicks. 'Dictators seem to delight in the magnificence of wide roads,' I reflected as we drove along the very broad, ruler-straight road to Moscow. The surroundings of this east–west axis road seemed to me as bleak and dreary as are now those of its Berlin counterpart in the Tiergarten, whose present state [in 1950] is a direct and one hopes final consequence of the Moscow visit.

The whole delegation was billeted in the German Embassy or at the homes of individual members of it. After a hasty meal Ribbentrop drove immediately to see Molotov in the Kremlin. We were apparently in a great hurry. I ought to have gone with him, but my luggage containing the dark suit, regarded as essential even in Moscow, had gone astray on the way from the aerodrome and eventually turned up in another embassy building.

I availed myself of the opportunity to go around Moscow with my host's wife, who was fluent in Russian. With its large broad streets, squares with churches, overcrowded trams, crowded thoroughfares and fairly heavy motor and horse-drawn traffic, at first sight it bore an almost disappointing resemblance to other great European cities. Only when I looked more closely was I struck by the essential difference. Cheerfulness, which I was accustomed to see on the faces of the crowds in the streets of Berlin, Paris or London, seemed to be missing here in Moscow. The people stared seriously and almost absent-mindedly straight ahead. Only very rarely during my walk of several hours did I see a smiling face.

Just as laughter was absent from the faces, so was colour lacking from the clothing of the Muscovites. Occasional white headdresses alone brought a little life into the grey of faces and clothing. Almost everybody was clad cleanly and neatly, with hardly anybody in rags, yet a melancholy grey pall seemed to hang over everyone and everything. In the case of the houses this effect was due to the fact that they had not been cleaned or painted for a long time. Many of them produced an effect similar to that of the district around the Schlesische station in Berlin immediately after the First World War and the 1918 Revolution.

Some new skyscrapers, built on the American model to house ministries, were impressive. I felt the same admiration as is expressed by all Western visitors who visit the famous underground railway system in Moscow. The line did not run far, but its stations, and their ornamental marble and good lighting, the comfort and cleanliness of the ultra-modern carriages and the superb ventilation put the tube systems of Berlin, London, Paris and Madrid to shame. The Muscovites sitting nearby stared at me silently with expressionless faces. As my companion explained, they recognised me at once as a foreigner by my clothes, especially my leather shoes. Had I been wearing my white sand shoes from Norderney I would have been less noticeable, for grey or white canvas shoes seemed at that time to be the height of fashion in Moscow.

I had thought of committing a capitalist act in the communist capital by making some purchases, but here I was out of luck. In shops whose windows displayed a few articles the daily quota had long before been exhausted. Even before the outbreak of war the shortage was as acute as it became in Berlin during the war, and my companion was answered with the Russian equivalent of 'We haven't got it and we won't be getting it' – the refrain in all Berlin shops towards the end of the war.

After I had got back to the Embassy late in the afternoon Ribbentrop came in from the Kremlin. He was positively bubbling over with enthusiasm about Molotov and Stalin who, so it seemed, had joined the discussion later. 'Things are going splendidly with the Russians,' Ribbentrop kept exclaiming as he ate. 'We shall certainly arrive at an agreement before the evening is out.'

The demarcation line separating the Russian and German spheres of interest in Poland that was to become so famous and involved a new partition of that country, had apparently already been discussed at the afternoon session. Ribbentrop put an enquiry through by telephone from the Embassy asking Hitler whether he agreed to the Baltic ports of Libau and Windau coming within the Russian sphere of interest. Within half an hour Hitler's affirmative answer had arrived.

Immediately after his hasty meal Ribbentrop rushed back to the Kremlin with Schulenburg and Dr Gaus, head of the Legal Division. To my regret I was not taken along with them. Hilger, who was acting as Russian interpreter, had now been detailed to make the reports on the discussions in my place. 'I don't want a new face to crop up suddenly amongst those taking part in the negotiations,' Ribbentrop explained. I was somewhat aggrieved to realise that the luggage lorry had deprived me of the opportunity of making Stalin's personal acquaintance. (I was to get to know Molotov at very close quarters when he came to Berlin in 1940 for discussions with Hitler, and on that occasion I resumed my old job of recording the meeting.)

When Ribbentrop and his companions reappeared at the Embassy upon conclusion of the negotiations, I learned the substance of the Kremlin talks. Everybody was in the best of spirits. In elaborating the individual points of the discussion, Ribbentrop enthused about Stalin and his 'aides with strong faces' to anybody who cared to listen. He seemed particularly happy about the spheres of interest allotted to Germany and Russia in Eastern Europe, details of which were kept secret for some time afterwards. That same night I had a look at the secret protocol dealing with this matter signed by Ribbentrop and Molotov. The introductory words, highly ominous in the political situation as it then was, read: 'In the event of a territorial and political reorientation …' and provided that of the Baltic States, Finland, Estonia and Latvia should fall into the Soviet sphere of interest. For the 'territory of the Polish State', the demarcation line should follow 'approximately the course of the rivers Narev, Vistula and San.' The question whether an independent Polish State should continue to exist was to be determined later between the two parties. 'With regard to south-east Europe …', I read with intense interest, 'Soviet Russia emphasises her interest in Bessarabia. Germany for her part expresses complete lack of political interest in these territories.'

The intentions of the two contracting parties could scarcely have been expressed more clearly. I realised that we had not been unreasonable when we drank our farewell toast to peace at Königsberg.

Ribbentrop and his delegation then enthusiastically described the little celebration that Stalin had improvised after the agreement had been signed. Stalin had concerned himself personally 'like a good paterfamilias' with the welfare of his guests. In accordance with Russian custom, one toast followed another. Stalin had led off by drinking the health of Hitler with the words, 'I know how much the German people love their Führer. I would therefore like to drink his health.'

I was also interested to hear what the others who had been at the talks had to say about Stalin's observations on the questions of the hour. Naturally, 'Britain is to blame for everything,' had been Ribbentrop's refrain. Stalin had concurred, and made some remarks about Britain's military weakness, adding, however, that no matter how weak she might be, Britain would fight hard and tenaciously. He seemed to rate the strength of France higher than did Ribbentrop. With regard to Italy, Stalin posed the question, interesting in view of subsequent developments, whether the Italians had annexed Albania with certain ideas in the back of their minds regarding Greece.

Stalin was very uncommunicative with regard to Japan. When Ribbentrop offered German mediation, Stalin did not decline it but said in his forthright way, 'I know the Asiatics better. They want rough handling occasionally.'

Having followed the conclusion of the treaty with Russia as intimately as I did, I found it of great interest to read in Churchill's war history the statement thst Stalin made to him at the Kremlin in August 1942. The Russians, Stalin said, had the impression that the British and French were not resolved to go to war if Poland were attacked, but rather that they hoped to scare Hitler off by a united front composed of Britain, France and the USSR. The Soviets were convinced, however, that Hitler would not allow himself to be scared off. Churchill quotes this statement in connection with the week-long negotiations through which an Anglo-French mission in Moscow was then attempting to lure the USSR into the 'diplomatic front' against Germany. We did not see the members of this mission during our stay although they were present in Moscow at the same time. They left empty-handed.

'The two contracting parties undertake to refrain from any act of force, any aggressive action and any attack against one another.' Thus ran Article I of the Non-Aggression Pact between Germany and the Union of Soviet Socialist Republics, which, signed by Molotov and himself, Ribbentrop displayed during the early hours of the morning with a beam of delight.

We left for Berlin at 1 p.m. on 24 August having spent only twenty-four hours in Moscow. Even by present-day standards this was fast work. By this surprise move in the diplomatic contest Hitler and Stalin had checkmated Britain and France.

Before leaving Moscow I went to see Red Square and the Lenin mausoleum. A long queue of Russian peasants was waiting patiently in front of the mausoleum to see Stalin's waxen predecessor in his glass coffin. In their bearing and expression the Russians looked like devout pilgrims. 'Amongst

Russian country folk,' a member of the embassy told me, 'anyone who has been to Moscow and not seen Lenin doesn't count.'

The great wall of the Kremlin was an impressive sight; so too was the Kremlin itself with its many towers, on which I had seen the great red stars gleaming the evening before.

Our delegation was so large that two Condor machines were required to transport everybody. One was to take Ribbentrop directly to Hitler at Berchtesgaden while the other flew to Berlin. As I was the only 'tourist', having been present but without portfolio, I was assigned a seat in the Berlin machine, which was not scheduled to take off until an hour after the first one. I thought that there would also be this interval of one hour when we made the intermediate stop at Königsberg, and calmly watched Ribbentrop's plane take off – followed immediately by the second Condor. In the course of my work amongst the VIPs of Europe I have often been photographed, and I have always regretted that no camera was present to record that moment as I stood there with a foolish look watching my aircraft depart.

In the course of a brief visit to the aerodrome restaurant, I had discovered that both Condors were being given fighter cover. In the last few days such was the tension developing between Poland and Germany that civilian Lufthansa machines received Polish anti-aircraft fire.

'Railway connection with the Reich was suspended today,' a bystander told me when I enquired about trains.

I hurried to the flight controller. 'Run to the other end of the field as quickly as you can. A reserve machine is taking off empty for Berlin at any moment.' I trotted off and gesticulated wildly at the aircraft, the engines of which were already running. I was relieved to see that the propellors slowed slightly. A little door at the end of the Ju 52 opened, the radio operator helped me in and I sat panting in the nearest seat. We took off at once.

'May I see your pass?' the pilot asked. 'As things are, one can't be too careful.' He also mentioned the Polish AA fire. 'We are not so grand as those others,' – meaning Ribbentrop and the delegation – 'We get no fighter cover, and so we fly far out over the Baltic where the Poles can't get at us unless they chase us with fighters and then force us to land.'

As a precaution I prepared my papers for destruction. I had to make sure they would not fall into Polish hands in the event of a forced landing. Nothing happened, however, and I landed in Berlin a half hour after Ribbentrop, who had been redirected to Berlin because Hitler was on his way there. My error might have had serious consequences had I not been present to act as his interpreter upon his arrival.

This whole episode brought home to me how near war between Poland and Germany really was. The newspapers and radios reported the insults and accusations; one could sense how disaster was steadily approaching step by step.

During my absence in Moscow a colleague had accompanied the British Ambassador to Berchtesgaden where Henderson handed Hitler a personal letter from Chamberlain. The Prime Minister said, amongst other things:

> Apparently the announcement of a German-Soviet agreement is taken by some circles in Berlin to indicate that intervention by Great Britain on behalf of Poland is no longer a contingency that need be reckoned with. No greater mistake could be made. Whatever may prove to be the nature of the German-Soviet agreement, it cannot alter Great Britain's obligation to Poland which His Majesty's Government has stated in public repeatedly and plainly, and which it is determined to fulfil.

Chamberlain added these words to his warning:

> It has been alleged that if His Majesty's Government had made its position clearer in 1914, the great catastrophe would have been avoided. Whether or not there is any force in that allegation, His Majesty's Government is resolved that on this occasion there shall be no such tragic misunderstanding.

This was plain enough; but Chamberlain, painfully disillusioned by Hitler's march into Prague and now become a new man by virtue of it, expressed himself still more clearly and unmistakably in the following words:

> If the need should arise, His Majesty's Government is resolved and prepared to employ without delay all the forces at its command, and it is impossible to foresee the end of hostilities once engaged. It would be a dangerous illusion to think that if war once starts it will come to an early end even if a success should have been secured on any one of the several fronts on which it will be fought.

Chamberlain continued this clear and unambiguous warning with a proposal for friendly negotiations, and for a truce in the German-Polish propaganda campaign. He also suggested that direct negotiations between Germany and Poland should be entered upon forthwith.

In view of the grave consequence to humanity which may follow from the action of their rulers, I trust that Your Excellency will weigh with the utmost deliberation the considerations which I have put before you.

I found the English text of this letter on my desk when I returned from Moscow.

In his reply Hitler made violent accusations against Poland. He referred to the German proposals regarding Danzig and the Corridor, and concluded with sharp criticism of Britain:

The unconditional guarantee Britain has given to Poland, whereby under all circumstances she would come to that country's assistance in any conflict without regard to its causes, could be interpreted in Poland only as an encouragement to initiate forthwith a reign of terror against the one and a half million Germans living there.

Cruelties insupportable to a great power such as the German Reich, breach of obligations with regard to the Free City of Danzig, economic strangulation ... such were the other main points of Hitler's letter, which concluded:

I have therefore to inform Your Excellency that if the military measures announced by Britain are carried out, I shall immediately order the mobilisation of the German Wehrmacht.

The next morning, 25 August, I was summoned to the Chancellery to translate for Hitler some especially striking passages from the statements made by Chamberlain and Halifax in the two Houses of Parliament. 'I do not attempt to conceal from the House,' Chamberlain said in the Commons, 'that the announcement [of a German-Soviet Non-Aggression Pact] came to the Government as a surprise, and a surprise of a very unpleasant character. In Berlin, the announcement has been hailed with extraordinary cynicism as a great diplomatic victory which removes any danger of war since France and ourselves would no longer be likely to fulfil our obligations to Poland. We feel it our first duty to remove any such dangerous illusion.'

Halifax's statement in the Lords was easy to translate since it was almost identical. These words made Hitler pensive, but he said nothing.

I noticed that Chamberlain's letter and his statement to the Commons had made a certain impression on Hitler when, at about two in the afternoon the British Ambassador was summoned to the Chancellery. Hitler was comparatively calm and told Henderson that he had thought over the latter's words uttered at Berchtesgaden about Anglo-German understanding and wished to make a final suggestion for an Anglo-German settlement. He referred expressly to the statements by Chamberlain and Halifax that I had translated for him that morning, and he got rather worked up doing so. After listing a long series of charges against the Poles, including firing at civilian aircraft, he shouted, 'The Macedonian conditions on our Eastern frontier must cease!' The Danzig problem and the question of the Corridor had to be settled under all circumstances, he said.

'Yesterday your Prime Minister made a speech in the House of Commons that does not alter the German attitude in the least. The only result of that speech can at best be a bloody and unpredictable war between Germany and Britain. This time Germany will not have to fight on two fronts, however, for the agreement with the Soviet Union is unconditional and represents a long-term adjustment of German foreign policy.' He concluded his speech for the prosecution with a sentence of particular interest in the light of subsequent events: 'Russia and Germany will never take up arms against each other again.'

There followed his now famous proposal for a guaranteed existence of the British Empire, and even an offer of help 'in any part of the world where such help might be needed'. Limitation of armaments, frontier guarantees in the West and other items rounded off this astonishing offer. Nothing further was said on the Polish question except for Hitler's declaration: 'The German-Polish problem must and will be solved.'

The proposals contained in this conversation were extracted from my report and I had to hand the remnant of it to Henderson at the British Embassy the same day. At Hitler's suggestion Henderson took them to London the following morning, 26 August, using a German plane being laid on for him.

Soon after the British Ambassador's visit, Attolico appeared. Hitler had already written to Mussolini hinting that probably very soon he would be compelled to proceed against Poland and that he hoped for 'Italy's understanding.' He waited for the Duce's reply with ill-concealed impatience, and was extremely disappointed when Attolico told him that his instructions were still on their way from Rome. Hitler was so anxious for an early reply that he sent Ribbentrop out to telephone to Ciano. It was apparently a matter of the greatest importance to make sure of Mussolini's 'understanding' before taking serious steps against Poland. Ribbentrop returned a short while later having failed to contact Ciano. Attolico was then dismissed with scant courtesy.

Because a visit by the French Ambassador was expected immediately afterwards, I remained in Hitler's office and so witnessed the effect on him of the formal pact of mutual aid just concluded between Britain and Poland. The Press Section had sent him the report, which I read over his shoulder, and then I watched him sit brooding at his desk until the French Ambassador, Coulondre, was announced.

Coulondre was the successor to François-Poncet, who had been transferred to Rome some time after the Munich Conference. I had known Coulondre for more than ten years; he had been head of the Foreign Trade Section at the French Foreign Office, and had therefore sat opposite me at innumerable session of the long Franco-German trade negotiations.

In the course of these negotiations, the elegant, dark, southern Frenchman had always struck me as a man of goodwill, concerned to defend the interests of his country with circumspection and skill, while at the same looking beyond the frontiers of France. I was delighted when he came as Ambassador to Germany, not only because I had a high personal regard for him, but also because I knew from experience that he had the diplomatic talent necessary in the critical period from 1938 to 1939 if disaster was to be averted.

Just as a year before at the time of the Sudeten crisis I had been struck by the statesmanlike wisdom and great diplomatic skill that François-Poncet had displayed, so now Coulondre his successor stood up to Hitler at these critical talks on 25 August 1939.

The Führer made very much the same statement as he had to Henderson four hours earlier. He raged against the Poles, whose provocation he described as intolerable.

He said that even the danger of a war with Britain and France would not prevent him from defending German interests. He would regret it especially if France and Germany were involved in war since there was no point of conflict between the two neighbours now that he had renounced formally all claims to Alsace-Lorraine. Whereas Hitler had confirmed his statement to Henderson in writing, he contented himself with asking Coulondre to report his views to Daladier personally.

In this conversation with Coulondre, Hitler got heated only when attacking the Poles, and expressed lively regret when he touched upon the possibility of war between Germany and France. I had the impression that he was repeating mechanically what he had said to Henderson, and that his thoughts were elsewhere. It was obvious that he was in a hurry to bring the interview to an end. At the end of his own statement when he half rose from his seat to indicate the end of the conversation, Coulondre did not let himself be dismissed so easily. Gravely he asked permission to reply immediately to some of Hitler's statements. Like François-Poncet he spoke forcibly.

I have often recalled his concluding words: 'In a situation as critical as this, *Herr Reichkanzler*, misunderstandings are the most dangerous things of all. Therefore to make the matter quite clear, I give you my word of honour as a French officer that the French army will fight by the side of Poland if that country should be attacked.' Then, raising his voice, he went on, 'But I can also give you my word of honour that the French government is prepared to do everything for the maintenance of peace right up to the last, and to work for moderation in Warsaw.'

'Why then did you give Poland a blank cheque to act as she pleased?' Hitler retorted angrily.

As Coulondre was about to reply, Hitler jumped up and launched into another attack on Poland. 'It would be painful for me to have to proceed against France, but that decision does not depend on me,' he said, and held out his hand to Coulondre, thus terminating the interview. He had talked with him for scarcely half an hour.

The next caller was already waiting outside. It was Attolico who had now brought Mussolini's urgently awaited answer to Hitler's intimation that he was about to intervene actively in Poland. 'In one of the most painful moments of my life,' Mussolini wrote, 'I have to inform you that Italy is not ready for war.'

The letter was a bombshell. Hitler seemed to have forgotten Ciano's clear indication at Berchtesgaden a few days before that Italy was not prepared militarily. Hitler was bitterly disappointed at this sudden and to him completely unexpected defection of his ally.

'According to what the responsible heads of the services tell me,' Mussolini continued, 'the benzine supplies of the Italian air force are so low that they would last only three weeks of fighting. The position is the same with regard to supplies for the army, and supplies of raw materials. Only the head of the navy has been able to acquit himself of culpable negligence; the fleet is ready for action and supplied with sufficient fuel. Please understand my situation.'

Hitler dismissed Mussolini's envoy with an icy gesture saying he would reply to the letter immediately. 'The Italians are behaving just as they did in 1914,'

I heard him say when Attolico had gone, and for the next hour the Chancellery resounded with disparaging remarks about the 'disloyal Axis partner'.

I remained at the Chancellery, since new talks might take place at any moment. During the next few days I was there almost night and day. Until the outbreak of war, there followed an unending stream of conversations between Hitler and the ambassadors. Thus, as well as attending at the diplomatic conversations, from behind the scenes I was able to more or less find out the whole course of events. There was much coming and going in all the rooms and passages of the Chancellery, with the military element predominating.

When I left Hitler's room with Attolico and took my leave of him, Keitel passed me swiftly on his his way to see Hitler. While still wondering which of the various groups I should join standing in the hall, Keitel came rushing out from Hitler's room again. I heard him speaking excitedly to his adjutant and caught the words, 'The order to advance must be delayed again.'

The rumours then had been correct, though due to pressure of work over the last few days I had paid them little attention. An order to move up had actually gone out to the services. Talking to the officers waiting in the hall, I picked up some more details. They all wanted to know whether my classroom would re-assemble.

'If you can tell me that the order to move up is cancelled,' I replied, 'then I would say that a resumption of my class at Munich is not impossible.'

'There will be frighful confusion, and a good deal of swearing on the frontier roads,' a major was saying, 'if the troops on the march are to be ordered back right now.' He added, 'You diplomats are to blame for this; you should have thought things out beforehand, and not sent us off just as everything started to look different.' It was harsh but deserved criticism of the 'diplomat' Hitler. In the Third Reich not even a Foreign Minister could take decisions, let alone the despised diplomats of the Foreign Office.

That same evening, 25 August, Hitler wrote a brief and cool reply to Mussolini. He asked for particulars of the raw materials and weapons needed by Italy in order to make war. The following day we translated Mussolini's answer, brought by Attolico. The demands were so exorbitant that Germany could not possibly have met them. It was quite clear that Mussolini was taking evasive action. Italy again came in for abuse – but not Mussolini.

We had to translate yet another letter from Hitler to Mussolini. He asked his ally to keep his decision to remain neutral a strict secret, and to give every appearance of preparing for war in order to intimidate the western powers. A few hours later Attolico presented Mussolini's agreement to do both.

Over the next few days, verbal or written contact with ambassadors in Berlin and statesmen in London, Paris and Rome continued almost without intermission. It was a sort of long-distance conference by telephone and telegraph and, as interpreter and translator I was kept just as busy as I had been the previous year at Munich when the negotiating parties faced each other across a table.

'If Poland is attacked, the honour of France insists that she fulfil her undertakings,' Daladier wrote to Hitler in a letter brought by Coulondre.

'Would not France act in just the same way if, for instance, Marseilles had for a time been severed from the mother country and its return to France were refused?' Hitler replied.

'Everything turns upon the nature of the settlement with Poland and the methods by which it is reached,' I read, as I translated to Hitler London's reply to his comprehensive offer to Great Britain. 'On these points, the importance of which cannot be absent from the Chancellor's mind, his message is silent, and His Majesty's Government feels compelled to point out that an understanding on both is essential if further progress is to be achieved.'

After again emphasising Britain's determination to carry out her undertaking to Poland, the note declined to discuss Hitler's grandiose offer to collaborate with the British Empire: 'His Majesty's Government could not, for any advantage offered to Great Britain, acquiesce in a settlement that would put in jeopardy the independence of a State to whom they have given a guarantee.'

It proposed as the next step the resumption of direct negotiations between the German and Polish governments, regarding which 'definite assurances from the Government of Poland' had already been received. The note concluded with the following unequivocal words:

A just settlement of these questions between Germany and Poland may open the way to world peace. Failure to reach it would ruin the hopes of a better understanding between Germany and Great Britain, would bring the two countries into conflict, and might well plunge the whole world into war. Such an outcome would be a calamity without parallel in history.

This note was handed in by Henderson on the evening of 28 August. Hitler's reaction was surprisingly quiet. He appeared to have an interest in the British proposal in some way. We translated Hitler's reply during the hours that followed until late in the night. It was not restrained: 'Barbarous atrocities that cry to heaven', 'persecution of the German population in Poland', 'the murder of Germans settled in the country, or their compulsory deportation in the most cruel circumstances', 'a state of affairs that is intolerable to a great power' – these are some samples that indicate the general tone.

'These conditions have now compelled Germany, after being a passive spectator for months, to take necessary active steps to protect legitimate German interests,' our translation ran. 'The present demands of the German Government accord with a revision of the Treaty of Versailles that has always been recognised as necessary – namely the return of Danzig and the Corridor to Germany, and safeguards for the German population in the remainder of Polish territory.'

Hitler too was not lacking in clarity: 'Under these circumstances,' he wrote, 'the German government accepts the British government's offer of mediation under which they will arrange that a Polish plenipotentiary would be sent to Berlin. It expects the arrival of a Polish envoy on Wednesday 30 August 1939 and will prepare its proposals at once.'

Henderson read this document carefully at a further interview with Hitler the next day, 29 August. 'It sounds like an ultimatum,' he commented, on account of the short time allowed for the arrival of the Polish plenipotentiary, 'the Poles are given only twenty-four hours to make their plans.'

Hitler disputed Henderson's pertinent remark on grounds as threadbare as those he had given at Godesberg in his memorandum about the Sudeten question. 'The time is short,' he said, 'because there is the danger that fresh provocation may result in the outbreak of fighting.' Because of constant incidents, the danger of an explosion did actually seem to be growing hourly.

Shortly afterwards Attolico came to see Hitler again. Mussolini reported that the British government had expressed to him on various occasions its willingness to negotiate. I had the clear impression from this message that Mussolini wanted to take the initiative in calling a conference. Hitler obviously realised this but felt no inclination to accept any mediation from 'disloyal' Italy. He replied to Attolico with marked coldness that he was already in direct communication with the British, and had stated that he was ready to receive a Polish plenipotentiary.

On the following day, 30 August, comparative peace reigned after the British Embassy advised Ribbentrop in the early hours that the British government considered it 'unreasonable' to expect that they could arrange for a Polish plenipotentiary to arrive in Berlin the same day. Our time was employed in drafting Hitler's proposals regarding the settlement of the Danzig and Corridor questions. When I saw these proposals I could scarcely believe my eyes. They contemplated a plebiscite in the Polish Corridor under the supervision of an International Commission of British, French, Italian and Russian representatives; they left Gdynia to Poland and awarded only Danzig to Germany; they gave Poland an international road and railway through territory that would become German. They were inspired by a spirit that had little in common with National Socialist methods and the ideas expressed previously by Hitler. It was a real League of Nations proposal. I felt I was back in Geneva.

Shortly before midnight on 30 August, that is to say just before the expiry of the German ultimatum regarding a Polish envoy, the British Embassy telephoned the German Foreign Office unexpectedly advising that Henderson wanted to hand Ribbentrop the British government's reply to the Hitler document of the previous day.

The conversation that ensued was the stormiest that I ever experienced during my twenty-three years as an interpreter. The atmosphere was highly charged, the nerves of the two men worn down by the protracted negotiations in which they had been involved together of late. Ribbentrop had come straight over from the Chancellery and was obviously in a state of almost shivering excitement.

What have they decided over there now? I asked myself as Ribbentrop, pale of face, lips set, eyes shining, sat himself opposite Henderson at a small table in Bismarck's former office at Wilhelmstrasse 76. He had greeted Henderson with an icy expression and stiff formality. The conversation was conducted partly in German, for Henderson liked to speak our language although he was not exactly a master of it. In this critical discussion he would have been able to express himself with more clarity and ease in English. On previous occasions he had often shown this tendency to break into German, and I assume therefore that he meant it to be a friendly gesture on this occasion too.

Henderson began by recalling the messages that had reached us in writing from the British Embassy that day, beginning with the statement that it was 'unreasonable' to expect the British government to be able to produce a Polish plenipotentiary in Berlin within twenty-four hours.

Ribbentrop flared up. 'The time is up,' he said with affected calm. 'Where's the Pole your government was to provide?'

In addition, Henderson handed over a personal communication from Chamberlain to Hitler that stated that the British had made representations in Warsaw to prevent frontier incidents. He also mentioned the British advice to Poland to practise restraint, and requested that Germany should adopt a similar policy.

'The Poles are the aggressors, not we!' Ribbentrop retorted, getting more excited. 'You have come to the wrong address.'

When Henderson then put forward his government's suggestion that in dealing with Poland the Reich should follow the normal procedure and transmit the German proposals through the Polish Ambassador in Berlin, Ribbentrop lost his self-control completely. 'That is out of the question after what had happened,' he shouted at Henderson, 'We demand that a plenipotentiary should come here to Berlin who has full powers to act on behalf of his government.'

Henderson too was beginning to lose the calm, typically British composure that made up his normal character. His face flushed and his hands began to tremble as he proceeded to read the official answer to Hitler's memorandum. The British note passed fairly quickly over the proposals regarding Anglo-German relations and concentrated on the Polish dispute. To avoid incidents, both parties were urged to refrain from aggressive troop movements during the negotiations.

As the individual points were read out, Ribbentrop interrupted Henderson continually. 'That's an unheard-of suggestion,' he said angrily at the recommendation of a temporary cessation to troop movements. Then he crossed his arms and looked at Henderson challengingly: 'Have you anything more to say?' he shouted, in order to indicate that Henderson might continue.

Then for full measure Henderson made a verbal addition to the British note. The British government, he said, possessed information to the effect that Germans were committing acts of sabotage in Poland.

'That's a damned Polish government lie!' retorted the infuriated Ribbentrop. 'I can only tell you, Herr Henderson, that the position is damned serious!'

Henderson in turn now lost his cool. Lifting a forefinger in admonition, he shouted, 'You have just said "damned". That's no word for a statesman to use in so grave a situation.'

This took Ribbentrop's breath away. One of the 'cowardly' diplomats, an ambassador, and an arrogant English one at that, had dared to reprimand him as he might a schoolboy. Ribbentrop jumped up from his chair. 'What did you say?' he roared. Henderson had also risen to his feet. Both man glared at each other.

According to diplomatic convention I too should have risen; but to be frank I did not know how an interpreter should behave when speakers passed from words to deeds – and I really feared that they might do so now. I therefore remained quietly seated and pretended to be writing in my notebook. Above me I could hear the two fighting cocks breathing heavily. The least that can happen now, I thought, is that the Foreign Minister of the German Reich will throw the Ambassador of His Britannic Majesty out the door. In the course of years an interpreter acquires a taste for grotesque situations, but I found nothing comic in this scene, it was extremely embarrassing for the only spectator.

Fortunately it did not come to fisticuffs. I went on scribbling in my notebook, heard more heavy breathing to my right and left and then first Ribbentrop, and next Henderson, resumed their seats either side of me. I raised my head and could see from their expressions that the storm had blown over.

For a while the conversation proceeded in relative calm. Then Ribbentrop drew a paper out of his pocket containing Hitler's 'League of Nations' proposals for the settlement of the Polish dispute. He read them out to Henderson in German without hurrying over them particularly as he was wrongly accused later of having done. On the contrary, he elaborated on some of the points. Then came the surprise.

Henderson asked whether he could be given the text of these proposals for transmission to his government. According to normal diplomatic usage that would follow as a matter of course, and I was rather surprised that Henderson should bother to ask at all. Expecting that Ribbentrop would hand him the paper without further ado, I could scarcely believe it when with a rather embarrassed smile he replied, 'No, I cannot hand you these proposals.'

Henderson must have thought he had misheard, and he repeated his request. Again Ribbentrop declined. Tossing the document on the table he said, 'It is out of date, anyhow, since the Polish plenipotentiary has not appeared.'

This made me agitated. Suddenly I saw the game that Hitler and Ribbentrop were playing. At that midnight hour of 30 August finally I understood that Hitler's high-sounding proposals were only for show, and were never intended to be pursued seriously. The point of refusing to hand the document over to Henderson was that the British government would be bound to pass the proposals to the Poles, who might well have accepted them. As an interpreter, seldom have I regretted so much that I could not intervene in a discussion. The interpreter who says something on his own account is guilty of an unpardonable sin. By so doing, he cannot but create confusion in the minds of the respective partners that the remark came from the other, and naturally there was nothing for me to do but sit grinding my teeth while a chance of peace was deliberately sabotaged before my eyes. So this, I reflected, was what Hitler and Ribbentrop must have been discussing at the Chancellery.

I made one last desperate attempt to transmit the contents of the document to Henderson, gazing at him fixedly and willing him silently to ask for an English translation of the German proposal. Ribbentrop could scarcely have refused this, and I would have translated so slowly as to enable Henderson to take notes. But the British Ambassador did not react, and there was nothing left for me to do but make a thick red mark in my book at the place where I had jotted down Ribbentrop's refusal as a sign that in this hour the die was cast for war.

The supposition I formed as to why Hitler's proposals were handled in so peculiar a manner was later confirmed by Hitler himself in my presence.

'I needed an alibi,' he said, 'especially for the German people, to show them that I had done everything to maintain peace. That explains my generous offer about the settlement of the Danzig and Corridor questions.'

Next day, late on the afternoon of 31 August, I was present at one of the briefest interviews I have ever known. The Polish Ambassador, Lipski, called on Ribbentrop and handed him a short communication stating that the Polish government had accepted the British suggestion of direct negotiations between Germany and Poland, and would send the German government a reply to its proposals forthwith.

'Have you plenipotentiary powers to negotiate with us now on the German proposals?' Ribbentrop asked.

'No,' Lipski replied.

'Well, then there is no point in our continuing this conversation,' said Ribbentrop, and the ultra-short interview was at an end.

Just before this, Attolico had seen Ribbentrop to offer Mussolini's services as mediator once again. Apparently Ribbentrop also lacked authority to negotiate, for he said he had to ask Hitler. Attolico returned in half an hour for the reply; it was in the negative. Ribbentrop said that the next move must come from France and Britain; Germany's demands had been communicated to them.

Activity in the corridors and offices of the Chancellery was again at high pressure. I was on hand there waiting for more work when on the evening of 31 August I heard that Hitler had finally given the order for the invasion of Poland, and that troops were to cross the frontier at 5.45 a.m. the next day:

By order of the Führer and Supreme Commander, the Wehrmacht has taken over the active protection of the Reich. In accordance with its instructions to check Polish aggression, troops of the German army have counter-attacked early this morning across all German-Polish frontiers. Simultaneously, squadrons of the Luftwaffe have flown missions against military objectives in Poland. The Kriegsmarine has taken over the protection of the Baltic.

So ran the first military communiqué of the Second World War, issued on 1 September 1939.

Hitler's hoarse and excited voice addressing the Reichstag rang from the loudspeakers on the morning of 1 September:

Last night for the first time, Polish regular troops also fired on our own territory. Once again I have donned the tunic which was to me the holiest and most beloved of garments, I shall take it off only after victory – or I shall not live to see the end.

That evening the British and French Ambassadors requested an immediate and joint interview with the Foreign Minister. Ribbentrop refused to see them together and made an appointment at 9.30 p.m. for Henderson and 10 p.m. for Coulondre.

Henderson had brought the British note, which I translated for Ribbentrop:

Through its action the German Government has brought about a situation in which the Governments of the United Kingdom and France must proceed to fulfil their obligations to support Poland. Therefore unless His Majesty's Government receives from the German Government satisfactory assurances that the German Government has ceased all aggressive action, and that it is prepared to withdraw its troops from Polish territory, His Majesty's Government will without delay carry out its obligations to Poland.

Ribbentrop behaved as though he understood no English and remained perfectly calm. Apparently he had shot his bolt with Henderson the previous evening. Once again he was apparently not authorised to make a reply and confined himself to a promise to transmit the communication to Hitler.

Directly afterwards, Coulondre handed in the almost identical French note. I had to translate this one too, for Ribbentrop had suddenly been robbed of his ability to understand French. As Henderson had, Coulondre asked for an immediate reply, to which Ribbentrop could only answer that he would submit the matter to Hitler.

Next day, 2 September, the British and French radio stations reported 'General mobilisation ordered in Britain' and 'Mobilisation in France.'

The same morning, Attolico hastened to the Foreign Office. 'Mussolini has suggested to both London and Paris that Germany and Poland conclude an immediate armistice,' he said breathlessly. Mussolini's proposal was that the fronts should be stabilised at their present positions and that an international conference should then meet to consider German–Polish questions and other frontier revision demands.

Half an hour later he was received by Ribbentrop, who put the single question: 'Were the notes that Britain and France handed in yesterday ultimatums or not? If they were, the question of considering the Italian proposal is out of the question.'

I can still see Attolico, no longer in his first flush of youth, running out of Ribbentrop's room and down the steps to consult Henderson and Coulondre.

In my opinion, the notes had been ultimatums, and I did not believe that my 'school class' would meet again as the result of Mussolini's eleventh-hour intervention. To my surprise, however, only half an hour later Attolico came running back as breathless as he had left. 'No, the notes were not ultimatums but warnings.'

Evidently the western powers also trafficked in ultimatums that were not ultimatums, as Hitler had the previous year and again only a few days since.

In the afternoon Attolico came to see Ribbentrop once again, and I became more hopeful.

I have never been able to find out exactly how Hitler reacted to the Italian proposal, but towards evening we learnt that the British government was insisting upon the evacuation of the territory occupied by German forces.

At 8 p.m. I was summoned to the Chancellery where a crushed Attolico was informing Hitler that the British government would not accept Mussolini's proposal unless Polish territory was evacuated. He added that the French government had deliberated for some considerable time whether or not to accept the Italian proposal, but finally fell in line behind Britain.

It was after midnight on the morning of 3 September 1939 when the British Embassy telephoned to say that Henderson had received instructions from London to forward a communication from his government at 9 a.m., and he asked to be received by Ribbentrop at the Foreign Office at that time.

It was clear that this communication could contain nothing agreeable, and that it might possibly be a real ultimatum. Consequently, Ribbentrop showed no inclination to receive the British Ambassador personally later that morning. I happened to be standing near him.

'Really, you could receive the Ambassador as my representative,' he told me. 'Just ask the British if that will suit them and say that the Foreign Minister will not be available at nine o'clock.' The British agreed, and therefore I was instructed to receive Henderson next morning – that is, in five hours time, it now being 4 a.m.

The pressure of work over the last few days had been such that on that Sunday 3 September 1939 I overslept, and had to take a taxi to the Foreign Office. I could just see Henderson entering the building as I drove across the Wilhelmsplatz. I used a side entrance and stood in Ribbentrop's office ready to receive Henderson punctually at 9 a.m. Henderson was announced as the hour struck. He came in looking very serious, shook hands but declined my invitation to be seated, remaining standing solemnly in the middle of the room.

'I regret that on the instructions of my government I have to hand you an ultimatum for the German government,' he said with deep emotion and then, both of us still on our feet, he read out the British ultimatum.

More than twenty-four hours have elapsed since an immediate reply was requested to the warning of 1 September, and since then the attacks on Poland have intensified. If His Majesty's Government has not received satisfactory assurances of the cessation of all aggressive action against Poland and the withdrawal of German troops from that country by eleven o'clock British Summer Time, from that time a state of war will exist between Great Britain and Germany.

When he had finished reading it Henderson handed me the ultimatum and bade me goodbye with the words, 'I am sincerely sorry that I must hand such a document to you in particular, as you have always been most anxious to help.'

For my part I also expressed my regret and added a few heartfelt words. I always had the highest regard for the British Ambassador.

I took the ultimatum to the Chancellery forthwith where most of the Cabinet and party leaders were collected in the anteroom near Hitler's study anxiously awaiting my arrival. There was something of a crush and I had difficulty getting through to Hitler.

'What news?' anxious voices asked.

'Classroom dismissed,' I replied and entered the adjacent study where Hitler was seated at his desk, Ribbentrop to his right near the window. Both looked up expectantly when they saw me. I stopped at some distance from the desk and then slowly translated the British ultimatum. When I finished there was complete silence.

Hitler sat immobile, gazing before him. He was not at a loss, as was stated afterwards, nor did he rage, as others allege. He sat completely still and unmoving.

After an interval that seemed an age, he turned to Ribbentrop, who had remained standing by the window. 'What now?' he asked with a savage look, as though implying that his Foreign Minister had misled him about the probable British reaction.

Ribbentrop answered quietly: 'I assume that the French will hand in a similar ultimatum within the hour.'

As my duty was now performed, I withdrew. To those in the anteroom pressing round me I said, 'The British have just handed us an ultimatum. In two hours a state of war will exist between Britain and Germany.' In the anteroom too, this news was followed by complete silence.

Göring turned to me and said, 'If we lose this war, then God have mercy on us!'

Goebbels stood in a corner, downcast and self-absorbed. Everywhere in the room I saw looks of grave concern, even amongst the lesser party people.

Coulondre handed Ribbentrop an identical ultimatum soon afterwards, which was to expire at 5 p.m.

By an ironic stroke of fate, when I left a blacked-out Berlin that evening in the Foreign Office special train for the east, it was from the same platform of the same station as when I had left my native city in 1917 as a soldier in a goods train.

Dr Paul Schmidt in 1950. (W.J. Pellkan, Munich)

Paul Schmidt with the German delegation in London in 1936. (*The Times*)

Sir John Simon (then British Foreign Minister) and Mr Anthony Eden (then Lord Privy Seal) with Hitler at the Chancellery in Berlin. Paul Schmidt acted as their interpreter. (*Planet News*)

The historic tea party at Berchtesgaden in 1938, showing Mr Neville Chamberlain and Hitler, with Paul Schmidt at the rear between Hitler and Sir Neville Henderson, British Ambassador. (Wide World Photos)

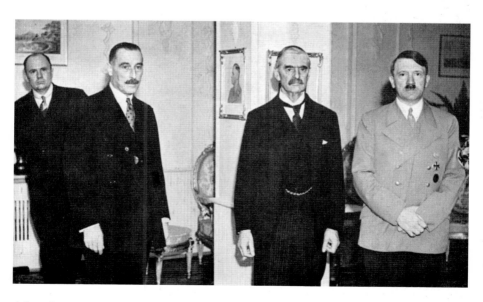

After the tea party: Paul Schmidt is on the left. (*The Times*)

The second meeting at Godesberg: Paul Schmidt talks with Hitler and
Chamberlain. (Wide World Photos)

After the Godesberg Conference in 1938: Chamberlain and Hitler leave the conference room of the Hotel Dreesen followed by Paul Schmidt. (Wide World Photos)

Ribbentrop witnesses the signature of the Polish Frontier Treaty in 1939.
(Wide World Photos)

Pétain greets Hitler: Paul Schmidt is between them; Ribbentrop is on the right.
(Associated Press)

Hitler and Mussolini at the famous Brenner Pass meeting. (Associated Press)

Hitler shakes hands with Franco on the Spanish frontier. (Associated Press)

SIX

3 SEPTEMBER 1939 TO END OF 1940

As I travelled towards the secret destination, the GHQ in the east, on the night of 3 September 1939, it seemed to me that my function as an interpreter had come to an end. The language of weapons that must now settle matters between the peoples of the world needed no translation. But in this I proved to be mistaken.

The HQ turned out to be in Pomerania, close to the Polish border. I was there not as an interpreter, but in the minister's department of the Foreign Office. Some months previously I had been transferred from the Languages Service, in which I had worked since joining the Foreign Office in 1923. The move was made in the beginning of 1939, and was designed to ensure that

I should be available exclusively to Ribbentrop as his interpreter. He took jealous care that no other member of the Cabinet or Department should take part in foreign policy activities, and therefore he always declined to allow others to make use of my services as had been the Foreign Office practice previously. 'Unfortunately I cannot spare Dr Schmidt from my ministerial office,' was his invariable reply to such requests.

I much regretted my loss of freedom in being thus chained to the ministerial office, and also disliked having my work restricted to dealing with files. A wide range of confidential matters came my way it is true, but these were of no great interest to me. As an interpreter I was familiar with all that was disclosed when the great men conferred, and I had become so indifferent to secrets that I no longer sought them out but expected rather that they would find their way naturally to my ears – as in fact they did. So my work lacked even this attraction.

If I was no conventional bureaucrat, neither was the German HQ my idea of a conventional HQ. At the beginning of the Second World War the 'Great Headquarters' consisted of three trains: the Führer-train, the Wehrmacht GHQ train and the Heinrich-train, which housed the civilians attached to HQ. These latter included Himmler (hence 'Heinrich'), Ribbentrop and Lammers. 'Heinrich' was a travelling exhibition of railway development. It displayed the evolution of the railway coach from ancient decorated carriages 'in which Charlemagne had travelled' to Ribbentrop's newly built streamlined saloon. It was made up of almost every variety of model that had ever rolled on German tracks. 'That's some crazy express,' Hitler once said when he saw the 'Heinrich' steaming past with its short, high grand ducal saloon, the old wooden restaurant cars and the super-modern telecommunications coaches in touch with the whole world.

If this arrangement had gone on, conditions would have become impossible, owing to the continual friction between Himmler, Ribbentrop and Lammers. Had the three 'enemy brothers' been forced to travel together in a single train in later years, it would doubtless have exploded from the internal stresses, if the conflicting views of its occupants about the political and geographical routes they wanted to travel had not wrenched it to pieces beforehand. In the early period, however, they were all more or less going in the same direction and even used to pay visits to each other's saloons in the evenings where they put up a show of the greatest cordiality.

The little band from the Foreign Office that accompanied Ribbentrop lived in a Mitropa sleeping car and worked in one of the wooden restaurant cars. The restaurant car accumulators were so weak with age that when the train stopped anywhere, even for half an hour, the lighting would slowly but surely dim and then fade out. Then we would resort to candles stuck in the neck of empty bottles 'like in a bunker at the front' said the few with actual front experience or 'as though we were dining at Savarin's' (the five star restaurant behind the Eden Hotel in Berlin) said most of the 'cowardly pacifists', as Ribbentrop frequently referred to his diplomatic staff.

The Foreign Minister himself disturbed us but little. He sat in his saloon-car office directing operations. This took the form mostly of hour-long telephone conversations with the Foreign Office in Berlin, in the course of which he tended to become wildly excited, his yells resounding far across the lonely railway siding into which we were usually shunted.

Ribbentrop kept me on the run with jobs from morning till night, for I was then the only senior official of the ministerial bureau with him. I had to maintain routine communication with the Berlin office, and often needed all my capabilities as interpreter. Ministerial rebukes to the Under Secretary in Berlin such as: 'Tell that ox ... ,' would have to be rephrased into the conventional form of ministerial disapproval customary in our offices, as would instructions rained down on all the 'cowards', 'lazybones', 'dunderheads' and 'people who don't seem to know there's a war on' who worked in his office. It was all very exhausting.

One of my duties was to make a daily report on the military situation. Each morning I stumbled along the railway track to the Führer-train a few hundred yards away carrying a large General Staff map rolled up under my arm. As I stood rather helplessly before the large-scale operational map, painfully drawing in the new front lines on my copy, one of my acquaintances on the General Staff would usually take pity on me. With skilled accuracy he would draw in the red and blue arrows, racing forward or bent round (where attacks had been repulsed), all beautifully neat, with the necessary explanations.

On my return to 'Heinrich' I would feel my importance grow at each step over the sleepers until I entered the Foreign Minister's office to deliver a situation report according to all the rules. I do not know what Ribbentrop got out of it though my colleagues seemed to be fairly impressed as I scooped in whole areas with the flat of my hand, spread out my fingers to mark the advancing spearheads or represented an encirclement with curved hand. For several days I was called Napoleon.

My martial glory was short-lived, for a General Staff colonel arrived to act as permanent liaison officer for our group. My activities were once again confined to telephone conversations with 'idiots', or to brief written messages to the 'idlers' and 'halfwits' in Berlin.

For some time this headquarters, in the sidings of a small frontier station whose name escapes me, was an ideal target for air attacks. A heavy flak battery had been sent up to protect us, and 'Heinrich' had its own particular protection in the shape of two miniature flak mounted on open goods trucks at either end of the train. Foreign Office staff were trained as gunners, one night one of them fired his weapon accidentally while loading it which culminated a long investigation next morning.

In the latter part of September I got myself into hot water, as was eventually bound to happen in the strained atmosphere: the occasion was the invasion of Poland by Soviet troops on 17 September 1939, news of which we had been awaiting with some impatience.

One of Ribbentrop's main concerns was to see that the control of propaganda for digestion abroad was in his, and not Goebbels' hands. This led to constant friction between the two and absorbed a great deal of Ribbentrop's time and nervous energy, even at the most critical junctures of the war.

On the night of 16 September, Ribbentrop had kept us all busy until 2 a.m. At 5 a.m. I was instructed to inform him that Russian troops had entered Polish territory. I gave him the news, which had been anxiously awaited, three hours later. Ribbentrop was beside himself with rage that I had not woken him at 5 a.m.: 'The German and Russian armies are rushing towards each other – there may be clashes – and all because you were too slack to waken me,' he shouted. I tried in vain to calm him by pointing out that a demarcation line had already been agreed upon, and that German and Russian military authorities were in direct communication. It did no good. At the time Ribbentrop was shaving in his sleeping compartment. He stood there with lathered face, brandishing his razor, and clad only in bathing trunks – a costume in which even the statesman of a great and victorious nation can look very funny. 'You have meddled with the course of world history!' he thundered. 'You do not have the experience for that!'

Shortly after I learned that the row had nothing at all to do with world history, but revolved around Ribbentrop's private war with Goebbels. It was Goebbels and not the Foreign Office press chief who had given out this item of news to the international press in Berlin.

After about two weeks of an unreal existence in railway coaches, FHQ was now transferred to the luxurious Casino Hotel at Zoppot on the Baltic near Danzig. As we sat at breakfast on the hotel terrace, we could watch the bombardment of the Polish base at Hela, 18 miles away at the other end of Danzig Bay, by two old German pre-Dreadnought battleships-of-the-line, *Schlesien* and *Schleswig Holstein*. With their tall funnels and high superstructure they transformed the whole scene into the picture of a naval engagement of times long past, especially when the Polish shore artillery retaliated and waterspouts arose around the ships. Our hotel was beyond the range of the Polish guns, otherwise not much would have been left of that fine building. Punctually at noon the 'naval engagement' was broken off, the ships withdrew to Neufahrwasser and the whole performance was repeated at the same time next day.

On 20 September 1939, Hitler made a major speech in the artistic Artushof of the beautiful city of Danzig, where he was accorded an enthusiastic reception by the citizens of that town. 'I stand for the first time on ground that German settlers acquired 500 years before the first white men settled in the present State of New York,' he said. 'For a further 500 years this ground was, and remained, German. It will, let everybody be assured, always remain German.'

This was the first and only occasion on which I heard a speech of Hitler's from start to finish without having something to do with it officially as interpreter. I was particularly interested to see how events in which I had myself participated were put before the public.

'I worked out the new plan,' Hitler declared, referring his proposals for the settlement of the Polish question. 'It was read to the British Ambassador; it was read to him sentence by sentence and, in addition, my Foreign Minister gave a detailed explanation.'

My mind went back to the stormy interview between Ribbentrop and Henderson when 'the explanation' had almost been put over amidst fisticuffs. Although I listened most carefully, I heard no indication of the fact that Henderson had been refused a written copy of the proposals.

'Poland chose war, and now she has it ... Eighteen days have passed. Never before in history could the saying be more exactly fulfilled: "The Lord broke them into pieces, man, horse and chariot."' So spoke the victorious Hitler describing the Blitzkrieg on Poland. He was triumphant and 'uncompromising', as the German press later described his speech.

'Should the war last three years, the word "capitulation" will not be heard – nor will it after four, five, six or seven years,' I was horrified to hear how long he was thinking it might last. He continued in this boasting, aggressive tone for some time. I realised that there was certainly no immediate prospect of my again interpreting between him and Chamberlain, although this had been suggested at Göring's instigation by a Swedish business man, Dahlerus, in my presence taking notes, in a conversation with Hitler that took place even after war had broken out.

On 26 September 1939 we all returned to Berlin, though Ribbentrop left for Moscow the next day by air without me.

On 1 October Ciano appeared and had two long conversations with Hitler at the Chancellery and a further talk at the Foreign Office with Ribbentrop, now returned from his brief visit. Nothing essentially new emerged: the representative of 'apostate' Italy was received with disdain by both Hitler and Ribbentrop, more especially the latter. Hitler was so elated by the success of 'lightning war' in Poland that he was glad of a new audience, and went on for hours recapitulating all the phases of the campaign and giving detailed accounts of the prisoners and booty taken. Ciano's expression reminded me of the refrain of Willy Prager's popular song in Berlin pre-1933, 'So genau wollen wir das gar nicht wissen' – 'We don't want to have all the details' – and neither was it the first or last time that the expression on the faces of Hitler's and Ribbentrop's visitors reminded me of it.

Ribbentrop was extremely pleased with himself – not over the Polish campaign, but over his success in Moscow. He raved enthusiastically about the Russians as he had done to me on his first visit to the Russian capital, until the Italians also 'didn't want to have any more of the details'. At a dinner he gave at his Berlin Dahlem villa, Ribbentrop really exceeded himself. Marked by often long and icy silences during which Ciano would address himself to me, he remarked that he felt as much at home in the company of the 'strong-faced men' surrounding Stalin as he did with old party members. He had made this remark once before at the Reich Chancellery in my presence to an audience of veteran party members and he had come in for heavy criticism. These were men who held Ribbentrop in contempt because he had delayed joining the NSDAP until shortly before Hitler assumed power.

When I translated this remark, Ciano gazed blankly at his plate; no 'ally' could have shown his displeasure more clearly. Ribbentrop frequently displayed a considerable lack of diplomatic tact and behaved on this occasion abominably. 'The Russians at the Kremlin rather reminded me of the Duce's Guard of Honour at the Palazzo Venezia,' he added innocently – and for the rest of the evening Ciano spoke only to me.

I had frequent opportunities to talk to Ciano elsewhere than this frigid dinner party. I came to know and have a regard for this man who, despite his frequently arrogant and somewhat uncivilised behaviour on official occasions, perceived the trend of events with great clarity and did not allow himself to be blinded by the fine words of Hitler and Ribbentrop. He had come to Berlin this time in an effort to improve German–Italian relations, which had cooled noticeably in Rome. His sceptical verdict on our opening successes in no way altered the opinion he had expressed to me at Salzburg in August, namely that once Britain and France embarked upon war, the end would not be swift and the outcome more than uncertain.

Soon after Ciano's departure, the Languages Service entered upon one of those major campaigns that recurred throughout the course of the war. Nominally, I was no longer attached to this important and busy Foreign Office Section; nor was I its head, but instead was made responsible for everything to do with foreign languages, and was given absolute authority in this work. If I advised Hitler or Ribbentrop of my need for technical necessities to complete a task successfully, they would always arrange for me to have it.

When in wartime Germany a speech or announcement was to be broadcast 'in thirty languages', the preparatory work would already have been done by an organisation unknown to the public; even within the Foreign Office it was looked at somewhat askance owing to its mixed composition. Over the course of several years, Privy Councillor Gautier made the Languages Service into a splendidly functioning precision instrument capable of handling the most difficult of translation jobs. Even during the war, the Service was a League of Nations in miniature. Its personnel included British, French, Spanish, Portuguese, Yugoslav, Bulgarian and other nationals. In later years it had branches in Paris and other European cities. For a major assignment, as many as 150 people would be employed.

Secrecy was assured by a method similar to that employed by the Americans for the German currency reform of 1948, when the German experts were put to work under lock and key in an unknown place. In October 1939 the Languages Service occupied two floors of the vacant Adlon Hotel in Berlin sealed hermetically from the outside world. Here, as on a desert island, the 'little League of Nations' could live and work days at a time; the telephone was disconnected, the approach to the floors was guarded and outside below the windows the watchful eyes of plain clothes police saw to it unobtrusively that the island remained an island.

The big speech that Hitler made at the Kroll Opera House on 6 October 1939 was translated into many languages at the Adlon. It was one of those speeches in which one would have preferred 'not to have had all the details' and consisted of a precise and in-depth account of the Polish campaign, the story of the German attempts at a settlement, of attacks against Britain and 'the Western plutocracies', and it had all the usual trappings of speeches of this kind – technical facts and statistical information alternating with lyrical rhetoric and furious tirades of hate.

The tail end of the speech was of great interest to the Languages Service, from whose members one could often get an indication of the likely reaction of foreign countries. These seemed to us the important points: 'Clarification of the foreign policy aims of all European States': 'No further revision necessary except with regard to the return of the German colonies … which is in no way immediate'; 'Reorganisation of markets and a final settlement of the means of exchange'; 'Reduction of armaments to a reasonable and economic level'; 'A European Constitution that will give all peoples a sense of security and therefore ensure peace.'

Reaction abroad, at least as far as the leading politicians were concerned, was nevertheless completely negative. Hitler's words, after the experiences of March and August 1939, no longer had credit:

> Hitler was certainly relying on His Majesty's Government willingly accepting the decision of battle in Poland, and that his offer of peace to Mr Chamberlain and his old colleagues, once they had saved face by a declaration of war, would get them out of the fix in which they had been put by the warmongering elements in Parliament. He was also not at all sure that Chamberlain and the entire British Empire might not now be intent upon a bloody fight to the finish, even if it meant that they themselves went under.

This is more or less how in his memoirs Churchill summed up the reaction to Hitler's peace offensive.

'The position is now clear. Britain and France have rejected the Führer's proffered hand of peace. They have thrown down the gauntlet and Germany has taken it up.' So said an official statement edited by Ribbentrop on 21 October 1939, which we translated in the Languages Service. The war with Poland was won, but the peace offensive had failed.

In a speech to the Italian Chamber in mid December, Ciano avenged himself for the rough handling he had been accorded in Berlin. He said that the so-called Pact of Steel, signed with so much ceremony in Berlin the previous year, provided that Germany and Italy should remain permanently in close touch in order to safeguard the peace of Europe for a period of from three to five years. In order to achieve this aim, no political questions were to be raised that might provoke new crises. The Pact of Steel had been concluded in the same spirit as the Anti-Comintern Pact, and made no provision for the possibility of an agreement between Germany and the Soviet Union, and about which Italy had first had notice as the German Foreign Minister was actually getting into the plane for Moscow.

'The British Ambassador congratulated me on the speech,' Ciano noted in his diary. Ribbentrop was furious when he read it, and in addition to Ciano's highly critical remarks about Hitler's action, a letter from Mussolini was received in Berlin on 4 January 1940 in which the Duce tried suggesting to Hitler that he needed to reach an understanding with the western powers, and hinted that he himself could act as mediator. He considered that a pre-condition would have to be the continuance of an independent Polish State. He went on to point out that great powers fell not through attack from without, but lack of unity within. Britain and France would certainly never cause Germany to capitulate, but neither could Germany bring the democracies to their knees. It was a delusion to believe so.

In this letter I first noticed the tendency, later increasingly apparent in talks between Hitler and Mussolini, of the latter's desire for coming to terms with the West, and to turn against Soviet Russia. 'I feel it my duty to add,' Mussolini wrote, 'that any further developments of your relations with Moscow would have catastrophic results in Italy, where anti-Bolshevik feeling, particularly amongst the Fascist masses, is unanimous and hard as granite'. That this was an allusion to Ribbentrop's gushing enthusiasm for the Kremlin's 'hard-faced men' could not have been plainer. 'The solution to your *Lebensraum* problem lies in Russia, not elsewhere.'

I do not know what kind of reception Hitler gave to this critical letter from Mussolini. He cannot have been particularly pleased about it, for he took two months to reply. It was not until the beginning of March, 1940 that the German Foreign Minister carried Hitler's answer to Rome. I accompanied Ribbentrop on this visit.

Early in March before we left, however, there took place the weird interlude of the visit to Germany of Roosevelt's emissary Sumner Welles from the US Foreign Office. His European tour including Berlin, London, Paris and Rome gave rise to all kinds of sensational rumours throughout Europe.

In Germany, people felt a stirring of hope, although the press hardly mentioned Sumner Welles' presence in Berlin. Hitler was well aware of the

German people's craving for peace and had only very reluctantly agreed to receive Roosevelt's envoy. Neither Hitler, Ribbentrop nor the Foreign Office knew of a reason for this unexpected visit.

In the long talks they had with Sumner Welles, Hitler, Göring and Ribbentrop were all on the defensive. With varying degrees of skill, they sought to demonstrate Germany's strength, power and determination to fight. They were at pains to avoid showing any sign of a readiness to compromise, which Hitler, with his inferiority complex, always feared might be interpreted as a sign of weakness.

I found Sumner Welles an exceptionally intelligent man, if not a very imaginative diplomat. He showed the Germans no cordiality in his conversations. Tall and slim, of aristocratic bearing, he would sit like a block of ice and begin each conversation by defining his mission, namely that the United States was interested in the creation of lasting peace in Europe, and not in a temporary truce; his government had sent him to ascertain what were the possibilities of such a peace. He could, however, make no proposals, nor could he undertake any obligations on behalf of the United States. He reminded me of the French Ambassador to London, René Massigli, who on a similar mission during Franco-German negotiations in the 1920s opened the discussion with the words, 'I am no more than a pencil with two ears.'

Even if Hitler had been eager to start peace talks, the frigid, reserved attitude of the American envoy would hardly have encouraged him. As the German attitude was in fact just the reverse, the speeches that attracted so much interest were almost similar renderings by Hitler, Ribbentrop, Göring and Hess. As an interpreter I was in a position to notice this and it certainly lightened my work. There were of course differences in tone and minor detail.

It was the 'diplomat' amongst these leading national Socialists who behaved most undiplomatically. Sumner Welles said that the 'most astonishing experience of his whole mission' was his meeting with Ribbentrop, who received him 'without even the trace of a smile and without a word of greeting,' and suddenly could not understand English. In my opinion Göring, as on other occasions, was the most skilful and most natural.

It would be pointless to relate the details of these conversations. Once can only say that that bore no relation to the hopes of peace they aroused in Germany – and I realised that hope had been aroused from the repeated anxious questions of my friends and acquaintances.

Sumner Welles was a good deal more friendly in personal conversation. On the long drive to see Göring at Karinhall, he told me much of interest about his experiences in South America. 'I often had to use interpreters at conferences there,' he said, 'so I am in a position to know what a good interpreter you are.' Sumner Welles left Germany on 3 March 1940 and with his departure I had the impression that the last chance for a peaceful halt to the war had disappeared.

Cordell Hull, at this time US Secretary of State, made the following interesting remark in his memoirs: 'The President stated to me expressly that Welles had come to him secretly on several occasions and pleaded to be sent abroad on a special mission.' Cordell Hull was opposed to this as it would be bound to arouse false hopes, but against his express advice the journey was undertaken.

As I mentioned earlier, a few days after this American visit I left with Ribbentrop and a large delegation for Rome to deliver Hitler's reply to Mussolini's critical letter received in January. Both the contents of the reply and what Ribbentrop said to Mussolini personally at the Palazzo Venezia showed that Germany was determined to settle her problems by war and emphasised that Italy's place was at Germany's side. Ribbentrop also dropped a hint of forthcoming military operations against the western powers. 'In a few months,' he predicted, 'the French army will be annihilated and those few British who remain on the Continent will be there as prisoners of war.' At first Mussolini listened very thoughtfully to Ribbentrop's highly coloured descriptions of German strength and his urgings on the necessity of an adjustment by force of arms. Then to my astonishment he came out with the remark that he too was of the opinion that Fascism might fight side by side with National Socialism.

In a second conversation the following day, Mussolini had now suddenly turned pro-war. He was ready to plunge into the conflict at Germany's side, I heard him say, except that he must decide for himself when the appropriate moment would be. Ribbentrop was obviously reassured, for he had come to Rome very doubtful as to the sentiments of the 'disloyal' Axis partner. He felt that the right moment had come to put forward the suggestion of a meeting between Hitler and Mussolini at the Brenner, which Hitler had authorised him to make. Mussolini accepted with enthusiasm.

The great event of this visit to Rome, as far as I and most of our delegation was concerned, was the audience with the Pope, which took place the following day. Mussolini was particularly pleased about this – in his conversations with Hitler and Ribbentrop he had frequently urged Germany to establish good relations with the Catholic Church, often citing his own success in the matter.

Three papal cars took Ribbentrop and ourselves to Vatican City. The Swiss guard, with ancient helmets and halberds, formed a cortège within the Pope's palace, and the whole audience took place with the solemn ceremony reserved for great occasions at the Vatican. Pope Pius XII was better known to us as the Nuncio Pacelli, having represented the Holy See in Berlin in the 1920s. He had a long conversation with Ribbentrop in German and then addressed some friendly words to the delegation, speaking very warmly of his time in Berlin. He then dismissed us with convincing good wishes for ourselves and our country but omitted the apostolic blessing.

None of the statesmen I got to know in my long career made so deep an impression upon me in so short a time by appearance and bearing alone as Pope Pius XII. His tall, slim form with narrow spiritual face standing before us in Papal robes impressed me as a being already to some extent no longer of this world.

What Ribbentrop discussed in private with the Pope I do not know, although he emerged apparently quite impressed and seemed not dissatisfied with the interview. On the other hand he did get very annoyed with Cardinal Maglione, whom he went to see after the Papal audience. 'If he had continued to talk to me as he did,' Ribbentrop told us, 'I would have got up and walked out. I had already reached for my hat.'

We were back in Berlin on 13 March, but a few days later we travelled south once again for the Brenner meeting of 18 March 1940. This was the first of a series of such rendezvous that took place periodically during the war. It was the fourth time that Hitler and Mussolini met for talks face to face.

The frontier railway station at Brenner, 4,500ft above sea level and within 300 yards of the then German frontier, is well known to all German travellers to Italy. The snow still lay deep as Hitler's special train drew into the left hand platform, finding Mussolini's train already stationed opposite. The Duce and Ciano greeted Hitler and Ribbentrop on the platform, and escorted them to Mussolini's carriage where discussions began immediately.

These Brenner conferences attracted much outside attention, as they often appeared to herald some new development. All traffic over the Brenner Pass had to come to a standstill. Whether it was a question of international passenger expresses or urgently needed coal trains, the two dictators held up the entire traffic. The conferences could not be described as discussions in the proper sense of the word: 'Hitler's Brenner Monologues' would be a more appropriate term, for the Führer always spoke for 80 to 90 per cent of the time while Mussolini would only manage to get in a few words at the end. The personal relationship between them appeared to be friendly enough and continued to be so right up to the last meeting before the fall of Mussolini on 20 July 1943. They did not meet on equal terms, however; already by 1940 Hitler had taken over the leadership and forced Mussolini into the role of junior partner.

On this occasion a self-important Hitler gave the attentive and admiring Duce a detailed description of his successful Polish campaign and spoke of his preparations for the great struggle with the West. Numbers and figures piled up. Hitler had an amazing ability to carry in his head troop strengths, casualty figures and the state of reserves as well as technical details about guns, panzers and infantry weapons. He seemed less interested in the Luftwaffe and Kriegsmarine. In any case, he was able to smother Mussolini with facts and figures to such an extent that the Duce goggled in wonder like a child with a new toy.

I was struck particularly by the fact that Hitler avoided giving Mussolini any precise information about his forthcoming military plans. I knew that all preparations had been made for an offensive in the West, the date for which had been set several times and then postponed. I also knew of the planned attack on Norway and Denmark, which occurred on 9 April, three weeks later.

Hitler had no confidence in the discretion of the Italians – indeed he had worked out a theory that Italy was to blame for the outbreak of war. I heard him say more than once: 'The House of Savoy told the British Royal Family that Italy would not enter the war. As a result the British thought that without undue risk they could conclude the alliance with Poland that led to the war.'

To my surprise – and, as I learned later, to the consternation of his associates – Mussolini used the few minutes left to him to reassert his intention to come into the war.

Ciano's diary entry for 19 March the next day says: 'He (Mussolini) resented the fact that Hitler did all the talking, he had in mind to tell him many things and instead he had to keep quiet most of the time – a thing which, as dictator, or rather the doyen of dictators, he is not in the habit of doing.'

What caused Mussolini to change his mind about entering the war is not clear. As Ciano once said, and I had seen for myself, undoubtedly he allowed himself to be 'fascinated' by Hitler's spate of words at the Brenner meeting. A contributory cause was that the Allies, with a clumsiness that seems incomprehensible, had cut off his coal supplies coming round by collier from Holland. In doing this they not only wounded Mussolini's pride, but put Hitler in the position of being able to allow these coal deliveries to be made overland through Germany.

Some three hours later the special trains drew out of the little station, and normal traffic resumed.

On Mussolini's instructions, Ciano had asked me urgently to let him have a copy just as our train was leaving, and I dictated the draft during the return journey. As had happened with Chamberlain at Obersalzberg, so now there were difficulties about Mussolini seeing my report. Hitler was very much opposed to handing it over to the Italians. 'One never knows,' he said to me, 'who may read this document on the Italian side and what Allied diplomats may be told.' For the next few days Mussolini importuned the German Ambassador in Rome for my report continually, and in the end Hitler agreed to send it although, as happened on many similar occasions, he drafted an abbreviated version himself.

In these cases, Hitler never interfered with statements made to him. With regard to his own statements he would make no alterations but deleted items about which he had second thoughts. What remained contained no inaccuracies but was often incomplete at many essential points. Thus a report would often exist in two versions, both of them with my signature, one for home, the other for foreign consumption, and in most cases even I could only distinguish between them by comparing them with my original notes. Historians will later have to ask themselves whether the report they are handling is Hitler's abbreviated version, or the fair copy corrected by Ribbentrop for the German archives, or the original that I dictated from my shorthand note as interpreter. In the case that my reports were not wanted by Hitler's conversation partners, he would generally take no further interest in them, though Ribbentrop usually went through them carefully.

The Italians spotted that my report on the Brenner meeting had been abbreviated by Hitler. 'Mackensen brought the Brenner report from Berlin,' Ciano noted in his diary on 1 April 1940; 'It is not in the verbatim style of Schmidt's other reports, there has been a fairly considerably shortening.'

Three weeks after the Brenner meeting, Ribbentrop instructed me to re-intern the Languages Service in the closed Adlon Hotel. On the night of 8 April 1940 we translated the German memorandum to Norway and Denmark that preceded the occupation of those two countries. 'The government of the Reich possesses irrefutable evidence that Britain and France intend the surprise occupation of certain territories of the northern states in the immediate future ...'

I translated this document regarding Germany's impending assault on the neutrality of the Scandinavian countries with bitter feelings, for I looked on the statement about the British and French intentions as a mere pretext.

What I did not know then is recorded in Mr Churchill's memoirs: 'On 3 April the British Cabinet implemented the resolve of the Supreme War Council, and the Admiralty was authorised to mine the Norwegian 'Leads' on 8 April ... As our mining of Norwegian waters might provoke a German retort, it was also agreed that a British brigade and a French contingent should be sent to Narvik to clear the port and advance to the Swedish frontier. Other forces should be despatched to Stavanger, Bergen and Trondheim, in order to deny these bases to the enemy.'

We made a translation of the German memorandum for Mussolini too; a short letter from Hitler accompanied it. This was the first information he gave his dictator colleague about the venture.

The following month on the afternoon of 9 May, I was summoned unexpectedly by Ribbentrop together with the head of our Press and Radio Section. 'The attack against the west on the whole front from Switzerland to the North Sea starts early tomorrow,' Ribbentrop told us. I was to pack together the Languages Service once again for the translation of a new government memorandum, and for Ribbentrop's statements to the press. Ribbentrop went on to say, 'If news of this offensive leaks out through one of your sections, the Führer will have you shot. I shall not be able to save you.'

This time the Languages Service did not gather at the Adlon, which was regarded as not safe enough, but in the staterooms of the former Palace of the Reich President. Ribbentrop had spent millions on having it modernised, and it was now his official residence. He told me personally to collect the individual Languages Services groups into certain Foreign Office rooms as unobtrusively as possible, and then conduct them through twisting passages and by the backstairs into his palace in such a way that nobody would know precisely where he actually was − 'lest anyone should throw a note to an accomplice in the street,' Ribbentrop said, suddenly become a VIP in hiding.

All this was duly done, and that night the staterooms of the Foreign Minister's palace, with their costly candelabras, genuine gilding, luxurious furniture, paintings, Gobelin tapestries and deep pile carpets were transformed into busy offices.

The various language groups worked in separate corners. Above the rattle of typewriters I could hear the phrases of the memorandum addressed to Belgium and the Netherlands being thrashed out in English, French, Italian and Spanish: 'In this battle for survival forced upon the German people by Britain and France, the Reich government declines to remain inactive and wait for the war to be carried through Belgium and the Netherlands into German territory. Accordingly it has now ordered German troops to safeguard the neutrality of those countries with all the military resources of the Reich,' said Hitler's version of protecting neutrality.

In the middle of the night there was great excitement when Ribbentrop was told that the Dutch military attaché had transmitted the news of the forthcoming invasion to his government. 'Has someone in the Languages Service made contact with the outside world?' Ribbentrop asked me nervously. 'Go quickly through all the rooms and see if all the translators are still there.' While I was making my count, he sent his police adjutant on the same mission. 'You'd better do a count too,' he told him. 'Schmidt knows languages, but I don't know what he's like at counting.' Nobody was missing.

At dawn Ribbentrop lost a major battle in his private war when Goebbels broadcast the proclamation, which the Foreign Minister had intended to announce himself. 'My whole Broadcasting Section is dismissed without notice for inefficiency!' he screamed, livid with rage, while through the loudspeaker in the background the mellifluous tones of his arch-enemy could be heard reading out the fateful memorandum.

To complete the picture of utter confusion that our conduct of foreign affairs would have presented to an impartial observer, Ribbentrop handed the already broadcast memorandum to the unfortunate Belgian Ambassadors and the Dutch Minister, making a wordy statement as he did so. He also made a grotesque statement to the press in which he said that we had anticipated a 'new act of aggression and desperation whereby the present governments in France and Britain seek to save the threatened existence of their Cabinets.'

In the following weeks events succeeded one another at lightning speed. Within a few weeks Holland was occupied, the Belgian army under King Leopold had capitulated, the British had succeeded in escaping at Dunkirk and the French had been swept back by the German flood. Brussels and Paris were occupied undamaged, their governments having sensibly declared them open cities.

Ribbentrop set up his 'field HQ' in the well-known Château d'Ardenne Hotel near Dinant. It was sad to see the luxurious surroundings of the famous hotel gradually becoming victim to weeds, and sad, too, to live in grand suites without light, water or employees.

On 10 June Ciano handed François-Poncet the Italian declaration of war, for Mussolini had at last decided 'to assist in the war at Hitler's side'.

'You can probably guess why I have sent for you,' Ciano said to François-Poncet.

'I have never considered myself particularly intelligent,' he replied, 'but I have just enough understanding to grasp that now you want to hand me a declaration of war.' This story went the rounds with us after Italian colleagues had passed it on with unconcealed joy at the French Ambassador's ready answer.

The Spanish Foreign Office informed us on 17 June that the French government at Bordeaux had asked the Spanish Ambassador to request from the German government an armistice.

That afternoon we flew with Hitler and Ribbentrop to Munich, where Hitler and Mussolini had a short discussion next day in the Führer-building on the Königsplatz, in the same room in which the conference with Chamberlain and Daladier had taken place in 1938.

Hitler was surprisingly conciliatory, being in favour of not subjecting France to oppressive armistice conditions. Mussolini wanted to demand the handing over of the French Fleet, but Hitler was emphatically against it. 'If we make that demand,' he said, 'the whole French Fleet will defect to the British.' Hitler also rejected Mussolini's suggestion of joint armistice negotiations. 'I would not think of burdening our negotiations with Franco-Italian animosity,' he explained afterwards to Ribbentrop.

I noted with some surprise that Hitler's attitude to Britain seemed to have changed. Suddenly he was wondering if it really would be a good thing to destroy the British Empire. 'It is, after all, a force for order in the world,' he said to the rather nonplussed Mussolini. Even his fanatical rage against the Jews seemed to have abated. 'One could found a State of Israel in Madagascar,' he observed to Mussolini when they were discussing the future of the French colonial empire.

It is interesting in this context to note a situation assessment that Churchill had passed to Roosevelt three days previously on 14/15 June 1940, which he revealed in the second volume of his war memoirs:

A declaration that the United States will enter the war if necessary might save France. If not, French resistance could collapse in the next few days leaving us alone. Although the present Government and I personally would never shrink back from sending the British Fleet across the Atlantic if the resistance here were broken, nevertheless a situation could arise during the fighting in which the present ministers no longer had the matter in their hands and the British Isles could receive easy terms and so become a vassal state of the Hitler Reich.

A pro-German Government would be formed to conclude a peace treaty, one thinks, and it might give a very groggy or starving population almost irresistible arguments for submitting to the will of the Nazis.

The fate of the British Fleet would, as already mentioned, be decisive for the future of the United States because if the British Fleet joined those of Japan, France and Italy and the great German industrial Power, Hitler would have overwhelming naval power in his hands.

If we are defeated then you will perhaps be left with a United States of Europe under Nazi mastery, and this combination of states would be numerically much stronger, much more powerful and far better armed than the New World ...

As soon as the Munich talks were over, we flew back to the Franco–Belgian frontier. On 20 June I was summoned to Hitler's HQ in a small village in eastern France to be given the text of the armistice conditions: a French version had to be ready to hand over to a French delegation at Compiègne next day. The small Italian-language group was working in the vicinity of Hitler's HQ as they had to be available for the translation of letters to Mussolini, and I had arranged some time before that one of them should also be a good translator into French; fortunately I had also arranged for another translator to be flown out from Berlin. With this miniature Languages Service I worked through the night of 20 June in the tiny, candlelit French village church. I found it a rather lugubrious place to be translating the conditions to be imposed on France: below the draped altar the low voices of the translators mingled with the clatter of typewriters. What a contrast this was to the brightly lit rooms of Ribbentrop's palace where not so long ago the documents were translated for the war with France whose last act was now being prepared – here, among a babel of many languages and the monotonous run of duplicating machines.

Point I of the historic document stated:

The French government orders the cessation of hostilities against the German Reich in France, in French possessions, colonies, protectorates and mandated territories, and at sea. It decrees the immediate laying down of their arms by those French units now surrounded by German forces. French territory to the north and west of the line shown on the attached map will be occupied by German troops.

The French for such phrases as 'demobilisation and disarmament', 'transport material and transport routes', 'prohibition of radio transmissions', 'resettlement of the population' echoed in the nave.

The German government solemnly declares to the French government that it does not intend to make use of the French fleet during the war ... It solemnly and emphatically declares further that it does not intend to make any demands on the French fleet at the conclusion of peace.

This was Hitler's decision, which Mussolini had contested at Munich.

We were also obliged to translate some ominous conditions:

'The French government undertakes to hand over on demand all Germans in France named by the German government.'

I thought immediately of my former colleague Jacob, whose voice I used to hear reading the news on Radio Strasbourg after he had immigrated to France. I hoped he had got away from France in time – and so he had, for I later heard the voice I knew so well on the Boston short-wave German programme.

'Members of the French armed forces who are in German captivity will remain prisoners of war until the conclusion of peace.'

All the misery of long captivity that I remembered so well from the period of the First World War came back to me as I translated this condition.

From time to time Keitel and occasionally Hitler himself came to see us in the church in order to make sure that the work would be finished in time, or to make last-minute alterations in the German text. There must have been a conference room nearby where the armistice conditions we had translated were subjected to a final scrutiny. It was not until past midnight that the last sheet was sent over to us, and by dawn the task was completed, and a fair copy had been made for the French.

I drove back hurriedly to Château d'Ardenne in order to get a little rest after the strenuous night's work, for I was on duty at the armistice negotiations that were to start the same day, 21 June 1940. After two hours' sleep I was awoken by an orderly. I was to drive at once with Ribbentrop to Compiègne since fog made flying impossible. I hustled into my uniform and rushed out of the house to the car in which the impatient Ribbentrop was waiting for me.

'Drive as fast as you can,' Ribbentrop told the chauffeur, 'The interpreter must not be late for armistice negotiations!' We sped along 'without regard to casualties' at 75mph over the excellent motor roads of northern France, through the battlefields of the First World War and the villages and towns on which the Second World War had now laid its destructive hand in a tragic repetition of that event. For the first time since 1918 I saw the outward manifestations of war. It was a depressing sight; the clock seemed to have been put back, and the hopes I had cherished in the 1920s in my work for Stresemann, Briand and Austen Chamberlain – hopes to which I had still clung at Munich in 1938 – now seemed finally dissipated. Nevertheless, hope stirred anew on this journey through areas devastated by the new war. Was I not, I reflected, on my way to armistice negotiations? That afternoon the shedding of blood would come to an end between Germany and France at least. Perhaps it was the beginning of a better peace, I thought.

By 2 p.m. we were slightly ahead of our hellish schedule and stopped on a hill near Compiègne for a lunch consisting of one sandwich and a bottle of mineral water. Thus fortified, we drove into the historic forest where stood, in bright sunshine in the well-known clearing, the famous wooden railway restaurant car in which the armistice with Germany had been signed on 11 November 1918. I had often seen this car in Paris, where it was on show in the 1920s, but naturally I never dreamt that one day I should sit in it amongst the conquerors facing a French delegation.

Shortly after 3 p.m. I went alone to the restaurant car, which was empty. Along the centre, where travellers had dined before the First World War, a long plain table had been set up with five or six chairs on either side for the two delegations. My place was at the head of the table so that I could see and hear both the Germans and the French.

Soon afterwards Hitler arrived with Göring, Raeder, Brauchitsch, Keitel, Ribbentrop and Hess and sat at my right; a few minutes later there appeared the French General Huntziger, Ambassador Noël, Vice Admiral Leluc and Air Force General Bergeret. Hitler and his associates stood up without a word; both delegations made brief bows, then they sat down at the table and negotiations began.

Keitel read out the preamble to the armistice conditions. 'After heroic resistance ... France has been defeated. For that reason Germany does not intend that the Armistice conditions or negotiations should demean so courageous an enemy.' I translated into French from the text we had prepared during the night. 'The aim of the German demands is to prevent a resumption of hostilities, to give Germany security for the further conduct of the war against Britain, which she has no choice but to continue, and also to create the conditions for a new peace which will repair the injustice inflicted by force on the German Reich.'

When I had finished reading the French text, Hitler and his companions rose. The French stood up too, and after short bows on both sides, the majority of the German party left. The first act of the Compiègne drama lasted exactly twelve minutes. During this time the French and Germans had sat opposite each other with fixed stares like wax figures.

Of the Germans only Keitel and I remained in the coach. Then a few more German officers entered and the second act began. The actual armistice conditions were handed to the French by Keitel in both the French and German texts. The French read them carefully and asked for a short interval in which to consider them. Everybody left the coach. A small conference tent had been set up at the edge of the wood for the French; we Germans contented ourselves with a little clearing amongst the trees. After a time the French sent someone over to say that they were ready to continue negotiations. When we had all assembled in the coach once more the French stated that they would have to transmit the conditions to the government at Bordeaux before they could even comment on them, let alone sign them.

'Absolutely impossible!' Keitel said, 'You must sign at once.'

'In 1918 the German delegation was allowed to make contact with its government in Berlin,' Huntziger replied, 'and we ask for the same facility.' A lively discussion followed amongst the Germans. Keitel asked the German officer sitting next to him whether telephonic communication with Bordeaux was technically possible. The German officer did not know: after all, the two countries were actually still at war and divided by a front of iron and steel. Eventually an improvised line was in the process of being set up, and Keitel told the French that he was prepared to let them telephone. Negotiations continued for two hours meanwhile. A Staff officer then reported that the connection was in hand: a line had been laid from the wood to the coach, and a telephone apparatus installed in the former kitchen of the restaurant car.

'We'll have Bordeaux on the line in five minutes,' a signals officer reported. The German delegation withdrew to allow the French to telephone to their government from the kitchen undisturbed.

I was instructed to eavesdrop the conversation from a signals coach in the woods. A simple private had set himself up on the ground in front of this coach with a couple of accumulators, some dry batteries and a simple field telephone as an improvised telephone exchange. He kept shouting something into the instrument. At first I did not understand what he was saying, but then it dawned on me that he was talking French with a Berlin accent.

'*Ici Compiègne,*' I made out at last. He repeated it at least twenty times and suddenly he started: the other end had answered. '*Oui, mademoiselle, je vous donne la délégation française,*' I heard the corporal say, though still with a very thick Berlin accent. Once again here we had an extraordinary contrast: from the heart of a French forest, in the middle of a new war, somebody was ringing a 'mademoiselle' in Bordeaux as though it were the most natural thing in the world. It would be difficult for anyone to realise now, years afterwards, how unreal that scene in the forest of Compiègne seemed to me at the time.

Quickly I came back to earth and put on my earphones. 'Yes, General Weygand speaking,' I heard the French commander-in-chief say from Bordeaux. His voice was clear.

'Huntziger here,' came the reply, loud and clear, from the restaurant car kitchen, which I could see through the undergrowth. 'I am telephoning from the coach' – a pause – 'from the coach you know.' (Weygand had been present at the armistice negotiations in 1918 as adjutant to Foch.)

'Have you got the conditions?' Weygand asked impatiently.

'Yes,' replied Huntziger.

Weygand came back at once with 'What are they like?'

'*Les conditions sont dures, mais il n'y a rien contre l'honneur.*' (The conditions are hard but there is nothing dishonourable.)

During the next few hours several conversations continued between Bordeaux and Compiègne: in the intervals between them discussions went on in the restaurant car. The negotiations went on until dusk; Keitel grew impatient, but there were further technical questions to be dealt with. Next morning the discussions resumed at 10 a.m. and lasted nearly the whole day. Keitel was getting more and more irritable. At about 6 p.m., during an interval, I went to the French tent with his ultimatum. 'If we cannot reach agreement within an hour,' I read out, 'the negotiations will be broken off and the delegation will be conducted back to the French lines.'

Great excitement ensued amongst the French. There were further conversations with Bordeaux, again with Weygand, who was evidently attending a Cabinet meeting in the next room there. Huntziger, no doubt in order to cover himself, had asked repeatedly for authorisation to sign: this the French government finally gave him. At 6.50 p.m. on 22 June 1940, Keitel and Huntziger then signed the terms of the German-French armistice in the presence of the other delegates. Some of the French had tears in their eyes.

The French then took their leave, and only Keitel, Huntziger and I remained in the historic coach. 'I do not want to miss the opportunity to express to you as a soldier my sympathy for the grave hours that you as a Frenchman have just experienced,' Keitel said to Huntziger. 'Your painful position will be alleviated by the knowledge that the French troops fought bravely – a fact I desire to state to you expressly.' They both stood silent, each close to tears. 'You, General,' Keitel added, 'have represented your country's interest with great dignity in these difficult negotiations,' and shook hands with Huntziger.

I accompanied the French General out of the coach and was the last German to bid him and his delegation farewell. I was deeply impressed by the attitude that the French had maintained throughout this most difficult situation.

I can still remember every detail of those memorable June days of 1940. The only reason I regret not having been present as interpreter at the surrender negotiations of 1945 at Reims and Berlin is that I was unable to compare how the respective victors and vanquished of 1940 and 1945 acted on the two occasions.

On 6 July 1940 Hitler entered Berlin as the conquering hero. On the following day, a Sunday, he met Ciano at the Chancellery. Hitler seemed to have abandoned the sober thoughts that had played a part in his conversations with Mussolini in Munich shortly before the Armistice and that had their effect in the way the Armistice conditions themselves were framed. He was again the trumpeting, victory-conscious, belligerent German dictator I had known during the negotiations immediately preceding the outbreak of war, and especially in his conversations with Ciano in August of the previous year, when he had been utterly convinced that Britain and France would not fight.

A completely changed Ciano sat facing him at the Chancellery. The lightning victory over the French and British armies had obviously had its effect, and he seemed to have lost his high opinion about the western powers. Now he had gone to the opposite extreme, at any rate for the time being.

Ciano behaved as though the war were already won. He almost fell over himself in making open or hinted demands on behalf of Italy. He wanted to annexe Nice, Corsica and Malta, make Tunis and the greater part of Algeria into an Italian Protectorate, and occupy strategic bases in Syria, Trans-Jordan, Palestine and the Lebanon. In Egypt and the Sudan, Italy simply wanted to step into Britain's shoes while Somaliland, Djibouti and French Equatorial Africa were to become Italian territory. Ciano was not in the least backwards about expressing such wishes. Hitler ignored them all and simply replied with a long victory monologue.

Ciano left to visit occupied France, and we met him again on 10 July in Munich, where Hitler and Ribbentrop received him together with the Hungarian Premier, Count Teleki and Foreign Minister Count Czaky. The conversation took place in the Führer-building and dealt with disputes between Hungary and Romania. These were settled a month later at Schloss Belvedere in Vienna by the so-called Vienna Arbitration Award.

'The Führer is going to make a very magnanimous peace offer to Britain,' Ribbentrop told me some days later, adding, 'When Lloyd George hears of it, he will probably want to give us all a hug.' He had evidently discussed this offer in great detail with Hitler and seemed to be fully confident of its effect upon the British. 'I should not be surprised,' he said in conclusion, 'if we were not all soon seated at a peace conference.'

I recalled Hitler's words to Mussolini in June, and the way in which he had just recently ignored Italy's exaggerated demands, and I began to feel some hope that in this hour of victory he might after all prove himself one of those statesmen who by their magnanimity have produced a lasting peace.

'Make sure that the offer is translated into English as perfectly as possible,' Ribbentrop enjoined me as he went away. I would certainly do my utmost if an end to blood-letting was the issue at stake. I had been informed that Germany's enemies often translated German statements very inaccurately and capriciously, and I decided to combat this by getting in first by broadcasting my English-language version from our own radio stations. After some experimentation I had developed a relatively simple system for transmissions that on this first run caused quite a stir in the then neutral United States.

On 19 July while Hitler addressed the Reichstag, I sat in a small studio of the Berlin broadcasting station with the English text of his speech before me. A colleague sat at my side listening through earphones to Hitler's speech, and indicating on my text with his pencil exactly where Hitler had got to. I remained silent for the first two or three sentences so that Hitler's words were heard first of all in German on the British and American frequencies. Then I pressed a button, which connected my microphone to the transmitter, and proceeded to read the English text. I spoke more rapidly than Hitler, who was often held up by applause and so on, and as soon as my colleague's pencil showed me that my translation had overtaken the original I disconnected my microphone so that Hitler's voice could be heard for another two or three sentences, after which I switched myself on again. In this way, at the moment when Hitler left the tribune in the Reichstag, the whole English-speaking world was in possession of the full and correct English text.

This new technique was a smash hit in America where my translation was carried by a large number of stations. Many newspapers marvelled at my achievement; the fact that they could hear Hitler making his speech in German led them to assume that the translation was impromptu. Others were puzzled as to how it was achieved technically. The London *Times* claimed wrongly that the BBC had already been using this system for some time.

Gratified though I was at my technical success, I was profoundly disappointed by the context of the speech. It was interminably long and enlarged upon the favourable course that events had taken for Germany – to such an extent that even many Germans would have said, 'kindly spare us any more details', not to mention foreigners to whom hearing it gave them no pleasure at all. I looked in vain for Ribbentrop's magnanimous peace offer that would have induced Lloyd George to give us all a hug. There was this single passage, high-sounding but completely bereft of any substance:

> In this hour I feel I owe it to my conscience to make another appeal to reason to Britain. I believe I may do so because I am not asking for something in defeat but as a victor asking for reason. I see no cause which makes the continuation of this war necessary.'

Nothing more. Not the slightest hint of any concrete suggestion. I had often noticed at negotiations that precision was not a strong point of Hitler's. Nevertheless, it was incomprehensible to me that he should believe that such a meaningless, purely rhetorical observation would have any effect on the sober British. I was of the opinion then that between telling Ribbentrop of his peace offer and making the speech, Hitler must for some reason have changed his plan. As far as I could see, the only reason why he should do this would be his grievance and annoyance at the adverse reaction of the British press to the very first rumours of a peace offer. I presumed that this was inspired by the British government, and I assessed it as the sign of a certain amount of war weariness, much more evident amongst all the combatants in the Second World War than it had been in the First. In the event of a tempting offer from Hitler, British war weariness might possibly have led to consequences that would have endangered their prosecution of the war. Part of Churchill's letter to Roosevelt, quoted earlier in this chapter, might hint at this.

It was from sheer pique that Hitler must have refrained from making the generous offer that might have weakened British resistance. In the little studio, when I read into the microphone sheet after sheet of the English text as it reached me from the Languages Service, I realised with growing concern that the peace offer predicted so bombastically by Ribbentrop was proving to be a provocative, vainglorious speech that would further strengthen the British will to fight. Some years afterwards, I was able to form a very good idea of what the British reaction must have been when I observed a similar situation in Germany. At the Casablanca Conference in 1943 when Roosevelt, to the surprise of his own Foreign Minister, unexpectedly demanded unconditional surrender to all the Allies jointly, he gave renewed vitality to the German will to resist, instead of undermining it by the deadly poison of an offer to negotiate.

During the following weeks two new subjects, south-east Europe and Spain, cropped up in the conversations that I interpreted at Berchtesgaden, Vienna and Rome. Henceforward they were to play an important part in my work.

Relations between Hungary and Romania had become more and more strained each month until at last Hitler intervened, anxious to avoid any complications in south-east Europe. He summoned Ciano and Ribbentrop to Obersalzberg on 28 August and directed them to settle the dispute between the two countries by an arbitral award.

I was particularly interested in Hitler's reason for wishing to prevent a conflict between Hungary and Romania. 'At all costs I must secure the supply of oil from Romania for carrying on the war,' he told Ciano.

'Bad weather alone has so far prevented us from proceeding vigorously against Britain,' he remarked in the further course of the conversation, 'We need at least two weeks of good flying weather to put the British Fleet out of action and leave the way free for a landing.'

On 30 August I was again in the Golden Chamber, the little round room at Schloss Belvedere in Vienna where the arbitral award between

Hungary and Romania as decided by Ciano and Ribbentrop was to be announced.

As before, it was a matter of delineating a new boundary. The new frontier between Hungary and Romania divided the ethnographically complex Romanian Transylvania, half of it being restored to Hungary, which had possessed all of it prior to the First World War. It was just as problematic an arrangement as the thickly pencilled boundary fixed a year before between Hungary and Czechoslovakia.

Eight men sat at the round table listening attentively as I read the award. On my right were Ribbentrop, next to him Ciano, then Minister Vitetti; on my left were the Romanian Foreign Minister Manoilescu and the Minister Valer Pop; opposite me sat the Hungarian Prime Minister Teleki and his Foreign Minister Csaky. When I spread out the map of Transylvania on the table with the new boundary line marked on it the Romanian Foreign Minister fainted. The new boundary had claimed its first victim, and he was not to be the last.

'With effect from today, Germany and Italy undertake to guarantee the integrity and inviolability of Romanian territory,' I read out after my neighbour, thanks to medical aid, had recovered. This was the notorious German guarantee to Romania to which the Soviet Foreign Minister Molotov was to react so angrily in Berlin some months later.

The next day, Ciano and Ribbentrop went hunting.

The question of Spain was discussed three weeks later on 19 and 20 September by Mussolini and Ribbentrop at the Palazzo Venezia in Rome. The German Foreign Minister put forward the view that they could count with fair certainty on Spain entering the war in the short term. He was indulging himself, just as he was in his statement that a landing in England was imminent and could be carried out easily. 'A single division will suffice to bring about the collapse of the whole British defence system,' he told Mussolini, who watched him with incredulous amusement. It was a typical Ribbentrop remark. I had to translate hundreds of the same sort, and in time got the impression that his listeners no longer took him seriously.

On 23 September we were back in Berlin where the following morning the Spanish question appeared in the shape of Serrano Suñer, Franco's brother-in-law. He was then Minister of the Interior and became Foreign Minister a month later. It was perfectly clear from the conversation with him that Ribbentrop's remarks in Rome had been exaggerated. Germany naturally wanted to bind Spain more closely to the Axis; I also knew that plans existed to take Gibraltar that could only be achieved if permission were granted for German troops to march through Spanish territory. Only oblique references were made to all this in the Berlin conversations, even when Suñer was received by Hitler himself on 25 September.

I can still clearly picture one further remarkable scene in Ribbentrop's office. Hanging by the window overlooking the old park behind the Wilhelmstrasse was a map of the French colonial empire in Africa. Suñer and Ribbentrop were standing in front of it. 'Help yourself' was in effect the gist of what Ribbentrop said, and the Spanish diplomat did help himself. He took the port of Oran; he wanted the whole of Morocco and large areas of the Sahara, and needed French West Africa to round off the Spanish West African colony of Rio de Oro. Ribbentrop eagerly sold him the goods that were not his to give; apparently no price was too high for Spanish collaboration.

It is of interest, incidentally, that Franco stated that with the same object in mind, Churchill offered him the French territory in North Africa during the war, although answering a question in the House of Commons by the Labour MP Mr Stokes on 22 June 1949, Mr Eden replied that 'As far as Mr Churchill and I are concerned, I can state categorically that we never gave any such assurances.'

In the conversation with Suñer, Ribbentrop confined himself to making certain economic requests with regard to Morocco, and asked for U-boat bases in Rio do Oro and on the island of Fernando Po opposite the Cameroons. Contrary to the grand generosity of Ribbentrop, Suñer proved miserly. He looked thoughtful about the requests regarding Morocco, and without in any way committing himself seemed to think that U-boat bases might be approved, but he declined outright the request for one on Fernando Po 'for historical reasons' and 'on account of Spanish public opinion'.

This brought the first chill to the warm friendship between Franco and Hitler. The real change came in October, in the sunnier south, when the two dictators met to discuss matters on the French–Spanish frontier, and could not agree. We know from Ciano's diary entry of 1 October 1940 that Suñer complained to him 'drastically' of the tactlessness with which the Germans treated Spain. Hitler and Mussolini, for their part, referred to Suñer as 'a crafty Jesuit'. The cordial friendship that has always reputedly existed between the Spanish and German peoples was not in evidence here.

'Japan recognises and respects the leadership of Germany and Italy in the creation of a new order in Europe,' ran Article I of the Tripartite Pact between

Germany, Italy and Japan, which I solemnly read out on 27 September in the reception hall of the New Chancellery, dressed up as though for a musical revue for the signing by the representatives of the three States, Ribbentrop, Ciano and the Japanese Ambassador Kurusu.

'Germany and Italy recognise and respect the leadership of Japan in the creation of a new order in Greater Asia,' ran Article II. Article III, meant as a broad hint to the United States, read: 'They further undertake mutually to support one another with all political, economic and military means if any of the three contracting parties is attacked by a power not at present involved in the European War or in the Sino–Japanese conflict.'

'A military alliance between the three most powerful states on earth!' Ribbentrop called it. Then the Foreign Ministers appended their signatures, the Japanese Ambassador using a brush to form elegant Japanese characters one below the other. Immediately above the signatures stood the words, 'Done in triplicate original texts, in Berlin, on 27 September 1940 in the XVIII year of the Fascist era corresponding to the 27th day of the 9th month of the 15th year Syowa.'

A week later, on 4 October 1940, international traffic across the Brenner was again suspended for three hours. Hitler held forth in the Duce's saloon carriage. His main theme was France, which he wanted to mobilise somehow against Britain. Spain was hardly mentioned, not so much for the coolness caused by Suñer's visit as because of tactical considerations of which I only became aware some days later. The battle against Britain in the Mediterranean also played a large part in this Brenner monologue, and I got the impression that the invasion of England was to be given up in favour of a Mediterranean offensive. Mussolini looked very interested. He was obviously pleased that Hitler should thus enlighten him as to his future plans, at any rate in broad outline. It did not happen often, and even on this occasion he found little opportunity to contribute to the conversation himself. At last Hitler's flow of words ceased, and the flow of international traffic across the Brenner was resumed.

'Drive to the station quickly, there's going to be an air raid warning very soon,' the Foreign Office telephone exchange told me on the evening of 26 October. I was starting on a long journey in the course of which I was to cover more than 4,000 miles in a few days. My first destination was Hendaye on the frontier between France and Spain. From there I was to go via Mannheim to Florence, and then return to Berlin. At that time British air attacks on Berlin were still pretty harmless. They did little damage and caused only very few casualties, but usually lasted all night. The RAF would send over only two or three bombers at a time, at short intervals. In this way they succeeded in depriving 4 million persons of their night's rest.

The British were droning overhead when I entered our special train at the Lehrter station, but we stayed in it and awoke next morning in Hannover. The following night we stopped at a small station in Belgium near a tunnel in which the train was to shelter in case of an air raid. It was a well thought-out scheme but did not always work too well. I once had the experience during an air raid of being in a train whose engine was so weak that it could only just drag itself into the tunnel and left the carriages outside, while huge clouds of smoke billowing from the tunnel drew attention to the target. The British ignored it, 'regarding a gasholder as more important a target than the Reich Foreign Minister' as one of our junior members remarked.

We made a wide circuit around Paris and reached Montoire in central France next evening. Meanwhile Hitler had arrived in his special train, and he had a short conversation in his saloon with Laval, then French vice-premier. It was the first time that I had translated for Laval since conversations at the Berlin Chancellery in 1931. He greeted me very warmly, with obvious relief at seeing at least one familiar face; and during the conversation with Hitler called on me as witness to the fact that as early as 1931 he had favoured a policy of closer association with Germany. Nothing new of any significance emerged during this talk at Montoire in which Ribbentrop also participated, and the atmosphere was fairly friendly. It dealt almost exclusively with arrangements for a meeting with Marshal Pétain, which took place at the same spot two days later on our return from Hendaye.

We travelled on towards the Spanish frontier that same night, our two special trains arriving at the little station the next afternoon. I had stopped here on a previous journey in 1928 when I accompanied Stresemann to the League of Nations Assembly at Madrid. As at the Brenner conversations, the negotiations were to take place in Hitler's saloon car. Franco's train, which was to arrive on the wider Spanish gauge at the next platform, was a full hour late but since it was a lovely day nobody minded; Hitler and Ribbentrop stood chatting on the platform.

I heard Hitler say to Ribbentrop, 'At the moment we cannot give the Spanish any written promises about transfers of territory from the French colonial possessions. If they get hold of anything in writing on this ticklish question, with these talkative Latins the French are sure to hear something about it sooner or later.' He added the interesting reason, 'In talking to Pétain,

I want to try to induce the French to start active hostilities against Britain, so I cannot suggest to them such cessions of territory now. Quite apart from that, if such an agreement with the Spanish became known, the French colonial empire would probably go over bodily to de Gaulle.' These few sentences showed me more clearly than any long memorandum could have done the whole nature of the problem underlying the forthcoming meeting between the dictators, and they revealed one of the reasons why it was a fiasco.

The Spanish train appeared at about 3 p.m. on the international bridge over the Bidassoa river, which forms the boundary. Military music, inspection of guards of honour, all the familiar ceremonial of a dictators' meeting, took place, and immediately afterwards the fateful discussion began that was to end all sympathy between Hitler and Franco.

Short and stout, dark skinned with lively black eyes: in the pictures I had seen of him he had always looked much taller and slimmer. If he were wearing a white burnous, it occurred to me, he might be taken for an Arab, and as the discussion in Hitler's coach proceeded, his hesitant, tentative way of putting forward his arguments seemed to confirm this impression. It was clear to me at once that Franco, a prudent negotiator, was not to be nailed down.

Hitler began by giving a most glowing account of the German position. 'Britain is already beaten decisively,' he said, concluding that part of his exposé that dealt with the German prospects of victory, 'only she is not yet prepared to admit the fact.' Then came the clue word: Gibraltar. If the British lost it, they could be excluded from the Mediterranean and from Africa. Hitler now played his trump. He proposed the immediate conclusion of a treaty, and asked Franco to come into the war in January 1941. Gibraltar would be taken on 10 January by the same special units that by new methods had won the Eben Emael fort on the Albert Canal with such surprising speed. The German methods of attack, of which an important part was the exploitation of 'dead ground' (ground that the traverse or elevation of the guns masks from the field of fire) that had in the meantime been brought to such technical perfection that the operation was bound to succeed. As I had already heard, German units in southern France had an exact model of the fortress of Gibraltar and were carrying out exercises for capturing it by this method.

Hitler offered Gibraltar to Spain there and then, and somewhat more vaguely, colonial territories in Africa also.

Sitting huddled up in his chair, at first Franco said nothing at all. From his impenetrable expression I could not make out whether he was taken aback by the proposal or just quietly thinking out his reply. Finally he undertook evasive action similar to that of his Italian counterpart at the outbreak of war. Spain was in sore straits for food. The country needed wheat, several hundred thousand tons immediately. Was Germany in a position to deliver this, he asked, with what seemed to me a slyly watchful expression. Spain needed modern armaments. For operations against Gibraltar heavy artillery would be required; Franco mentioned a very large figure for the number of heavy guns that he wanted from Germany. Then too he must protect his long coastline against attacks by the Royal Navy. In addition, he was short of anti-aircraft guns. How was Spain to insure against the loss of the Canary Islands, which would have to be expected? Apart from this, it was not consistent with Spanish national pride to accept Gibraltar as a gift, taken by foreign troops. The fortress must be taken only by the Spanish.

I was much interested in an observation Franco made in reply to Hitler's statement that panzer units from the Gibraltar bridgehead could clear the British out of Africa. 'To the edge of the great deserts, very possibly,' Franco said, 'but central Africa is protected against major land attacks by the desert belt in the same way that an island is by the open sea. As an old African campaigner, I am quite clear about that.'

Hitler's high hopes, amounting to almost a certainty, of being able to conquer Britain were also discouraged. Franco was of the opinion that Britain might possibly be conquered, but then the British government and fleet would continue the war from Canada with American support.

As Franco made these remarks in a quiet, gentle voice, its monotonous sing-song reminiscent of the muezzin calling the faithful to prayer, Hitler became more and more restless. The conversation was obviously getting on his nerves. He even got up once saying there was no point in continuing the discussion, but sat down again immediately and renewed his attempts to win Franco over. Finally Franco said he was ready to conclude a treaty, but this was merely a façade for all its many conditions regarding the supplies of food and armaments and the actual time when Spain would eventually intervene actively in the war.

The meeting was then adjourned. Ribbentrop and Suñer continued talking in the Foreign Office train. The change in the German attitude about which Hitler had spoken to Ribbentrop before Franco's arrival did not escape the notice of the sharp-witted Suñer.

The formula advanced during Suñer's visit to Berlin amounted to: 'Spain will receive territory from French colonial possessions.' At Hendaye Ribbentrop had amended this to: 'Spain will receive territories from the

French colonial possessions to the extent that France can be indemnified from British colonial possessions.' The logical Suñer, recently appointed Foreign Minister, objected that Spain might then get nothing – that is, if it proved impossible to offer France compensation from British possessions.

That night, a dinner was served to the Spanish party in Hitler's great banqueting car, superbly illuminated by indirect lighting and brought specially from Germany for the occasion. Hitler and Franco were scheduled to depart leaving their Foreign Ministers to work out a formula on which they could agree, but after the meal the two principals plunged into discussion once more. They came no closer to a mutual understanding and so left two hours later than intended.

Right up to the following morning Ribbentrop continued to dismantle piece by piece what remained of German-Spanish friendship. Systematically he plagued and pressurised the increasingly recalcitrant Spanish Foreign Minister to accept formulae which the latter did not want. Finally Ribbentrop sent the Spanish delegation off to San Sebastian. 'The text must be here by eight in the morning,' the stern schoolmaster admonished them, 'I have to leave then as we are meeting Marshal Pétain.' The next morning, however, his pupils failed to reappear, and instead delivered their 'essay' through Under Secretary of State Espinosa de los Monteros, a friendly, gentle man and one-time ambassador to Berlin who spoke German like a Viennese, having been educated in that city. The schoolmaster described the work as 'unsatisfactory'. Just before we left Hendaye, another draft was concocted. This one provided for Spain's entry into the war after mutual preliminary consultation but contained nothing about deliveries of food and weapons. The Under Secretary of State promised in his charming way to lay the draft before Franco and to report the latter's decision to Germany.

Spluttering with rage, Ribbentrop drove off with me to Bordeaux, and its nearest aerodrome. As on the drive to Compiègne, we had to go hell for leather to reach Montoire in time for the talks with Pétain. All the way, Ribbentrop cursed the 'Jesuit' Suñer and the 'ungrateful coward' Franco 'who owes us everything and now won't join in with us'. The car springs seemed to join in the abuse.

We flew to Tours in very bad weather. Any other aviator but Bauer would probably have been unable to make a landing in the rain and fog, but he brought us safely down and we were in Hitler's saloon car at Montoire station on time to greet the old marshal of France when he was shown in. Despite his advanced years the simply uniformed marshal sat up very straight as he faced Hitler. His attitude was self-confident rather than servile, and he listened imperturbably to my translation. I spoke fairly loudly because I had been told that the marshal was hard of hearing. Beside him, a vivid contrast, sat small, dark Laval, with the inevitable white tie, gazing alternately at Hitler and Ribbentrop with searching eyes as I translated.

The talks started off as another 'railway monologue', Hitler enumerating a long list of French sins though showing no harshness. He repeated what he had said at Hendaye: 'We have already won the war; Britain is beaten and will sooner or later have to admit it.' He went on to say: 'It is obvious that someone has to pay for the lost war. That will be either France or Britain. If Britain bears the cost, then France can take the place in Europe that is her due, and can fully retain her position as a colonial power.' If this was to happen it was essential that France should even now protect her colonial empire from attack and reconquer the central African colonies that had gone over to de Gaulle. An indirect suggestion that France join the war against Britain was made when Hitler asked Pétain what France would do if she were attacked again by Britain, as for instance when French warships at Oran had refused to obey the orders of the Royal Navy.

Pétain understood the implication at once, for he replied that France was not in a position to conduct a new war. He put a question of his own to Hitler about a final peace treaty 'so that France may be clear about her fate, and the two million French prisoners of war may return to their families as soon as possible.'

Here Laval intervened in the discussion, pointing out the readiness with which France had met Germany's request for collaboration in other than purely military matters. The French were a peace-loving people. They had gone to war reluctantly and had never really fought well, as was shown by the large number of prisoners.

Hitler did not answer what must have seemed to Pétain and Laval the most important questions, and the French made no reference to Hitler's hint that France should enter the war against Britain. The great stakes for which Hitler had played had been lost as a result of the prudent reticence shown by Pétain and Laval. Pétain's monosyllabic utterances during the Montoire discussion had clearly been meant as a rebuff, nor had any better progress been made with Laval. Knowing the French as I did, my sympathies during that discussion were entirely with the underdog. I believe that on such occasions one is particularly sensitive to any false notes struck by the other side. I felt then, and feel today, that France had no cause to be ashamed of the attitude to the conqueror displayed at Montoire by these two Frenchmen. My impression was confirmed when I observed Hitler that evening apparently profoundly disappointed by the French aloofness. In the following months this disappointment continued to increase and culminated in an outburst of rage against Admiral Darlan, Laval's successor, at Christmas. Hitler then upbraided Darlan for an hour outside Paris in the same coach in which the discussion with Pétain and Laval that had taken place at Montoire.

The atmosphere in the two special trains as Hitler and Ribbentrop returned to Germany was by no means cheerful. Neither at Hendaye nor at Montoire had Hitler got what he set out to achieve, and there was to be another failure to add to it: soon after we reached the German frontier our embassy in Rome reported that the Italians were about to invade Greece. Hitler was beside himself; he regarded Mussolini's undertaking as quite unsuitable at that time of year. Ribbentrop, 'his master's voice', said to us at dinner: 'The Italians will never get anywhere against the Greeks in the autumn rains and winter snows. Besides, the consequences of war in the Balkans are quite unpredictable. The Führer intends at all costs to hold up this crazy scheme of Mussolini's, so we are to go to Italy immediately to talk to him personally.' In the tense atmosphere prevailing upon receipt of this news one could almost sense the swerve of the train as it turned southwards away from Berlin. 'The police hastened to the scene of the crime,' as they say in detective novels.

We passed through a prematurely snowy landscape as chilly as our mood and arrived at 10 a.m. on 28 October at the festively decorated station of Florence. We knew already that events had overtaken us, for two hours previously we had received news from our signals carriage of the Italian invasion of Greece. Mussolini greeted Hitler with a smug smile. He did not wait to leave the platform before announcing in our own style for similar occasions: 'At dawn today, victorious Italian troops crossed the Greco-Albanian frontier.' This was Mussolini's revenge for the innumerable coups of which Hitler had not informed him until the last moment by the expedient of despatching the Prince of Hesse, the royal courier, with the notification by special plane for Rome in the grey dawn.

Hitler controlled himself surprisingly well. On that occasion he was a good loser, as the British say, and there was not the slightest sign of mental gnashing of teeth in the friendly words he exchanged with Mussolini at the Palazzo Pitti.

Hitler went north again that afternoon with bitterness in his heart. He had been frustrated thrice: at Hendaye, at Montoire and now by Italy. In the lengthy winter evenings of the next few years these long, exacting journeys were a constantly recurring theme of bitter reproaches against ungrateful and unreliable friends, Axis partners and 'perfidious' Frenchmen.

During the remaining months of 1940 I got no rest. Early in November, Ribbentrop and Ciano met for hunting at Schönhof near Karlsbad. I found that kind of fancy sport most out of place in wartime. In the evenings I translated the political talks in the little castle Ribbentrop had 'rented'. 'We have already won the war,' the gramophone repeated endlessly – a refrain I translated with growing repugnance.

Ten days later on 12 November Molotov arrived in Berlin. I shall relate in greater detail in the next chapter the portentous and highly interesting discussions that Stalin's envoy had with Hitler during those November days.

On 18 and 19 November I worked at the Berghof, where Hitler received first King Boris of Bulgaria and then Ciano and Suñer. These latter two Foreign Ministers had already had long but quite fruitless conversations with Ribbentrop at Schloss Fuschl.

Another king required my services as interpreter: Leopold of Belgium, held prisoner of war in his own country, had an interview with Hitler on 19 November. A few weeks earlier the Crown Princess of Italy, the sister of King Leopold, had been received at the Berghof where during an informal tea party she had mentioned not only a number of Italian questions but also the difficult situation of her native country, Belgium. As was natural for a woman she had dwelt on the more human problems; in particular she had interested herself in the fate of the Belgian prisoners of war, and pleaded eloquently that they should be allowed to return to their homes. She painted a gloomy picture of the situation in Belgium regarding food supplies.

Hitler was most evasive. Had he been talking to a man, his replies to both questions would probably have been a curt refusal, but he was always much milder with women, especially if they were young and elegant, and advanced their cause with as much feminine charm and diplomatic skill as did the Princess of Piedmont. After a time she naturally became aware of Hitler's evasive tactics.

With true feminine ingenuity, she said finally, 'If you will not discuss these matters with me because I am a mere woman and do not understand politics, could you not talk to my brother Leopold about them some time? All these hardships that his people undergo weigh very heavily on his mind.'

I saw at once that Hitler was not in the least interested in such a meeting; an irritable frown showed that he felt he had been trapped. He hesitated, then his brow cleared and he said that he was prepared to receive King Leopold, but he assented in such a way as to suggest that nothing would come of the matter. The Crown Princess was satisfied with her success. On the car journey back to Munich she made me recapitulate the whole conversation; I formed the impression that she wanted to give her brother a very exact report on it.

When I fetched King Leopold a little while later from the small inn below the Berghof for his interview with Hitler, I felt it to be unlikely that he had known beforehand about his sister's move.

As he walked beside me, tall and slender, he seemed to me like a student who goes to extra tuition to please his parents though he sees no point in it himself. He mounted the famous Berghof steps with slow reluctance, showing none of the expectancy of such visitors as King Boris, Lloyd George, Chamberlain and the Duke of Windsor.

I could see that Hitler had to force himself to assume the air of somewhat frosty friendliness with which he received Leopold. The King's expression as he sat down in Hitler's office was an odd mixture of displeasure and expectation, and I felt that he secretly regretted his sister's initiative. Hitler tried to improve the atmosphere by a few personal questions. The companionable phrases it was his custom to employ on these occasions gave away his Austrian provincial schooling. 'I regret the circumstances under which you have to visit me here. Have you any personal wish that I could grant?'

'I have no wishes for myself personally,' Leopold replied with the condescending tones of a monarch addressing the revolutionary dictator of the people, though the dictator now faced him as conqueror: he indicated clearly by this remark that he intended to make other, non-personal requests. To begin with, however, he took pains to get Hitler into a more amenable mood to receive these requests by thanking him for what he had already done. He expressed gratitude among other things for the permission granted by the Germans for the return home of the Belgian refugees, and added his personal thanks for the favours accorded to him, especially the return of his children from Spain. Leopold was not a good diplomat, though, for his words of gratitude did not sound all that convincing.

Hitler then began one of his long monologues about the political situation. This conversation developed better than I had at first feared. In the middle of his delivery, rather unexpectedly Hitler asked Leopold how he envisaged future relations between Belgium and Germany: Leopold replied with a question of his own: Would Belgium recover her independence on the conclusion of peace? Hitler, who disliked all definite questions, embarked on a long dissertation about the future of Europe. King Leopold stuck to his point: he asked for a more precise definition of Belgian independence, adding that he was thinking in particular of independence in internal affairs (a clear reference to German support for the Flemish–Dutch-speaking regions of Belgium).

By this time Hitler was visibly annoyed at such persistence and he launched a fairly violent attack on Belgium's previous attitude, the violation of her obligations as a neutral and so on. In future, Belgium must orientate herself politically and militarily towards Germany.

'Am I to understand that Belgium's political independence would be guaranteed as a quid pro quo for a military and political agreement between Belgium and the Reich?' Leopold asked. In his immediately following remarks he laid such stress on Belgium's love of independence that at once he cast doubts on the feasibility of this solution. He demanded unconditional independence, giving as his reason that Britain had long ago formally acknowledged that independence and that out of sentiment the Belgians would turn to the side that guaranteed their independence under all circumstances. This was more than ever so at a time when BBC broadcasts worked on Belgian public opinion on this vulnerable point.

From this moment on Hitler was deaf to Leopold's requests. He was obviously annoyed that the Belgian King, unlike other heads of states, had not agreed willingly to the suggestion of collaboration with Germany. Foremost among Leopold's requests was the return of the Belgian prisoners of war. 'We need their manpower for ourselves,' Hitler told him, 'the officers will naturally remain in captivity until the end of the war.' Leopold made further desperate attempts to secure some small concession from Hitler over the matter of food supplies and with regard to the internal administration of Belgium. On both these points Hitler was obdurate. They now became mutually antagonistic, Leopold being more and more monosyllabic and occasionally seemed not to be giving the conversation his full attention after the rejection of his requests. He allowed Hitler's flood of words to flow over him with a disdainful expression, offering no more than an occasional formal gesture. As I had seen happen so often before, the conversation became empty of all content.

Hitler would probably have liked to put an end to the visit at once, but arrangements had been made to give the King and his entourage tea, and so although the conversation was broken off long before the appointed time,

Leopold was kept for tea. This was served in the same great hall with the vast window in which a few weeks before the King's sister had pleaded hopefully for this interview, which had now proved so unsatisfactory to her brother and so disappointing to Hitler.

At tea Hitler produced a final inducement to persuade the King to reconsider his suggestion for closer collaboration between the two countries. In the course of a long monologue about the New Order in Europe, he indicated that if Belgium turned to Germany he would not only guarantee her complete military protection, so that she would scarcely require there to be a Belgian army in future, but that Belgium might also acquire certain extensions of territory as far as Calais and Dunkirk. I interpreted this conversation as it took place, naturally being very careful over the translation of this suggestion. The King remained silent. Had he even been listening? Had he lost interest in the conversation? I could not make it out. I saw only a completely apathetic, disappointed man sitting before me, a boy longing for school to be over. This was not to be, for Hitler had got into his stride and went on for a considerable time, endlessly repeating what he was saying.

My impression of this conversation was borne out by later developments. Hitler never saw Leopold again; everything in Belgium remained as it had been. The administration was not changed and the position regarding foodstuffs was as bad as ever; Belgian prisoners were not liberated until the end of the war; Leopold himself remained a prisoner and was even taken to Germany, despite his protests, shortly before the war ended. Hitler never forgave him for having refused his offers at the Berghof. 'He is no better than the other kings and princes,' I heard him say occasionally, although before the visit he had sometimes spoken of him appreciatively: 'King Leopold prevented pointless bloodshed in 1940'.

My report on this conversation played a part in 1945 in the discussions in Belgium about the King's return to the throne. It was known as the 'Schmidt Report'. I learnt about this only much later, almost by accident. It turned out that only one of my reports on the actual conversation had been found by the Allies, and that what was perhaps the most important report, the one which contained Hitler's offer at the tea party, had apparently been lost. I was questioned by a Belgian representative about the conversation between Leopold and Hitler, but owing to the mystification sometimes practised in 1945 with regard to the interrogation of German officials I got neither a sight of my own report nor was I told what was really at issue. I could easily have cleared up any obscure points had I known what it was all about.

Later I learnt that the accuracy of my report had been questioned. I was supposed to have reported some of the King's words so as to please Hitler, and not as spoken verbatim. This was complete nonsense. In the first place, in the ordinary way Hitler no longer saw my reports at the time, and secondly I am not clairvoyant and could not have known that my reports would be involved in 1945 in the controversy surrounding the Belgian throne. I had the impression then, as I also have today, that Leopold yielded nothing to Hitler, and I reported accordingly. All that anybody needed to do was to take the trouble to read my report in the original German and with the necessary political understanding.

From the Berghof I went with Ribbentrop to Vienna where on 20 November Hungary joined the Tripartite Pact. The customary ceremonies were observed at Schloss Belvedere – signatures were once again written and painted in Japanese character and again I had to read out the complicated conclusion with the dates given in the German, Fascist and Japanese manner.

Two days later we were back in Berlin. General Antonescu, the Romanian Head of State, had his first interview with Hitler on 22 November. Though his appearance suggested a Prussian Staff officer, this Romanian had been educated in France: in later years he would become one of Hitler's closest intimates and was kept even more closely in the picture than Mussolini. He was the only foreigner from whom Hitler ever asked for military advice when he was in difficulties.

Antonescu was anti-Bolshevik and even more anti-Slav to the marrow, making no attempt to conceal his attitude when in Berlin. He was fanatically opposed to the Vienna arbitration award that had given Hungary Transylvania, which he called 'the cradle of Romania'. Before he saw Hitler, it was drummed into him that he must not say a word against the award. He spoke for two hours about nothing else. 'That always impressed me,' Hitler said in my presence frequently on later occasions. To me as interpreter, with his French way of speaking, Antonescu was a kind of rhetorical counterpart to Hitler. He made long speeches just like Hitler, usually starting off at the creation of Romania, and somehow relating everything he said to the hated Hungarians and the recovery of Transylvania. This hatred of Hungary made him congenial to Hitler, for the Führer also despised the Magyars.

The actual occasion for Antonescu's visit was the great show that was put on, with the usual theatrical effects, to celebrate Romania's accession to the Tripartite Pact. This was followed two days later on 24 November by another performance in the great chamber of the New Chancellery to celebrate the accession of Slovakia.

That year, such a turbulent one for me, ended true to form. On the afternoon of Christmas Eve I was crossing the Wilhelmsplatz on my way home. Just before I reached the underground station a colleague shouted out, 'Safe journey!' In surprise I asked him what he meant. 'Why, don't you know you're flying to Paris today?' he replied. I hurried back to the office. My namesake the flight captain was on the telephone. 'We must take off soon if we are to reach Le Bourget before dark,' he said. Half an hour later we were flying over the Havel lake, the flight captain, mechanic, radio operator and I. 'Quite the wrong direction to be taking on Christmas Eve,' we told each other in annoyance.

The purpose of my journey was to interpret between Hitler and Admiral Darlan in Hitler's train, somewhere north of Paris. Hitler showed none of the Christmas spirit; for half an hour reproaches hailed down on the French admiral. 'Why was Laval dismissed?' Hitler shouted, 'It is the work of anti-German intriguers around Marshal Pétain.'

Hitler complained bitterly about Pétain, who had declined his invitation to attend the interment of the remains of the Duke of Reichsstatt, Napoleon's son. As a grand gesture, Hitler had had these brought from Vienna. The reason for Pétain's refusal had somehow come to the Führer's ears: the old Marshal feared that the Germans would kidnap him. 'It is contemptible to credit me with such an idea,' Hitler roared, beside himself with rage, 'when I meant so well.'

Darlan scarcely had the chance of uttering three sentences in reply, but what he did say was not without interest. Before the German armistice conditions were made known, he had considered whether to sink the French Fleet, to take it over to Africa or America, or even to place it at the disposal of the British. When he heard the armistice conditions, he felt that France could still play a role in Europe and for this reason he had opted to serve under Pétain. Incidentally, Darlan impressed me with his marked hostility towards Britain on this and other occasions.

Hitler terminated the interview abruptly. I travelled back to Paris with the French admiral and noted with inward satisfaction that the whole scene had slid off the back of this creator of the modern French navy like a breaker off the oily skin of an old walrus. On the journey he entertained me in radiant manner with the most delightful stories as though nothing at all had happened; his complete indifference impressed me.

The day after Christmas, I flew back in the old AMYY Ju 52, unrecognisable in new war paint. These had been strange Christmas celebrations with which to bring an eventful year to a close. The intense diplomatic activity of 1940 represented the final flare up of National Socialist policy before the end; during the following years matters of foreign policy gradually receded into the background of my sphere of activity as an interpreter. I had to acquire a new vocabulary, and learn to speak in foreign languages about panzers, self-propelled assault guns, motor torpedo boats, types of aircraft and fortifications. The increasing gravity of the situation slowly but surely pushed the political phrases into the background.

SEVEN

1941

I must go back a few weeks to November 1940 to include in this chapter Molotov's Berlin discussions with Hitler where they have their proper context. They were the prelude to the conflict with the Soviet Union in 1941 just as clearly as the march on Prague in March 1939 had been the decisive event that led to the break with the West. In November 1941, the infinitely more consequential fiasco of the talks with Molotov was added to the failure of Hitler's approaches to Spain and France at the meetings with Franco at Hendaye and Pétain at Montoire.

Some days before Molotov's arrival it was discussed whether the Soviet national anthem – then still identical with the Third Internationale – should be played to greet him at Berlin Anhalter station. Ribbentrop gave me a very severe look when I joked that a large number of German spectators might join in with the German version, which no doubt many of them could still remember from the recent past. However, caution prevailed and only the usual march of welcome, the *Präsentiermarsch*, was played at the station, which had more flowers and greenery decorating it than Soviet flags and hammers and sickle emblems. The train bearing the Soviet delegation arrived on the morning of 12 November 1940.

The ceremony of welcome was identical with that of other State visits. There were the same handshakes, introductions, inspections of guards of honour and driving in open cars to the guest apartments at Schloss Bellevue in the Tiergarten. One difference struck me greatly as I drove with 'my' Russian through the streets of Berlin: the populace remained perfectly silent. This might perhaps have happened on the occasion of other visits had no welcoming applause been organised by the party – especially in the 'Via Spontana', as some of us like to call the Wilhelmstrasse on these occasions.

Little time was wasted on formalities. The talks began soon after the Russians arrived, first Molotov and Ribbentrop, then Hitler and Molotov. There was no cordiality, and at the end of those two fateful days the relationship between the two countries was left severely strained.

Ribbentrop had vacated Bismarck's historic office at Wilhelmstrasse 76 some time ago. He had probably never felt quite at home there. The Foreign Minister's new office in the former presidential palace was fairly comfortable compared with some of the other elaborately decorated rooms, which looked as though they had been designed for Hollywood. In this office on 12 November 1940 the People's Commissar for Foreign Affairs of the Soviet Union, Molotov, and the Foreign Minister of the German Reich sat opposite each other at a circular conference table. Dekanosov, Deputy People's Commissar for Foreign Affairs, frequently mentioned post war in connection with German affairs, was also present. A younger member of the Soviet Embassy staff in Berlin, 'Little Pavlov' as we called him, acted as Russian interpreter. I have seen photographs of him standing beside Molotov and Stalin at many conferences since the war, where he also translated into English. Hilger was the German interpreter and I was present only as an observer to draw up the report. Thus I was able to observe everything in peace and make my notes in comfort on both days of the negotiations.

Ribbentrop was at his most forthcoming with 'the men with strong faces'. Ciano would probably have rubbed his eyes if Ribbentrop had ever smiled at him in the friendly way he did at the Soviet Foreign Minister. Only at the end of long intervals did Molotov reciprocate when a rather frosty smile would glide over his intelligent, chess-player's face. This rather short Russian with lively eyes behind old-fashioned pince-nez reminded me of my old mathematics teacher. It was not only his appearance: Molotov had a certain mathematical precision and unerring logic in his way of speaking and presenting his arguments. In his precise diplomacy he dispensed with flowery phrases and, as though he were taking a class, gently rebuked the sweeping, vague generalities of Ribbentrop and later even of Hitler. Dekanosov sat huddled up, listening with rapt attention to the discussion, to which he contributed nothing, with a completely expressionless face.

'No power on earth can alter the fact that the beginning of the end has now come for the British Empire,' said Ribbentrop to open the conversation. The old gramophone record grated on the ears. A little later Molotov replied to Ribbentrop's exaggeration with some irony, referring to 'that Britain which you assume is already beaten'.

'Britain is beaten and it is only a question of time before she admits her defeat,' Ribbentrop boomed on; 'If the British do not decide to admit their defeat at once, they will certainly be begging for peace next year ... Owing to the extraordinary strength of their position the Axis powers are not considering how they can win the war, but rather how they can most swiftly bring to a close a war that is already won.' He went on for quite a while in this vein. What does Molotov think of it? I wondered as I saw him listening attentively with a blank face to Hilger's translation.

After this beating of the drum, Ribbentrop turned to the practical subjects that were to be discussed. The first of these was Japan. At that time Ribbentrop was still warmly advocating closer relations between the Soviets and Japan. Four months later, during the highly significant discussions with Japanese Foreign Minister Matsuoka, he and Hitler had already made a complete about-turn, and warned Matsuoka in the most emphatic terms against any closer relationship. I inferred accordingly that between November 1940 and March 1941, Hitler made the decision to attack Soviet Russia that sealed the fate of National Socialist Germany.

Ribbentrop now passed to a broader theme, which for the sake of brevity I shall call the 'Southern Motif'. Its general drift may be described as follows: 'Everything turns towards the south,' said Ribbentrop, and he assumed the statesmanlike expression that he reserved for great occasions. 'Japan has already turned her face to the south and will be occupied for centuries in consolidating her territorial gains.' I noticed how he linked the southern motif to Japan, for if Japan was kept busy for centuries in the south, she could not be a menace to Russia. 'For her *Lebensraum*, Germany will also seek expansion in a southerly direction, that is to say in central Africa, in the territories of the former German colonies.' Here the southern motif was combined with a note of reassurance bearing in mind the heavy emphasis on the easterly motif in *Mein Kampf*. 'With regard to Russia, Germany has set boundaries to her sphere of influence,' Ribbentrop added soothingly. 'Italian expansion also tends to the south, to the African Mediterranean coast' – and now he had reached the point to which his motif was leading. 'Will not Russia also finally turn southwards in order to acquire the natural outlet to the open sea in which she is so much interested?' It was clear to me that Germany was endeavouring to divert to the South Russia's century-old demands for access to the sea in the west, and was trying to liberate the Europe of Hitler's New Order from the threat now again prevalent in present-day Europe.

'What sea did you mean just now, when you spoke of access to the open sea?' asked Molotov with an innocent expression. Thrown somewhat out of his stride by this interruption, after a long diversion about 'the great changes that will take place throughout the world after the war' and the 'new ordering of affairs in the British Empire', Ribbentrop finally reached 'the Persian Gulf and the Arabian Sea' and an unmistakable reference to India. Molotov retained an impenetrable expression. He made no reference to these hints, at any rate not in Berlin at that time. Only after his return on 26 November did a telegram arrive from the German Ambassador in Moscow stating that Molotov agreed with the proposals regarding a four-power pact 'subject to the condition that the territory south of Batumi and Baku in the general direction of the Persian Gulf is recognised as a focal point of Soviet aims.' This was one of four conditions.

The next subject Ribbentrop touched upon was the question of the Dardanelles; he wanted a pact between the Soviet Union, Turkey, Italy and Germany to replace the old Montreux Convention.

His fourth theme dealt with Russia's accession to the Tripartite Pact. 'Could we not envisage some agreement between Russia and the Axis powers whereby the Soviet Union would declare itself in agreement with the aim of the Tripartite Pact; that is, the prevention of the war spreading and the early conclusion of world peace?' Ribbentrop suggested a further visit to Moscow for discussion of this question. 'Perhaps the presence of the Italian and Japanese Foreign Ministers at the same time would be useful. So far as I know both would be prepared to go to Moscow.'

In conclusion Ribbentrop also brought China into the discussion, letting it be understood cautiously that he would like to mediate between Chiang Kai-shek and Japan. 'I have by no means offered Germany's mediation, but … merely informed Marshal Chiang Kai-shek of the German view.'

Molotov was obviously conserving his forces for the main battle. He scarcely addressed the points raised by Ribbentrop, who in any case had not chosen his themes at random but only touched on the main questions the Russians had already raised at Moscow with the German Ambassador. They had expressed some criticisms and alleged various grievances. The methodical Molotov confined himself to asking some questions of his own.

'What does the term 'Greater Asian area' actually mean?' he wanted to know.

'This concept has nothing to do with the spheres of influence vital to Russia,' Ribbentrop hastened to reply.

'Spheres of interest must all be more precisely defined,' Molotov retorted. 'First we want to reach an understanding with Germany, and only then with Italy and Japan,' and added immediately, 'after we are exactly informed about the significance, the nature and the aim of the Tripartite Pact.' The gong then sounded for lunch.

In the afternoon, the talks between Hitler and Molotov began, Hilger and Pavlov continued as interpreters. Hitler set out first to anticipate certain Russian complaints of which he knew from conversations between Molotov and the German Ambassador. Molotov himself also took care to draw attention to them pointedly later in the discussion.

'Germany is at war, Russia is not,' said Hitler. Many of the measures taken by Germany were explained by the exigencies of war. For instance, in the struggle with Britain, Germany had found it necessary to advance into far distant territories in which, fundamentally, she had neither a political nor an economic interest.

Hitler then spoke in very general terms (as he always did) about Germany's non-political economic interests, especially with regard to the supply of raw materials. He recognised Russia's efforts to gain access to the open sea, without bringing in Ribbentrop's southern motif, and spoke of the need for Russo-German collaboration. To this Molotov heartily agreed. Hitler went on to call for battle against the United States which, 'not in 1945 but at the earliest in 1970 or 1980 would seriously imperil the freedom of other nations.'

With Hitler, Molotov was no silent observer as he had been with Ribbentrop; in his own way he entered very actively into the discussion.

He wanted much more precise information than Hitler had given him on matters concerning Russia; he wanted the i's dotted and the t's crossed. In a tone of gentle remonstrance he said that Hitler had made general statements to which he could, in principle, agree. He then proceeded immediately to ticklish points of detail.

Taking the bull by the horns he asked:

Does the German–Soviet Agreement of 1939 still apply to Finland? What does the New Order in Europe and in Asia amount to, and what part is the USSR to play in it? What is the position with regard to Bulgaria, Romania and Turkey, and how do matters stand with regard to the safeguarding of Russian interests in the Balkans and on the Black Sea? May I be given information about the boundaries of the so-called Greater Asia area? How does the Tripartite Pact stand with regard to it?'

The questions hailed down upon Hitler. No foreign visitor had ever spoken to him in this way in my presence. I remembered how indignant Hitler had been at Eden's questionnaire of May 1936 – which he had simply left unanswered – and I was intensely curious to see how he would now react to Molotov's questionnaire.

Hitler did not jump up and rush to the door as he had done in September 1939 when Sir Horace Wilson brought him Chamberlain's letter, nor did he say that there was no point in continuing the discussions as he had done to Franco just three weeks before at Hendaye. Instead he was all sweetness and politeness.

'The Tripartite Pact will regulate conditions in Europe according to the natural interests of the European countries themselves,' he said almost apologetically, 'and that is why Germany now approaches the Soviet Union, so that she can express her views on the territories that are of interest to her.' In no case would a settlement be arrived at without Russian collaboration. That applied not only to Europe but also to Asia where Russia, by the very definition of the Greater Asia area, would be brought in and could substantiate her claims. 'Here Germany plays a mediating role, in no circumstances will Russia be faced with a *fait accompli*.' In addition they were concerned to oppose any attempt by the United States to make capital out of the affairs of Europe. 'There is nothing for the United States in Europe, Africa or Asia.'

Molotov agreed eagerly with this last remark but was less prepared to commit himself on other matters. First of all he wanted more details before expressing himself on Russia's accession to the Tripartite Pact. 'If we are to be treated as equal partners and not mere dummies, we could in principle join the Triple Pact,' he said cautiously, 'but first the aim and object of the Pact must be more closely defined, and I must be more precisely informed about the boundaries of the Greater Asia area.'

Hitler avoided answering any more of Molotov's insistent questions at the intervention of the British. 'I fear we must now break off this discussion,' he said, 'otherwise we shall get caught up in an air-raid warning.' On parting, he assured Molotov that he would address his questions the next day.

Hitler's reference to an air-raid warning was not only a means of escape. I often noticed that he was much concerned for the safety of official visitors during air raids. For example, for the visit of Suñer he had had the cellars of the Adlon Hotel specially strengthened, while the big deep shelter under the Pariser Platz, next to the Adlon, which would later enable us to carry on emergency office work for the Ministerial office during the heavy raids of 1944 and early 1945, had been originally intended for use by official guests of the government. That evening Berlin was spared by the RAF, and the reception thrown by Ribbentrop for the Soviet delegation was held unmolested.

During the second conversation between Hitler and Molotov on the following day, Molotov insisted on pinning the debate down to concrete matters. The first flurry arose over the question of Finland.

'In taking over territory, we ourselves have always adhered to the secret clause of the Moscow agreement delimiting the German and Russian spheres of influence, which is more than one can say about Russia in every case,' Hitler began. This remark referred to the unexpected occupation of Bukovina by the Russians. 'The same goes for Finland,' Hitler went on, 'we have no political interests there.' Germany needed nickel and timber from Finland during the war, however, and could not allow any military complications with regard to Finland that might give the British the opportunity to involve Sweden, and thereby endanger the Baltic Sea. 'Germany has a life and death struggle with Britain on her hands,' Hitler said emphatically, 'and therefore cannot tolerate anything of that sort.'

'If good relations are maintained between Russia and Germany,' Molotov replied calmly, 'the Finnish question can be settled without war,' adding somewhat tartly, 'but in that case there must be no German troops in Finland, and no demonstrations against the Soviet government there.'

'I need not deal with your second point,' Hitler replied quietly but emphatically, 'for that has nothing to do with us.' He went on in sarcastic vein, 'In any case, demonstrations can be staged, and one can never tell who in fact instigated them.'

Hitler did not mince words as he would do in talks with his western partners. With regard to German troops who had crossed Finnish territory in transit to northern Norway, he said that he could give Molotov assurances on this point when general agreement had been reached on the whole question.

'When I mentioned demonstrations, I was also referring to the sending of Finnish delegations to Germany and the reception of leading Finns in Berlin,' Molotov said. 'The Soviet government considers it to be its duty to make a final settlement of the Finnish question.' No new agreement was necessary for this purpose since the existing Russo-German agreement had quite clearly assigned Finland to the Russian sphere of influence.

'We must have peace in Finland because of their nickel and timber!' Hitler was now getting cross. 'A conflict in the Baltic would put a severe strain on Russo-German relations, with unpredictable consequences.'

'It's not a question of the Baltic, but of Finland,' Molotov snapped back.

'No war with Finland,' Hitler repeated.

'Then you are departing from our agreement of last year,' Molotov answered obstinately.

This exchange never became violent but the debate was conducted on both sides with singular tenacity. Even Ribbentrop felt himself called upon to intervene soothingly. Then Hitler began to speak about the 'southern motif', endeavouring to change the Russian drive to the west into a drive to the south. He spoke of the British Empire's 'bankrupt's estate' that had to be divided up, and though he did not mention India by name he referred fairly unmistakably to a 'purely Asiatic territory in the south that Germany already recognises as part of the Russian sphere of interest.'

Molotov refused to be fooled, saying that he preferred to deal first with matters of more concern to Europe. 'You have given a guarantee to Romania, which displeases us. Is this guarantee also valid against Russia?'

'It applies to anyone who attacks Romania,' Hitler declared flatly, but added immediately, 'This question should nevertheless not become acute in your case. You have just made an agreement with Romania yourselves.'

'What would you say,' Molotov enquired, 'if we gave a guarantee to Bulgaria similar to the one you have granted to Romania and on the same terms, that is, with the despatch of a strong military mission?' Bulgaria, he said, was an independent country lying very near the Dardanelles, and therefore important to Russia.

'If you want to give a guarantee on the same terms as we did to Romania,' Hitler remarked, then I must first ask you whether the Bulgarians have asked you for a guarantee as the Romanians did from us?'

Molotov's reply was in the negative but he expressed the view that Russia could certainly reach agreement with Bulgaria, and emphasised that they had no intention of interfering in that country's internal affairs. He would be grateful if Hitler would reply to his question.

'I must talk it over with the Duce,' Hitler stated evasively. Molotov stuck to his point, and again requested a reply from Hitler 'as the man who decides all German policy.' Hitler remained silent.

In connection with Bulgaria the question of the Dardanelles was also discussed. As Ribbentrop had done on the previous day, Hitler wanted to take the opportunity of getting a revision of the Montreux Convention. Molotov on the other hand required 'more than a paper guarantee against any attack on the Black Sea through the Dardanelles'; here he was insisting on an agreement between Russia and Turkey alone. Flanking cover would be provided through the guarantee to Bulgaria, which would be given 'an outlet to the Aegean'.

Some days later, on 26 November 1940, our ambassador in Moscow informed us that Molotov was demanding 'military and naval bases in the Bosphorus region and the Dardanelles, secured on a long-term agreement,' and proposed the conclusion of a protocol 'regarding the military and diplomatic measures to be taken in the case of Turkey's refusal.'

Thus the subjects of chief importance to Russia, then as now, were broached.

On the afternoon of that day, Hitler and Molotov exchanged a further series of ill-tempered remarks upon such questions as Salonica and Greece: Hitler, like Ribbentrop, advocated Russo-Japanese rapprochement. Once again the RAF came to his aid, enabling him to put an end to the uncomfortable conversation by pointing out that there would soon be an air raid warning.

Molotov threw a banquet that evening at the Russian Embassy, which Ribbentrop, but not Hitler, attended. In the unaltered (except for the bust of Lenin) magnificent rooms of the old Tsarist Embassy on Unter den Linden with the most excellent Russian produce, especially of course caviar and vodka, were served. No capitalist or plutocratic (a word then current in the Third Reich) table could have been more richly spread. Everything had been most tastefully arranged. The Russians proved perfect hosts so that in spite of language difficulties it was a very good party. Molotov proposed a friendly toast to which Ribbentrop was just about to reply when the RAF intervened to break up the harmony of the Russo-German banquet. The guests left the Embassy hurriedly on receipt of the preliminary warning, most of them wanting to get to their quarters quickly by car.

Ribbentrop escorted Molotov to his air raid bunker. I did not take part in their conversation as I had only just reached the Adlon when the RAF bombers arrived but Hilger told me about it next day. As I had expected, in its essentials it was a repetition of the other discussions although Molotov on this occasion had been more communicative and had shown an interest in Romania, Hungary, Yugoslavia, Greece and Poland, as well as in Turkey and Bulgaria. Ribbentrop had been really shaken by a remark about Russian interest in the Baltic. Hitler and he referred constantly to this remark in many future conversations in which I took part with other visitors, when they sought to prove that it was quite impossible to get on with the Soviet Union. Molotov on this occasion had described the approaches to the Baltic as a matter in which Russia was not disinterested, and mentioned the Kattegat and Skagerrak.

Molotov and the Russian delegation left next day. I had not been present at such sharp interchanges as those which took place during the talks between Hitler and Molotov since the conversations with Chamberlain during the Sudeten crisis. I am convinced that it was during those days that decisions were taken that led Hitler to attack the Soviet Union. This was the last time that outward form and inner content bore any relation to each other. I attended many another discussion under a political sky dark with the gathering storm, but all were shadowy and unreal compared to the Hitler–Molotov talks.

There was, however, to be one exception: the talks that Hitler and Ribbentrop had four months later with another envoy from the east, the Japanese Foreign Minister Matsuoka. His musical name was on everybody's lips when he arrived in Berlin on a state visit from Japan. It was notable that the Berliners pronounced his name clearly without changing it into Berlinese as they had done for instance at the time of the Kellogg Pact, when President Coolidge and US Foreign Minister Kellogg were nicknamed Kulicke and Kellerloch. I often had occasion to drive through Berlin in an open car with Matsuoka during his visit in March 1941, and could thus observe the Berliners' reaction to the little man from Japan. 'Look, there's Matsuoka!' the crowd would shout. 'Watch out that the little man doesn't slip away under the car!' a fat Berliner once called out to me as I alighted. Matsuoka took this as an ovation and raised his top hat with Asiatic solemnity.

I had known Matsuoka since 1931 when he was chief of the Japanese delegation at Geneva representing Japanese interests at the League Council during the Manchurian conflict. When I saw him again in Berlin, I immediately recalled the scene when he had thundered 'anarchy in China!' in the crowded League of Nations hall.

On 26 March I waited at the Anhalter station 'with the leaders of party and state' for the arrival of the special train bringing Matsuoka. Such a '*Bahnhof*' (station), as we of the Foreign Office used to call these grand receptions, was always a sort of music hall spectacle on the diplomatic stage.

With the officials and party members all in uniform – and what uniforms richly decorated with gold and silver lace they were – the whole scene looked more like a film set. A long red carpet spread over the platform set the tone. Ranged along it were grouped the officials, according to their department and rank; at their head stood the Foreign Minister of the Reich, looking like a bored film star, acting out the part of statesman. Next to him stood the immensely tall *chef de protocol*, von Dörnberg who, like a Furtwängler, was the expert conductor of the diplomatic orchestra at such a '*Bahnhof*'. He was responsible for seeing that the soloists did not miss their cue. Above all, he had to arrange that the Reich Foreign Minister should be properly floodlit when east and west shook hands at the exact moment just after the train had stopped. Another condition had to be fulfilled if the scene was to come off exactly as laid down in the 'shooting script' – the front door of the guest's saloon coach must be exactly opposite the red carpet when the train stopped. As any engine driver knows, that needs some skill with a train of twelve to fifteen coaches; yet at each of the innumerable 'stations' in which I took part this trick was performed faultlessly by the *Reichsbahn*. For the purpose the whole train had to be carefully measured at the last station before Berlin Anhalter; it was necessary to calculate how much the buffers of the individual coaches would be compressed at a given brake pressure, and there were other technical problems involving the couplings and hooks as well. It always worked, however, even if sometimes, as on one of Mussolini's innumerable visits, the train stopped with such a jolt that the foreign VIP's knocked their heads against the window frames, and the smile prescribed at this point of the script had a pained expression.

There was no jolt for Matsuoka. His train, with himself visible at the window, slid in quietly and stopped dead opposite the red carpet so that the representative of the Far East ally could step on to the platform according to programme. The Reich Foreign Minister and his suite stepped forward solemnly to greet him. There followed the mutual introduction of colleagues, press flashlights, newsreel floodlights, applauding crowds, children singing and a short respite in the so-called 'Princes' Room' (the waiting room for state visitors at the Anhalter station), then more shouting on the station forecourt, military bands, national anthems, and an inspection of the guard of honour by the two ministers. The comic effect created by their differences in height was accentuated by the *chef de protocol*, over 6ft tall, who stood by them.

The dapper little Japanese with his solemn face, his short little black moustache and golden spectacles made one think of him as a lost child. What a different effect he made here, surrounded by the tall Germans, literally looking down on him, to that occasion in Geneva when I had looked up as he stood on the speaker's tribune to hear him snarl about 'anarchy in China!'

The enthusiasm of the populace had been carefully organised along the streets through which we drove to reach Schloss Belvedere. The producers, on this occasion party members, had thought of everything, including thousands of little paper Japanese flags, which, rushed up at the last moment, were distributed to the crowd in the 'Via Spontana'. Someone had seen it in the weekly newsreel, and had thought this a particularly delightful Japanese custom, and so Berlin promptly went Japanese.

Initially the Berliners' enthusiasm for Matsuoka was indistinguishable from that accorded to other state visitors, from Mussolini to the Croat leader the Poglavnik, as he was called. But during the days after his arrival when people in Berlin got a clearer idea of their little guest from East Asia through newsreels, radio and seeing him, interest became more human. With his instinct for comical situations, the Berliner saw the light opera effect in all these scenes and the longer the visit lasted the more pronounced was the Gilbert and Sullivan atmosphere in the streets through which Matsuoka passed.

The first meeting with Hitler took place the day following Matsuoka's arrival. The ceremony surrounding such receptions has often been described. In many particulars it was like a '*Bahnhof*', for the props were the same. The most notable feature of a reception was the walk along the 500ft-long hall of the New Chancellery; one could see immediately whether the visitor was at home on polished parquet. Here the tiles were dark red marble and not parquet but so smooth that the visitor was compelled to cover the distance to the great swing doors of the anteroom to Hitler's office with short, prudent, courtly steps. When these doors opened, only very few persons were admitted by Minister of State Meissner, Hitler's high master of ceremonies, who ruled here. Anyone else, no matter how fine his uniform, would be intercepted by Meissner's staff and diverted into other anterooms and kept more or less under observation.

On this occasion, apart from Matsuoka and Hitler, only the two ambassadors, Ott, our man in Tokyo, and Oshima, their man in Berlin, were present when the conversations began on 27 March 1941.

News had been received that morning that in Yugoslavia Zvetkovich and Prince Regent Paul, had been overthrown in a *coup d'état* and that Belgrade was in a state of siege. This news had caused Hitler to delay the meeting with Matsuoka at short notice.

I had witnessed Yugoslavia's joining the Tripartite Pact at Schloss Belvedere in Vienna just a few days before. Only after considerable German pressure had Yugoslavia given in and signed. Experts had advised against insisting on it as the Yugoslav government, having regard to prevailing sentiment, would probably not survive this unpopular measure. Foremost amongst those advising against it was German Ambassador von Heeren, but as happened so often on these occasions the opinions of the 'weakly diplomats' were ignored. Pressure was intensified, Zvetkovich signed at Vienna and only a few days later disaster ensued just as the 'weaklings' had predicted. I must add that after the solemnisation of the treaty I succeeded in drinking a *slivovich* with Zvetkovich, and in so doing won a bet that I would succeed with this Balkan tongue-twister.

While Hitler, intent upon revenge, had been making arrangements for the attack on Yugoslavia, Ribbentrop had preliminary discussions alone with Matsuoka. Almost as a matter of routine he gave the usual account of Germany's enormous military supremacy although he avoided saying that the war was already won. Since the Molotov visit he had toned down the refrain and now he was stating that Germany would scotch any attempt by the British to make landings on the European continent and establish a footing there. He added that Germany now had an enormous army reserve 'which can be committed at any time and at any place the Führer considers necessary.'

To anyone with ears to hear, especially if he was aware of Hitler's intention to attack the Soviet Union, the Russian motif could be heard in these words for the first time. With many different variations it ran through the whole

Matsuoka series of conversations. Combined with a modified southern motif, now changed into an endeavour to persuade Japan to attack the British in East Asia, it constituted the main theme of the talks.

'Strictly between ourselves, Mr Matsuoka,' Ribbentrop said at the end of this discussion at which he substituted for Hitler, 'I should like to inform you that present relations between the Soviet Union and Germany are correct, but not exactly very friendly.' This was a very mild understatement of the position as I knew it after the Molotov talks. 'After Molotov's visit,' Ribbentrop continued more outspokenly, 'during which we offered Russia accession to the Tripartite Pact, the Russians suggested conditions unacceptable to us. We were to sacrifice German interests in Finland, leave to the Russians strongly influential positions in the Balkans and grant them bases in the Dardanelles. The Führer will not enter into such arrangements.'

Matsuoka sat there inscrutably, in no way revealing how these curious remarks impressed him.

In the course of further conversations both Hitler and Ribbentrop returned constantly to this subject. They were obviously much concerned to eradicate Matsuoka's impression that harmonious relations existed between Germany and the USSR lest Japan should be inclined to work for closer friendship with the USSR. In view of the planned war with the Soviets this would not have fitted at all into the political framework as Germany saw it. I was especially interested to note how their statements gradually pointed more and more openly to the coming conflict with the USSR although it was never mentioned outright. Thus in another context Ribbentrop complained quite openly about the increasingly unfriendly attitude being shown by the Soviets towards Germany. 'Since Sir Stafford Cripps has been ambassador in Moscow, relations between Britain and the USSR have been very actively cultivated in secret. Sometimes even fairly openly.' Matsuoka pricked up his ears, and Ribbentrop continued in the rather overbearing tone he sometimes assumed: 'I know Stalin personally, and do not believe that he is inclined to adventures, though naturally I do not know for certain.' He had come to the point he was aiming for from the start and now broached it with a frankness which surprised me: 'If the Soviet Union should one day adopt an attitude that Germany regards as a threat, the Führer will destroy Russia.'

Even the inscrutable Matsuoka blinked at these words, such was his surprise at the prospect they opened up. Ribbentrop must have thought that his guest looked rather concerned, for he decided to administer a tranquiliser, stressing every word: 'Germany is absolutely convinced that a war against the

Soviet Union would result in a complete victory for German arms and the total destruction of the Red Army and the Soviet State.'

From the horrified look on Matsuoka's face Ribbentrop must have noticed that he had administered the wrong prescription, and been too frank, for he added very quickly, 'I do not believe, however, that Stalin will pursue a foolish policy.'

The southern motif was now brought in. 'The Tripartite Pact can best achieve its true aim of preventing the war from spreading, that is to say, by the expedient of frightening the United States from taking part in it, if its partners decide upon a common plan for the final conquest of Britain,' Ribbentrop explained and he combined this fairly obvious hint with the suggestion that Japan should occupy Singapore.

At this point the discussion was interrupted. A messenger summoned Ribbentrop to a conference with Hitler at which it would be decided to attack Yugoslavia.

I took advantage of the interval to speak to Matsuoka, telling him with what interest I had followed his activities over the Manchurian question at the time, and how I still remembered the Japanese delegation walking out of the League of Nations.

'Just so,' he replied. 'I was not very successful on that occasion; if we could have remained in the League and got the Japanese view accepted by the member States, my mission would have been a success. As it is, I regard our having left the League as a failure.'

I should have liked to answer, 'Not only *Japan's* leaving the League,' but that was a private opinion and irrelevant to the discussion.

The talks with Hitler postponed on account of the Yugoslav crisis began that afternoon of 27 March 1941. Hitler was again confident of victory, speaking of the successes of the German U-boat arm and the supremacy of the Luftwaffe. 'I advise you,' he told Matsuoka,' to take a look, while you're in Berlin, at the negligible damage wrought by the British air attacks, and compare it with the devastation we have inflicted on London. That will give you an idea of our supremacy in the air.' Although his Foreign Minister now showed more reserve in the matter, Hitler still maintained that Britain had already lost the war. 'It is now only a question of Britain being sensible enough to admit her defeat. Then we shall see the deflation of the persons in the British government who are responsible for Great Britain's senseless policy.' Britain had only two hopes left: help from the USA – 'but if it reaches Britain at all it will be too little and too late' – and from the USSR.

This remark brought Hitler to one of the two main themes. He treated it on the same lines as Ribbentrop had done, but not so clumsily. From time to time he used the same stock phrases as Ribbentrop had done; these were later repeated to Matsuoka by Göring and others. I was reminded of the stereotyped speeches when Sumner Welles visited.

In discussing the second main theme, the southern motif, Hitler observed that it seemed to him highly desirable to keep the United States out of the war. This was obviously a matter of grave concern to him, for he was to make the point constantly in the course of his conversation with Matsuoka. One of the most appropriate ways of attaining this objective, he suggested, would be a resolute attack on Britain, for instance the surprise capture of Singapore by Japan. Another such opportunity would not occur again soon, therefore Japan should act quickly. 'And she should have no fear of Russia with regard to this enterprise in view of the strength of the German army.'

All these weighty hints were given in a setting of magnificent rhetorical fireworks. No doubt Hitler himself took a rosy view of the military and political situation. As he often did, he juggled with facts and figures, seeming to carry in his head all the details of armaments production and strategy.

The little Matsuoka sat quietly opposite Hitler; so far, like many others who 'conversed' with the Führer he had not been able to get a word in edgewise. Finally Hitler stopped talking, feeling no doubt that he had prepared the ground adequately, and gave Matsuoka a challenging look. The latter had mastered English quite well during his long stay in the United States and the words came slowly and deliberately from his lips. He answered Hitler's point about Singapore evasively; personally he was convinced that the German view was the right one but, as he added with some emphasis, 'I can give no firm promise on behalf of Japan at the moment.'

Hitler's expression showed his disappointment quite plainly. Matsuoka went on to say that he himself was for quick action, but he could not put his view across in Japan yet. He continued with a surprisingly outspoken lament, highly unusual in such a conversation, about the opposition he had to overcome in Japan to his energetic all-out policy. This opposition came from the intellectuals, from the Japanese who had been educated in the United States or Britain and in whom the pure tradition had been corrupted by association with the Western world. Commerce and court circles were apparently all conspiring to hamstring Matsuoka. I felt, as I took notes, that I was hearing one of Goebbels' leading articles on difficulties inside Germany.

Matsuoka's remarks would have seemed to me even more intriguing had I known, as we do now, that at almost the same moment another Japanese envoy was complaining about him in talks with President Roosevelt on 14 March 1941. I refer to Nomura, the Japanese Ambassador in Washington, who said quite openly that his Foreign Minister talked too big because it had a good effect at home and he was motivated by personal ambition. Nomura said that Japan could not commit herself to ambitious plans such as those of Matsuoka's devising. Conditions in Europe were deteriorating, therefore Japan and the United States must collaborate in the cause of peace! With regard to Matsuoka's Berlin visit, Nomura said that it was no more than a gesture of courtesy to the German government, and that the belligerent remarks made by Matsuoka while on his way to Berlin were not to be taken too seriously. This did not quite satisfy US Secretary of State Cordell Hull. He has told us that he replied to Nomura: 'You must understand that Matsuoka's dallying with the Axis and his noisy statements on the way to Berlin, taken in conjunction with the concentration of Japanese naval and air forces in the neighbourhood of Indo-China and Thailand, have made a very bad impression here in the United States.'

As I have said, these interesting conversations were taking place in America without our knowing anything about them and at about the same time that Matsuoka was talking with Hitler at the Chancellery.

Despite his disappointing reaction to Hitler's suggestion of an attack on Singapore, Matsuoka did tell us that such an undertaking had been the subject of a detailed examination by the Service Departments, who regarded three months as the necessary time in which to complete the operation. Being a cautious Foreign Minister, he had preferred to reckon on six months. These long periods of time put forward by Japan were a further severe disappointment to the impatient Hitler.

Hitler's discussion with Matsuoka thus achieved nothing on the essential point of interest to Germany – Japan's taking part in the war against Britain. In further talks Ribbentrop tried frequently to extract from Matsuoka a binding statement, but Asiatic caution proved more than a match for the thick-skulled Westphalian.

In the course of his visit Matsuoka went to see Göring at Karinhall and duly heard the same line of talk as he had endured in his meetings with Hitler and Ribbentrop, though here perhaps more skilfully put over.

Karinhall had been further enlarged since my last visit. Along its rambling passages one sometimes got the impression of being in a small museum.

In Göring's study, with its vast seats and mighty writing table, and especially of course in the huge hall with its heavy ceiling beams, the little man from Japan seemed even more diminutive than he had in Berlin. When we sat down in the magnificent dining room, one whole wall of which was a window, one was almost surprised that Matsuoka, sunk into his seat, could see over the edge of the long, fabulous table with its heavy silver and floral decorations. His surroundings seemed to rather oppress Matsuoka. Gazing meditatively at the snowy landscape outside the enormous window, looking at the snow-covered pines of the Schorfheide, standing out like filigree work against the grey March sky, he said to me, 'This reminds me of the paintings we love in Japan. The marvellously delicate sight makes me feel quite homesick. Do you know that my name Matsuoka means pine hill?'

He was greatly interested in the marvellous floral decorations on the dining table. I had never yet known a state visit where the guests showed such a fond appreciation of these things. His love of nature was revealed in another way: he told me that he enjoyed his quarters at Schloss Belvedere so much because, although the Schloss was in the heart of the city, it stood in a great park and 'one could even hear birds singing.'

'In the evenings I sometimes used to make the men on guard outside the house rather uneasy,' he told me, 'walking on the terrace in my nightshirt listening to the birds.' I had to smile inwardly at this picture of the Foreign Minister of powerful Japan, expected in Berlin to hurl himself precipitately on Singapore!

Matsuoka's remarks to me that afternoon were not confined to the beauties of nature. Suddenly, he leant towards me so as not to be heard by the others and said, 'Do you know that abroad they say that he' – he indicated Göring by a movement of his head – 'is mad?'

Naturally I knew of these stories, but adopted the astonished expression prescribed by diplomatic custom for such situations – as illustrated in comics by question marks drawn above the astonished face. He must have seen this for he drew his chair a little closer and said, 'Oh yes, it's true enough. There are mental institution papers shown around with his name on them,' and he tapped his left hand with two tiny fingers as is the Japanese custom to drive home the point.

I said nothing, being somewhat embarrassed in my efforts to retain a serious demeanour. Words such as these, spoken by the guest of honour amidst festive surroundings and seated opposite the host at a fortunately very large table, belonged in a situation comedy. My rather long silence and pained expression from my attempts to keep a straight face aroused the sympathy of the good Mr Pine Hill, who sought to reassure me: 'But that need not mean anything, there are many people in Japan who say the same of me. They say, "Matsuoka is crazy"!'

Misfortunes seldom come singly: this weighty remark by the envoy from the East coincided with one of those silences that occur fairly often at such gatherings when nobody can think of anything more to say to his neighbour. Into this silence dropped the vehement words, 'Matsuoka is crazy!' Naturally everyone asked me what he had been talking about and I had to exchange the office of interpreter for that of diplomat, saying with a smile that we had been discussing the withdrawal of the sons of the Rising Sun from the hall of the League of Nations – and I was relieved that I could now laugh openly.

As a matter of course, Göring took Matsuoka on a tour of the house. He was like a big boy showing his possessions to a younger playmate, displaying with pride the treasures he had collected, the pictures, Gobelin tapestries, art antiques, sculptures and valuable old furniture. Göring led him through the whole house, starting at the cellar, where once he had shown the Duchess of Windsor how Elizabeth Arden's massage apparatus worked, and which now contained in addition an excellent swimming bath. 'I hope that one of these gentlemen in his beautiful uniform doesn't slip on the tiles and fall in!' Matsuoka whispered to me with a grin. Then we came to the large room on the ground floor where the model railway was set up.

'There's 300 square yards here,' said Göring, and he went to the control station to release a model of the German express *Der fliegende Hamburger* and a fast through-train in perfect miniature. Its 'safety record' was now second to none and the Duke of Windsor would no longer have had to stand on tiptoe to pick up the trains that had become derailed. 'The track is 1,000 yards long and there are forty electric points and signals,' Göring told Matsuoka, who was shyly admiring this splendid toy.

There were further conversations with Ribbentrop during the next few days. The subject matter was a repetition and so was the result. The only matter of interest was that Ribbentrop had to continually reassure Matsuoka, who had pointed out that the United States would come into the war if Japan attacked Britain. 'We have no interest in a war against the United States,' Ribbentrop declared. This did not completely reassure Matsuoka, who argued constantly that the English-speaking peoples must be reckoned as a single unit.

Matsuoka went from Berlin to Rome, and on his return stayed again for a short time in the German capital where he had further talks with Hitler and Ribbentrop. Nothing new came of them, and they in no way altered the fact that Hitler's endeavour to bring Japan into the war against Britain had failed.

When Matsuoka bade Hitler farewell, once more I had to translate into English for his benefit, "When you get back to Japan, you cannot report to your emperor that a conflict between Germany and the Soviet Union is out of the question.' I was fully conscious of the significance of these words and repeated them slowly twice to make certain that Matsuoka wholly understood their import. He looked at me very seriously and intently, and I felt sure that he realised what Hitler had meant.

I felt less sure of this a few days later when I heard of the neutrality treaty concluded with Stalin by Matsuoka on his return journey. However he might have taken this step just because he had realised in Berlin how critical the situation was between Germany and the Soviet Union, and wanted insurance in case a conflict did arise.

We were much impressed when we heard of a scene that occurred when Matsuoka left Moscow. Contrary to his usual practice, Stalin had been at the station, and after Matsuoka's departure he had turned demonstratively to the German Ambassador Graf von der Schulenburg. Putting an arm around the ambassador's shoulders he said, 'We must remain friends, and you must do all you can to further that end.' A few moments later Stalin turned to the assistant German military attaché, Oberst Krebs, and said to him, 'We shall remain friends with your country – whatever happens.'

While Matsuoka was in Moscow, as we now know, the British made an attempt to influence Japan. Churchill sent a letter to the Japanese Foreign Minister in Moscow in which he warned Japan against entering the war on the side of the Axis powers. The Anglo Saxon powers, the letter stated (bearing out what Matsuoka had himself maintained in Berlin) would always act together. The final victory of the Anglo Saxons was absolutely certain. Churchill like Hitler sought to influence Matsuoka by facts and figures. Britain and the United States produced 90 million tons of steel annually, the Axis less than half that amount and Japan scarcely 10 per cent of it, Churchill pointed out.

While Matsuoka was still in Europe, efforts were also made by the United States, with the support of certain circles in Japan, to detach Japan from the Axis. The Americans offered to act as mediators between Japan and China, and even to recognise the independence of Manchuria, which had been the occasion for Matsuoka's demonstrative departure from the League of Nations in 1931. It seemed that the United States was prepared to forget the whole incident and fall in with Japan's requirements.

After the highly significant talks with Matsuoka, in which the coming disaster was quite clearly evident, there followed some weeks of rather superficial, routine activity for me. This took place against the background of the war in the Balkans and preparations for the forthcoming attack on Russia, of which I had been aware for some time.

Early in May 1941 I was sent with Ribbentrop on a hasty journey to Rome to give the Duce an explanation of Rudolf Hess's surprising flight to Scotland. Hitler was as appalled as though a bomb had struck the Berghof. 'I hope he falls into the sea!' I heard him say in disgust. When we reached Rome, Hess had arrived in Britain. 'He's mad,' Ribbentrop told Mussolini, using the word seriously, unlike Matsuoka. On my return to Berlin I was asked by an old workman, who helped look after my garden, 'Did you know we are ruled by lunatics?'

On 2 June I interpreted again at an interview of several hours' duration at the Brenner. 'German U-boats will force Britain to capitulate,' was now Hitler's refrain. Not the faintest hint did he give the Duce of his intentions with regard to Russia. Hitler's complete silence about these plans, of which I now knew a good deal, particularly impressed me.

Hitler had more confidence in Antonescu, and on 12 June at the Führer-building in Munich he let him into the secret of the forthcoming action against the Soviet Union, almost going so far as to tell him the zero hour. Antonescu was delighted. 'Of course, I'll be there from the start,' he said, after Hitler had promised him Bessarabia and other Russian territory. 'When it's a question of action against the Slavs, you can always count on Romania.'

On 15 June the newly created Croatia joined the Tripartite Pact amidst great celebrations in the Doge's Palace at Venice. The lagoon city and old Venetian Palace, redolent of centuries of Mediterranean history despite the removal of its art treasures for safe keeping, constituted a dreamlike background to which the insignificant and theatrically staged accession of the little state formed a fantastic contrast.

The next scene was dramatically different. In the early hours of 22 June 1941, I waited with Ribbentrop in his Wilhelmstrasse office for the Soviet Ambassador Dekanosov, who since the afternoon of the previous day had been telephoning the Foreign Office every two hours saying that he had pressing business to settle with the Minister. As was usual on the eve of great events he had been told that Ribbentrop was not in Berlin. Then at 2 a.m.

Ribbentrop gave the sign, and Dekanosov was told that Ribbentrop wanted to see him at 4 a.m.

I had never seen Ribbentrop so excited as he was in the five minutes before Dekanosov's arrival. He walked up and down his room like a caged animal. 'The Führer is absolutely right to attack Russia now,' he said to himself rather than to me; he repeated it again and again as though he wanted to somehow reassure himself. 'The Russians will certainly attack us themselves if we do not do so now.' He went on walking up and down the large room in a state of great excitement, his eyes flashing, and kept repeating these words. At the time I attributed his attitude to the fact that he looked on himself as the creator of Soviet–German understanding, and now found it hard to have to destroy his own work. Today I can almost believe that on that morning he felt, subconsciously at any rate, that disaster would result from the decision he now had to communicate to the Soviet Ambassador.

Dekanosov was shown in punctually and, obviously not guessing anything was amiss, held out his hand to Ribbentrop. We sat down, and with 'Little Pavlov's' assistance Dekanosov proceeded to carry out his mission, which was to put to Ribbentrop certain questions for which he needed clarification on behalf of his government. He had hardly begun before Ribbentrop interrupted him with a stony expression and said, 'That's not the question now. The Soviet government's hostile attitude to Germany and the serious threat represented by Soviet troop concentrations on Germany's eastern border have compelled the Reich to take military counter-measures. As from this morning, the relevant counter-measures have been taken in the military sphere.' Ribbentrop did not mention the word 'war' or 'declaration of war'; perhaps he thought it too plutocratic, or perhaps Hitler had instructed him to avoid the word. Now he recited a short but fiery list of breaches, referring especially to the pact concluded by Soviet Russia with Yugoslavia just before the outbreak of war between that country and Germany. 'I regret that I can say nothing further,' he concluded, 'especially as I have myself come to the conclusion that in spite of serious endeavours, I have not succeeded in establishing reasonable relations between our two countries.'

Dekanosov recovered his composure quickly; he expressed his 'deep regrets' that developments had taken such a course. 'It is entirely due to the non-cooperative attitude adopted by the German government,' Pavlov translated, while I took notes for my report. 'Under the circumstances, there is nothing more for me to do but make the necessary arrangements with your *chef de protocol* for the transport home of my mission.' He rose, made a perfunctory bow and left the room accompanied by Pavlov and without shaking hands with Ribbentrop.

'It is how Napoleon's Russian venture may well have started,' I reflected, and felt ashamed of my imperfect knowledge of history. I telephoned the Languages Service and released them from the incarceration in which they had again been working all night at the old Hindenburg Palace.

For the next few weeks all attention was concentrated on military events on the Eastern Front and I was able to have a brief period of respite before taking up busily where I had left off. To begin with, there were conferences at Hitler's HQ *Wolfsschanze*, now in a wood near Rastenburg in East Prussia. In early August he talked to Antonescu almost exclusively about military questions, and for the first time I had to use the technical vocabulary I mentioned earlier. During the latter part of August Mussolini paid a brief visit of several days to the front, which I shall describe later, and in October 1941 Ciano came. Somewhat later Hitler received Dr Tiso, President of Slovakia. It was strange to see Hitler greeting this Catholic priest with friendliness; the short, stout Church dignitary stood facing a man who could hardly be called a friend of the Church of Rome. If Tiso wanted something for Slovakia, however, he would have called on the devil himself. Once he told us, 'When I get worked up I eat half a pound of ham, and that soothes my nerves.'

In November I was working at high pressure in Berlin where, to celebrate the anniversary of the 1936 Anti-Comintern Pact, Hitler had assembled numerous leading statesmen of the countries under German influence. These celebrations were held on 24 and 25 November, and provided the greatest show yet put on in the reception hall of the New Chancellery. On the afternoon of 25 November, Ciano, Antonescu and Serrano Suñer, as well as the Foreign Ministers of Hungary, Bulgaria, Croatia, Finland and Denmark, sat at a very polished long table laden with microphones, a magnificent Gobelin tapestry decorating the wall to the rear. Facing an invited audience of notables, they made a series of high sounding but meaningless speeches. This was Hitler's great review of his allies and vassals. He received each one individually, and gave each his special injection of courage. By the end of these two days I had almost lost my voice.

At the beginning of December I went with Göring to France for a meeting with Pétain at St Florentin-Vergigny, a little town north of Paris. The marshal, who appeared much aged since Montoire, was even more reserved than he had been previously. I could see no reason why this meeting should have been held at all.

While I was observing these meaningless activities from my interpreter's post at FHQ and in Berlin, the really decisive events were taking place elsewhere. During the night of 7 December 1941, the foreign broadcast monitoring service got news of the Japanese attack on Pearl Harbor, and when a second report to the same effect seemed to confirm the news, Ribbentrop was informed. He was extremely angry at being disturbed by these unverified reports. Next day I was told that Ribbentrop had said it was 'probably a propaganda trick of the enemy's for which my Press Section has fallen,' but at the same time he gave instructions that further enquiries should be made and the results reported to him in the morning.

The event was duly confirmed. Hitler and Ribbentrop had been taken by surprise by the Japanese, just as Hitler had surprised their ally Mussolini on similar occasions, only enlightening him at the very last moment. We 'fault finders' commented that it seemed to be the fashion among dictators and emperors.

On 8 December 1941 the United States declared war on Japan. Cordell Hull relates how Roosevelt and some members of the Cabinet including himself had discussed the previous evening whether or not war should be declared on the other Axis powers. They assumed, however, that Germany would certainly declare war on the United States, having gathered from an exchange of telegrams between Berlin and Tokyo that there was a definite understanding on this point. They had therefore decided to wait and leave it to Mussolini and Hitler to take the initiative, and they did not have to wait long.

I know of no understanding with Japan that might have compelled Hitler to declare war on the United States. From what Ribbentrop said at the time I got the impression that Hitler, with his inveterate desire for prestige, was expecting an American declaration of war and wanted to get his one in first.

On 11 December at noon I was once again in Ribbentrop's office in the Wilhelmstrasse, this time, six months later, expecting the US chargé d'affaires. When he came in he was not invited to sit and Ribbentrop, also remaining standing, read out a statement accusing the United States of breaches of neutrality and of making overt belligerent attacks on German U-boats.

> The government of the United States of America, beginning with violations of neutrality, has finally proceeded to overt acts of war against Germany … Under these circumstances, brought about by President Roosevelt … Germany regards herself as from today to be at war with the United States of America.

Handing the document to the chargé d'affaires with a sweeping gesture, the man obviously feeling his position keenly, Ribbentrop indicated with a stiff bow that the audience was terminated.

At the Foreign Office we all liked this American diplomat. I saw him to the door, shook his hand and gave him a friendly smile. The *chef de protocol* was waiting for him outside, and I was pleased to see him behave as I had done, seeking as far as possible to alleviate this unpleasant situation.

During this year the east had spoken to us twice in Berlin, and twice in Ribbentrop's office I had seen the start of a new war, connected directly or indirectly with the East. Seldom did I leave the Foreign Office so depressed as after this second declaration of war. At the time I underrated America, and I did not believe that the war between Japan and the United States, separated as the two countries were by the thousands of miles of Pacific Ocean, could be over as soon as eventually proved to be the case. My first reaction was: 'The war will now be endlessly protracted', and then I went on to think that victory was now impossible for Germany, which, as in the First World War, would again be fighting on two fronts. Despite these premonitions, I had no conception of the scale of the catastrophe to which the Reich was heading under Hitler's leadership.

EIGHT

1942 AND 1943

Soon after the memorable morning of 22 June 1941 when Ribbentrop notified the Russian Ambassador of the 'military counter-measures', the surroundings in which I did my interpreting were very different. Instead of working in magnificent palaces or at banquets, to an increasing extent I was now attached to Hitler's various headquarters in the east. He regarded his presence among his military colleagues as so important that even his foreign visitors were summoned to see him there.

Hitler's principal HQ, where most discussions now took place, was in East Prussia, hidden in a gloomy wood near Rastenburg. It reminded one of the fairy tale of the wicked witch. It was aptly known by the code name *Wolfsschanze* (Wolf's Lair).

The quarters occupied by Hitler and his military staff were in the heart of the forest, miles from any human habitation. They consisted of a dozen comfortable block houses, built partly of stone with wood panelling inside and furnished quite simply and in fairly good taste. The whole encampment was naturally fitted with all the most up-to-date telephone and wireless installations. There was even a cinema, which showed not only the latest newsreels but also British and American films – otherwise strictly forbidden in Germany – in order to alleviate to some degree the monotony of this sort of existence. Anyone coming from the sunny expanses of the surrounding countryside to this encampment in the gloomy East Prussian forest found the atmosphere oppressive. The electric light in Hitler's rooms often had to be on all day even in full sunshine. Hitler seldom went out – it was as though even the dim light of the forest was too bright for him – and his entourage only rarely emerged from the dark woods.

'It is dreadful to be surrounded by trees the whole time,' Hitler's liaison man with the Foreign Office said to me once, 'and never really to get out into the open.' I could well understand the oppressiveness of the twilight atmosphere at FHQ *Wolfsschanze*, although I rarely spent more than one or two consecutive days there, and I always heaved a sigh of relief as I escorted foreign visitors away from the dark forest. I commiserated sincerely with the many whose duties tied them to Hitler and his entourage, and who had to live for weeks, even months, like prisoners in the great wood. Most of them would gladly have exchanged this strange, artificial existence for life in the front line.

Conditions became even worse when HQ offices were transferred to surface bunkers owing to the increasing risk of air attack. Camouflaged grey and green, windowless, with 20ft-thick walls of reinforced concrete, they squatted in the wood like primeval monsters. Low corridors, like galleries in a coal mine, ran through these *montagnes synthétiques*, as Antonescu once aptly referred to them. The rooms were very small and one felt cramped in them, and the dampness from the mass of concrete, the artificial light and the perpetual buzzing of the ventilating machinery increased one's sense of unreality. It was in this milieu that Hitler, growing daily paler and more puffy, received his foreign visitors. The general effect was of the lair of a legendary evil spirit. Observers less grimly inclined thought it was like living in a film studio. A witty colleague once said to me, 'The woodland used in the Hansel and Gretel films we've just finished will be taken down tomorrow, and the day after we're going to start shooting *Anthony and Cleopatra*; the pyramids are up already.'

Over the years my activities had varied considerably, but one thing was always the same, and that was the way I was sent on journeys suddenly and without warning. On these occasions a voice on my office telephone would tell me, 'You must go to FHQ at once. The courier plane is leaving Staaken aerodrome in an hour.'

These courier aircraft were a crazy means of transport. They were not fitted out for passengers; one sat on a chest or packing case or, later on, would have to balance on a primitive wooden bench. There was a frightful draught and smell of fuel, and the noise was deafening. The pilot was usually Luftwaffe, less interested in his passengers than flying quickly to his destination. Closely following the straight line marked on his flight map he would hurl his passengers and freight through the storm clouds and hail showers. Even the strongest of men were apt to lose their breakfasts when using this spartan form of transport.

The speed of my movements was materially increased in 1941. Scarcely had I arrived at FHQ than I was informed that I was to fly to Ukraine next day with Hitler. He was meeting Antonescu to confer on him an decoration and discuss with him the current military situation. We had breakfast and lunch in East Prussia, having in the meantime flown from Rastenburg to Berdichev, conferred the order, had a political conversation and discussed the military situation with von Rundstedt and then flown back to Rastenburg.

At this time I also established long-distance records for an interpreter: in the second half of August I travelled 3,750 miles in a few days. It differed from my long journey of 1940 in that this time I travelled eastwards and with Mussolini. Owing to the shortage of staff, very noticeable in the Foreign Office as elsewhere, I sometimes had to come to the assistance of my friend the *chef de protocole* and act for him, and on several occasions I combined the two posts quite conveniently.

It was in the course of these varied duties that I was detailed to meet Mussolini at the Brenner (in my capacity as Chief of the Ceremonial Service). The order was given at such short notice that I was driven at 70mph all the way down the *autobahn* from Berlin to Munich station where a small special train had been laid on to get me to the Brenner. I remained with Mussolini until he was handed back to his countrymen at Tarvisio in Carinthia on the Reich frontier a week later.

From the Brenner we had gone direct to the East Prussian woods, where we met Hitler, then spent the following day in Brest-Litovsk, returning that night to East Prussia. We left the same night in the Italian special train for

Hitler's southern HQ near Kraków, flew from there next day with fighter protection to Uman in the Ukraine, where we jolted along in an old car looking for an Italian division that Mussolini wanted to see, finally found it and then flew back to Kraków. Here the special trains awaited us in a siding protected against air attack within an extremely long concrete tube, and I left that evening with Mussolini for Tarvisio via Vienna. After taking leave of him I was borne by train to Salzburg and returned to Berlin via the autobahn the way I had come.

It is obvious that this programme hardly allowed time for any serious discussion. Hitler and Mussolini did not even use the same special train and met only in the aircraft, in the jolting car and during short stays at FHQ. Meetings such as this one were therefore only a fantasy staged for the outside world. When Hitler and Mussolini were together, the latter expressed his own opinions even less frequently than he had at the Brenner meetings. When they sat opposite each other for an hour Hitler would ramble on about our forthcoming victory, or the strength of our position and the weakness of Russia and Britain, or the inevitability of final victory; overwhelm his guest with figures and military details; or call for Kluge or Rundstedt to deliver a military dissertation and exhibit the newest giant gun. Nevertheless I was surprised to observe that the final effect was always to produce a strengthening of Mussolini's morale, or that of his visitors, who were treated to a shortened version of the same programme. I had considerable doubts myself, even at the time, of the lasting effects of this high-powered propaganda. My own confidence would weaken markedly after I parted with one of these visitors, and I would reflect that back in his own country the visitor would share my pessimistic views. Indeed, he was bound to do so as the general situation from 1941 onwards persistently grew worse.

These meetings called for a vast amount of organisation. Everything had to be worked out to the minute; Mussolini's shaving time, during which his special train would stop, had to be allowed for accurately by the Reichsbahn; a number of locomotives, already scarce enough, had to be requisitioned and special personnel detailed; military staffs behind the front who had the misfortune to be visited had to waste their time in preparing shows and lectures when there were much more urgent things to do; and all this vast amount of futile activity was eventually condensed into stereotyped communiqués about 'comradeship', 'carrying the war to its victorious conclusion', 'the New European Order' and so forth. Indeed, I often had the feeling that all these elaborate arrangements were carried out only for the sake of the communiqués, whose purpose was to impress the German public and, even more, the outside world. Fantastic incidents sometimes occurred over their preparation.

On my way back to Tarvisio, for instance, at a station where our train was linked up to the Reich telephone network, I got a curt message for transmission to Mussolini:'The German Foreign Minister has withdrawn the agreed communiqué.' Immediately after receiving this, the train started off again and communication was broken off. Theoretically a radio signal could have been sent while the train was in motion, but having regard to the time it would take to encode the signal for relaying from Berlin to reach Hitler and Ribbentrop in their special trains and for the signal to be decoded, I suggested that it was simpler to deal with the matter instead when we got to the next place from where we could telephone. The Italians did not dare agree and immediately reported the message to the Duce. He exploded with rage and said to me in the greatest excitement, 'Have the train stopped at once. I shall not leave German territory until Ribbentrop's shameless conduct has been dealt with.' I had the impression that he would like to have pulled the communication cord there and then. 'We'll stop at the next station, and you'll telephone!' he commanded me with a look worthy of the Caesars. I explained that I could only speak on the through line, and that we had to wait until we reached the next available station enabling us to link into the main network. When we got there I established what had happened, and relate it now as typical of the fantasy of those years.

After Mussolini's departure, Hitler and Ribbentrop had also left in their respective trains. Ribbentrop had then read through the communiqué again, and noticed that the concluding paragraph read as follows:'Also taking part in the military and political conversations on the German side were ... Generalfeldmarschall Keitel and Reich Foreign Minister von Ribbentrop.' Infuriated that his name was put after that of Keitel (one of his many enemies), Ribbentrop rang through to my namesake Schmidt, head of the Press Section, and told him to reverse the order of the names. At the next station Schmidt dashed to Hitler's special train to report Ribbentrop's complaint to Hitler, at which Hitler began to rage at Ribbentrop's vanity. The Foreign Minister's disputes with Goebbels, Keitel and others had often been the cause of great annoyance to Hitler, but inexplicably he always gave in, causing Ribbentrop to become ever more arrogant. This time too, in the end Hitler said that he would allow Ribbentrop to be named first in the communiqué, and Schmidt returned much relieved to Ribbentrop's train at the next station and reported his success.

'What did the Führer say?' Ribbentrop asked rather anxiously, and when Schmidt gave him a toned-down version of the Führer's displeasure he declared suddenly, 'I withdraw my request. It shall stay as it was.' The communiqué was to be issued in Berlin within an hour and announced over the wireless and so the matter was most urgent. Schmidt decided to use the wireless telegraph to Berlin, from where the cancellation of the originating message was re-transmitted to me for communication to Mussolini.

Rather less unreal were the discussions Hitler had with Antonescu, who came to FHQ in East Prussia for the first time in February 1942. I have already related how Antonescu always began with a long-winded dissertation on the creation of Romania, which he described as 'the rock that has withstood the Slavonic flood throughout the centuries' and 'whose cradle is Transylvania'. On each visit he indicated pretty plainly his firm intention of one day recovering the whole of Transylvania by force of arms. Hitler took a secret pleasure in Antonescu's outbursts against the Hungarians, and even went so far as to hint that he might perhaps give him a free hand later in his plans of conquest.

'History never stands still,' Hitler said by way of mollifying Antonescu, who was complaining most emphatically about the 'injustice of the Vienna Award.' To make his meaning plainer, Hitler added: 'You, perhaps, will be able to turn over another new page of history.' Antonescu understood him well enough, for in later years he reminded Hitler more than once of his 'promise' about Transylvania.

On other matters too, Antonescu never minced words at these conversations. On one occasion when Hitler wanted to blame the Romanians, Hungarians and Italians for the Soviet breakthrough that led to the encirclement of 6th Army at Stalingrad, Antonescu contradicted him emphatically, and proceeded to a vehement criticism of German leadership – of Hitler by implication – using what seemed to me very telling arguments by a former General Staff officer, for in military matters Antonescu refused to be hoodwinked. As far as I could judge he was an outstanding strategist. He always turned up to meetings well supplied with volumes of statistics and charts in which all operational details were set out, ranging from casualties, neatly indicated in various colours to show categories and age groups, to ammunition requirements and artillery reserves.

With attentive and critical eyes Antonescu followed the daily conferences on the situation at the front as indicated on the big map in the room in which the attempt would later be made on Hitler's life by Stauffenberg. Army, navy and Luftwaffe experts described the position successively, and I translated their accounts into French. Antonescu was always given a general survey but, as the real position at the fronts grew worse, I heard the officers refer more often to these situation reports as 'show pieces', the foreign visitor being given a rosier picture of things than they actually were. I could not gather whether Antonescu, a professional soldier, saw through these tactics or not. At all events, he asked very few questions and always seemed to leave FHQ in better spirits than when he arrived. I would often hear from Bucharest a few days later after his return to Romania, however, that he showed no signs of any good effects from Hitler's pep talk, having in the meantime learnt from his own reports from the front that matters had been represented to him too favourably at FHQ.

Even if the communiqués were headed 'From the Führer's Headquarters', the meetings had not always taken place in the simple setting of the forest encampment in East Prussia or at one of Hitler's other HQ's in the east.

In the spring of each year there was a sort of Salzburg Season when, as far as the public was concerned, the meetings took place 'at FHQ' although actually they were held at the baroque Schloss Klessheim, which had formerly belonged to the Prince-Bishops of Salzburg and had been used by Max Reinhardt during the Salzburg Festivals before the *Anschluss*. One can say without exaggeration that especially after it had been completely renovated inside by specialists, this Schloss was an architectural jewel – quite different from what the general public pictured as the Führer's headquarters.

Mussolini and Ciano were at Salzburg on 29 and 30 April 1942 during the Salzburg Season and had discussions with Hitler and Ribbentrop in the apartments of the former episcopal residence, sometimes in pairs and sometimes all four of them together. A 'show situation' was put on for their benefit.

When they paired off I translated for Ciano, who knew no German, leaving Hitler and Mussolini to converse alone. As is known, the winter of 1941 brought the first difficulties of the Russian campaign. We were held up in front of Moscow and there was rising popular indignation about the inadequate supply of winter clothing for the army. Quite suddenly furs had to be collected from civilians and skiers equipment and clothing requisitioned so that any unprejudiced person got an extremely bad impression of the lack of foresight shown by the German leaders. In their conversations with the Italians, Hitler and Ribbentrop had somehow to gloss over these and other shortcomings. For this purpose Ribbentrop would proclaim from the rooftops that 'The Führer's genius has overcome the Russian winter'; Germany would press on to southern Russia and force the Soviets to capitulate by depriving them of their oil resources, which would make the British realise that they had better sue for peace. 'America is one big bluff.' 'France is unreliable'. Such were the themes of the Salzburg fantasy.

In his diary entry for 29 April 1942, Ciano vividly described the scene: 'Hitler talks, talks, talks. Mussolini, who is himself accustomed to speaking and must be almost silent here, suffers. On the second day, after the meal, when everything had already been said that could be said, Hitler went on talking for an hour and forty minutes about war and peace, religion and philosophy, art and history. Mussolini checked his watch, I followed my own thoughts … General Jodl had nodded off on a divan after an epic struggle against sleep. Keitel was a bit unsteady but managed to keep his head up, sitting too close to Hitler to follow his inclination. Those poor Germans, they had to endure this every day and there was certainly no word, pause or gesture they did not know by heart.' As interpreter I can certainly confirm this last statement, since my workload was lightened considerably by the seasonal replays.

At the following year's Salzburg 'performance' Ciano did not have to be bored. He had been demoted by Mussolini and to the great joy of Hitler and Ribbentrop, from whom Ciano had not concealed his increasingly critical attitude towards German policy, was sent as ambassador to the Holy See in February 1943. In one of those political trials that became the fashion, he was executed by firing squad on 23 December 1943 for his part in the overthrow of Mussolini.

At the beginning of April 1943 Mussolini appeared with his new foreign policy adviser, Bastianini, who was the complete opposite of Ciano – serious, almost grim, and quiet and reticent when he spoke. The scenes of the previous year, so aptly described by Ciano, were repeated; the only new element was the interesting fact that Mussolini now advocated emphatically coming to terms with the Soviet Union. 'To conquer Russia seems to me impossible,' was in effect what he said. 'Therefore it is better to make a compromise peace with the east and have our hands free for the west.'

Antonescu, who met us at Schloss Klessheim two days after Mussolini's departure, held exactly the opposite view. 'All out forces against the east,' was his advice, and therefore he advocated concluding a separate peace with the western powers.

On 16 April 1943, four days after Antonescu's visit, Horthy appeared. I have little information about his conversation with Hitler as I did not have to interpret and Horthy objected to my presence as a reporter. Before his talk with the Hungarian regent, Hitler had said to me, 'I want to have you there today when I talk to Horthy so that we can have an independent report made, otherwise Horthy distorts what I say.' When the regent arrived he looked at me rather disapprovingly and said to Hitler: 'I thought we were going to be talking alone without witnesses.' So I was sent out. I was never sorry to be spared a tedious job.

Before the end of the month we had two more visitors at Klessheim: the cleric Tiso (who ate a pound of ham when he was worked up) from Slovakia and Pavelich the Poglavnik, leader of the Croats. 'Never was a local mayor received with such honours by the head of state of a great power' was the comment on this visit in the corridors of Schloss Klessheim, for by this time the partisans already has such a hold in Croatia that the Poglavnik's authority scarcely extended beyond the town of Zagreb.

In the summer of 1942 Hitler's HQ was transferred to the Ukraine in another large, dark forest near Vinnytsa. The atmosphere at FHQ *Wehrwolf* was an improvement on Rastenburg, but for a normal person still grim enough. The block houses were the same but there were no bunkers.

Two hours away at Zhitomir was the 'field HQ' of Ribbentrop, who thought he should be near Hitler once the Russian campaign started, whereas Hitler kept him at a distance 'so that he doesn't keep coming and bothering me with his affairs'.

In East Prussia for the same reason Ribbentrop had had to accommodate himself some distance from Hitler's HQ. He stayed at Schloss Steinort near Angerburg, which belonged to the Lehndorf family while a large part of his staff lived and worked at the opposite end of the Schwenzeit Lake in the Hotel Jägerhöhe, which had been built for the ice yachting regattas of the winter Olympiad. This distance between the two staffs, both in East Prussia and the Ukraine, was responsible for a lot of lost time.

Ribbentop, who had no experienced in running a department, summoned the Foreign Office officials to East Prussia or the Ukraine for the most trivial reasons and then would leave them hanging around idle all day. It was a fantastic waste of time, valuable manpower and petrol.

Foreign ambassadors too were often summoned to HQ, and as many of them did not speak German well enough I had to make innumerable journeys to the Ukraine. A special sleeper train, the so-called 'service train', was made available for this purpose and left Berlin-Schlesien station every evening, earlier in the winter to avoid the air raids. It reached Warsaw the next morning, Brest-Litovsk at noon and the former Russo-Polish frontier in the evening. From there on, because of partisans and frequent damage to the track, this luxury train proceeded at a snail's pace to Vinnytsa and arrived the following morning. The foreign diplomats had to detrain at Berdichev at three in the morning, however, and make a two-hour drive by car to Ribbentrop's field HQ. He received them at 11 a.m., lunched with them at noon and then flew with them at 1 p.m. to Hitler's HQ. Here the conference would take place at 3 or 4 p.m., and last an hour or two. Then they had to return by car to Ribbentrop's field HQ where they dined, leaving at midnight for Berdichev and catching the Service Train back to Berlin at two a.m. This train pulled into Berlin at eight in the morning. on the second morning. Thus for a short discussion with Hitler, on what were nearly always trivial or irrelevant matters, ambassadors or other important persons would spend at least three days and four nights travelling. This example is characteristic of the methods favoured by Hitler and Ribbentrop. Not only the ambassador and I, but also usually an escort from the Protocol Section, were set in motion. On some occasions, as for instance when the new Turkish Ambassador presented his credentials, a whole saloon coach with attendants was attached to the 'service train', and Minister of State Meissner, as Hitler's master of ceremonies, had to escort the guest personally.

Hitler made several attempts to induce Turkey to come into the war on the side of the Axis powers. One of the baits he offered was the hint that Turkey might take over Turkish-speaking territories held by Russia. Neither Gerede nor his successor Arikan would discuss such a suggestion; both stated bluntly that Turkey had enough to do in fully developing their own country and had not the slightest interest in any acquisition of territory.

Hitler's efforts were also directed at preventing Turkey from joining the Allies. The Turkish Ambassador always denied this danger, but our Intelligence Service kept us well informed of the Allies' efforts to lure Turkey over in this respect. For some time the Intelligence Service had succeeded in obtaining photographs of documents from the desk of the British Ambassador in Ankara, and these 'Cicero' documents gave us remarkably useful information about the Allies' negotiations with Turkey. They were of particular interest to me because Turkey seemed to evade the Allies' vigorous efforts by methods very similar to those I had seen employed by Franco at Hendaye when Hitler had tried to get him to enter the war on Germany's side.

In April and again in August 1942 I went to France with a small delegation from the Languages Service to interrogate Canadian prisoners of war who had recently spent time in Great Britain and had been captured in the Dieppe raid, and British prisoners of war taken at Saint-Nazaire. I was attempting in particular to get information about the food and supply situation, the effect of German radio propaganda and the general mood prevailing in Britain. The *Wehrmacht* was very reluctant to let Foreign Office civilians have access to 'their' prisoners, and we were expressly forbidden to put any questions to them on military matters.

We elaborated a system whereby in the course of conversation with prisoners of war we touched on selected points and drew our conclusions from the prisoners' reactions and answers. In this way we ascertained that despite the U-boat war the food and supply situation in Britain could not be anything like as bad as wishful thinkers in Germany – led by Ribbentrop – said they knew it was. We learnt that the English-language broadcasts from Germany were listened to attentively, and we were told the best time to send them. 'If you want to, you yourselves can give your family news of your capture over the German radio,' we told the British. Despite the strict ruling against broadcasting, almost all of them were prepared to do so.

To the question of when their families in Britain would be listening so that their personal messages could be sent over German radio at that time, most replied, 'Our people listen first to the nine o'clock news, and then to the news from Germany at nine-thirty.' When we went on to ask whether they believed what they heard from Germany, all answered 'No!' but added, 'Neither do we believe all we hear from the BBC; probably the truth lies somewhere between the two.'

We were interested to find out that people in Canada were unlikely to hear our propaganda. When the Canadians captured at Dieppe wanted to send personal messages, we asked them whether their families had short-wave sets to receive messages from Germany. They said they had not, and that personal messages from prisoners of war were relayed by local transmitters. If this was so, it was a clever way of nullifying our attempts to exploit such messages for propaganda purposes because the local transmitters relayed the greetings and censored the propaganda.

All the prisoners made an excellent impression and behaved splendidly. I found it a melancholy experience to see behind barbed wire these men with whose language and history I was so thoroughly familiar, and whose peoples had always been so congenial to me. In the same situation in 1945 I sometimes reflected on my conversations with the British of Saint-Nazaire and the Canadians of Dieppe, and now and then divined a similar feeling of commiseration in my interrogators, especially amongst some from the US State Department. In the course of this brief assignment in France I had naturally learnt a good deal about interrogation methods and later made interesting comparisons. It was not without amusement that I discovered how their civilian staffs were regarded with the same suspicion by the American military as we diplomats had been by the Wehrmacht in 1942.

At Saint-Nazaire and Dieppe the other ranks and senior officers were the easiest to talk to, the young British lieutenants the most difficult to draw out. Only when one went on saying that Germany would certainly win the war would they contradict us. 'I should say the same in your place,' we would reply, 'but I can explain why Germany will win the war, whereas you cannot tell me why Britain will win.' This method never failed and always got the conversation going, usually with very interesting results. I was very greatly impressed by the complete confidence that all, from private soldier to general, expressed in their prospects of victory and by the absence of any fanaticism or any suggestion of hatred of Germany.

We had almost insuperable difficulties with the Canadians, not for their obstinacy but because these huge, hearty backwoodsmen with friendly blue eyes and jolly laughs revealing perfect teeth knew practically nothing about Europe, let alone Germany.

I once asked one of these fine lads, 'Have you ever heard of any Germans?'

He thought deeply for a long time and then said, 'Yes. General Rommel and Lili Marlene.'

As a matter of purely personal interest, at Saint-Nazaire one of the prisoners looked at me closely and said, 'Why, you are the Dr Schmidt who is always interpreting,' and explained that he had often seen my photograph in illustrated accounts of conference meetings. The same thing happened at Dieppe with a French-Canadian major, a ski manufacturer, to whom I was talking in French. 'I have followed your career in the press,' he said, 'and would have given quite a lot of money to have had a chat with you!' The major escaped eight days after our conversation, and two months later published in Britain an article about our talk. I am glad that he did not repeat some of the rather indiscreet remarks I made on the assumption that he would remain a prisoner until the end of the war, but he had taken remarks that I had made on the theme of 'who is going to win the war' at face value – I had only made them to draw him out.

These conversations also showed me how good were underground communications between France and Britain during the hostilities. As did the other members of the delegation, I always drew up a report on the interrogations – which as far as I know were never used, since they stated facts that did not fit in with the official view.

We used to work in a large lounge writing up our reports at the Hotel Bristol in Paris to where now and then the waiter would bring us drinks, at which we would usually stop dictation. Only a short time after my August visit to Paris, a London newspaper reported that certain orders, ostensibly found on a British officer who fell near Dieppe and used for propaganda purposes by Germany 'had in reality been forged by Dr Schmidt, the English expert at the German Foreign Office and a large staff in Paris.' Remembering the head waiter, I could see how this story might have come into being, and I was rather gratified that my knowledge of languages was rated so highly in London that I was thought capable of fabricating even official documents convincingly.

While the political world receded further into the mists of unreality, my work in Berlin was carried on under increasingly warlike conditions as British air raids gradually intensified. In the autumn of 1940 I had been deeply grieved to read the jubilant accounts in the Goebbels press of the air raids on London, where I had a large number of friends. I knew London as well as I knew Berlin and the many months I had spent there, and in Paris too, in the years before the war made me look on it as a kind of second home. 'How on earth shall I be able to look my English friends in the face again?' I used to think sadly when I read in the papers of the 'great conflagrations', 'widespread destruction' and the like, and Ribbentrop give gloating accounts of the raids to foreign visitors. I rejoiced at heart when I heard on the radio of the courage of Londoners, and read in the British press, to which I had access throughout the war, that they stood up to all their trials with that sane equanimity and humour that seems to be characteristic of the folk of all capital cities in all countries. I cursed the Hitler regime for forcing on me this battle with my conscience, for in the midst of war my heart was with 'the enemy' whom I could not regard as such.

In the years that followed I went through almost all the major air raids that Berlin had to endure, since I always seemed to be at home when the big raids were on. On raid nights when I sat in the cellar with other anxious people and we heard the bombs drop near our inadequate ceiling and waited with bated breath and heads ducked down for it to collapse, when the cellar door sailed through the room, the lights went out and the house swayed with the pressure from the blast, and everyone ran out because we expected next moment to be buried under the ruins, when we coughed up dust and smoke from our lungs and we shuddered to hear the walls falling in nearby, when all this went on, together with my fear for my personal survival I felt a paradoxical sense of satisfaction. During those nights I knew that I could look my English friends in the face. The burning districts of Berlin seemed to me to square the account, at any rate as far as the war in the air was concerned. Another result of these air raids was my feeling of pride in my fellow Berliners. In 1940 I had always heard with mingled satisfaction of the 'we can take it' of Londoners; now I knew that we Berliners were their equal. Here was a link between the citizens of the capitals.

Early in 1943 the Foreign Office was badly damaged. In November 1943 Wilhelmstrasse 74 was gutted by fire to the top floor: our offices were there. Buckets stood on the pile carpets, bitter cold entered through the temporary repairs to the windows, we worked wearing hat and coat, but we too 'could take it'. When it became insufferable we all repaired to our emergency office, a hut about the size of a railway carriage compartment protected above by 1.7m of concrete. A second group had a compartment about the same size located in the Adlon bunker.

It was not only a question of the building being reduced to rubble; the way Ribbentrop organised the department had long anticipated the structural damage inflicted by enemy action. He had not he slightest notion how to run a department of State, and created new departments and posts and appointing 'special commissioners' in the same manner in which the bomb-damaged buildings were propped up by crude repairs.

In the symbolic and actual ruins of our ministry the permanent officials of the Foreign Office lived and worked. They had the weary and laborious task of trying to extinguish both incendiary bombs of Allied origin and the 'incendiaries' hurled by Ribbentrop upon the German Foreign Office, once of fine repute, from his 'Field HQ'. Here and there they might succeed in putting out a fire, but just as they could not catch the bombs before they reached the ground, so they were not in a position to check the catastrophe to which Hitler's amateur policy was leading. Some were killed by bombs; some of the best fell victims of Hitlerian justice. The survivors were reproached after the war had ended with having failed to extinguish all Hitler's and Ribbentrop's 'incendiaries'.

So firm was the structure of the Foreign Department that it withstood Ribbentrop's bombardment for a very long time. It was not until 1940 that a purge of 150 higher officials to south-eastern Europe was ordered; as they were all specialists they were irreplaceable and had to be allowed to remain in office whether the powers that be liked it or not; many were 'dismantled' individually a good deal later. The clamp that held the structure of the department together was the Under Secretary of State Freiherr Erich von Weizsäcker. He enjoyed the high esteem both of his own officials and of all foreign diplomats, and combined the highest moral integrity with the greatest diplomatic competence. With a word, gesture or a significant silence at the right moment he could let us know what he wanted in a manner that could be understood neither by the receiving apparatus of such minds as Hitler's and Ribbentrop's, nor by his later accusers at Nuremberg. All the old, and some of the new, Foreign Office staff looked for guidance to the Under Secretary of State. With his quiet but nonetheless persuasive manner, it was he and his moral authority that strengthened our resolution to maintain Western European mental and moral standards insofar as we could under the Ribbentrop machine.

This Foreign Office administered by Weizsäcker, repudiated and despised by Ribbentrop who wanted nothing to do with it at Field-HQ, was for me a relic of the old Germany that I had valued and that had been respected abroad. In these three houses of the Wilhelmstrasse, though but ruins in the end, I definitely did not feel myself a 'stranger in my own country'. Here I could talk freely about everything with my colleagues, here a true community of spirit prevailed, here nobody betrayed another, either under Hitler or at other times. With tough resilience the old Foreign Office opposed the manifold assaults of Hitler and Ribbentrop with the intent of making itself available, after the foreseeable and inevitable catastrophe, as an expert salvage team.

Like all foreign ministries, the German Foreign Office was divorced from home politics. Political parties might fight at home, but the officials of the Foreign Office service had only their country's interest at heart. Governments came and went, Foreign Ministers changed, but however the scene might shift there was no change in the Foreign Office representation of Reich interests abroad. It was therefore quite natural that German diplomats should regard the National Socialist government as a phenomenon just as transitory as its predecessors, and allow themselves to be ruled only by the idea of serving their country as before. Any notion that the Third Reich might be a permanency evoked only a smile amongst us at the Foreign Office.

As soon as it became clear that in the realm of foreign affairs the conduct of policy by the National Socialists did not promote the general interest and to a constantly increasing degree ran counter to it, it aroused considerable opposition. By reason of its whole tradition and training, the Foreign Service found itself in ever sharper opposition to National Socialist foreign policy and its exponents as that policy became more reckless. The mistakes and dilettantism of the Hitler regime in foreign affairs were first evident to German diplomats and so it was amongst them that an opposition, varying according to individual temperament from passive to the most active resistance, was generated.

As a veteran member of the service, if something of an outsider since I was only a technical official and not a diplomat in the true sense of the word, I shared the diplomat's view of one's duty to country, especially as this attitude corresponded with my personal convictions. I was fairly well informed about the activities undertaken by the more energetic members to avert the misfortunes accruing from Hitler's foreign policy, and with my accurate knowledge of the conversations between statesmen I was able to give some helpful advice.

I had heard from my friends of Chief of the Army General Staff Generaloberst Franz Halder's command to the troops at Potsdam and Hof at the end of September 1938 to march on Berlin in case of a general mobilisation – an order withdrawn when the Munich Conference was called. I knew that the British statements of 1939 (given in detail in my description of the period), which left nothing to be desired as to outspokenness, could be ascribed largely to the influence of friends of mine in Berlin and London, diplomats who made every effort to bring home to the British that they would be understood by Hitler only if they spoke blunt words without beating about the bush. I also knew to the extent to which Weizsäcker and Attolico worked together with the object of doing everything they could to prevent war. I have given a notable example of this in my account of the events preceding the Munich Conference. I had shared in a great many of the disappointments these men had experienced repeatedly as their efforts, made at great personal risk, were frustrated by Hitler's obstinacy and blindness, and by the compliance and lack of understanding of other countries. I witnessed the human tragedies enacted during the war and thereafter. Writing in 1950, much has already become known to people both home and abroad through political writings, especially in connection with the Nuremberg trials. I am convinced that the whole truth about the part played by the best men of our Foreign Office under the Hitler regime will become known, and I can therefore confine myself to these brief observations.

The 'incendiaries' also descended on my smaller circle, the ministerial office. Quite early on, a high-ranking official was summoned for personal interrogation by Heydrich, and dismissed. After the events of 20 July 1944 he lost his life. Another man, a good friend of mine, was banished to East Asia in 1941 by Ribbentrop, who was no doubt aware of his critical attitude but unable to make a concrete allegation. For similar reasons, at the same time I was excluded from close collaboration with Ribbentrop and 'promoted' to be head of the ministerial office, but only the Berlin section. 'It's better for you to rest a little in Berlin between conferences after your strenuous work as interpreter,' said Ribbentrop's stooge, the notorious Under Secretary of State Martin Luther, who had formerly run a transport business. He was later sent to a concentration camp for 'disloyalty' to Ribbentrop. If anyone suggests I should have a rest I always agree, as I did then.

I always felt that to some extent I enjoyed a jester's licence, and expressed my views on the monstrous events through which I was living in the various languages at my disposal, in no way concealing my sympathy for the Western peoples whose languages I had mastered. Until the spring of 1945 I wore the international uniform of non-authoritarian Foreign Offices: a black homburg and the despised umbrella, which Chamberlain had first publicised widely in Germany. I was practically the only civilian to be seen in the Wilhelmstrasse. It was after 1945 before I learnt that these matters had not passed unnoticed as I had assumed, but had been documented religiously.

I caused considerable worry to our Personnel Section, which exhorted me constantly to be prudent or at least to join the party since not to do so might give rise to scandal. In view of my work at the highest levels of National Socialism, my remaining outside the party might justly be deemed proof of disloyalty. I had decided to remain outside of it if possible until 1940, and actually I succeeded in postponing my entry into the party until 1943. It was then high time to join, and when the purge set in after 20 July 1944 I was glad that in the end I had followed the kindly advice of the Personnel Section.

The words of the song had changed: instead of 'We have won the war', foreigners now heard 'We shall win the war' and finally 'We cannot lose the war.'

In January 1942 I went to Rome with Göring, who was to reassure Mussolini about the Russian campaign. This was when we had come to a standstill outside Moscow. 'Nothing more can be done this winter,' Göring told the thoughtful-looking Duce. Soon afterwards Mussolini switched the conversation to his plans for the conquest of Malta.

I also had business once more at the Führer-building in Munich. After the American landings in North Africa, Hitler, Laval, Ciano and Ribbentrop met on 9 November 1942 in the Munich Agreement conference room. Hitler spoke at great length, Ciano listened bored. Laval could contribute little as he was brought into the discussion only right at the end. Finally, as in 1938, Keitel entered the room with a large map. This time it was required in connection with the occupation of hitherto unoccupied France, which Hitler had ordered as a response to the landings in North Africa. The conference was nothing more than a briefing. 'It is the desire of the German government and its troops,' I translated for Laval's benefit from the appeal to the French people that Hitler was to make the following day, 'not only to protect the French frontiers together with members of the French forces, but above all to assist in preserving for the future the African possessions of European peoples from piratical attacks.' At the same time Hitler announced the occupation of Corsica and Tunis. Laval left Munich next day very depressed; he had tried in vain to keep Hitler from occupying the whole of France.

Laval was already the subject of much controversy both in France and Germany. As far as I could see from the conversations he had with Hitler and Ribbentrop, he justified Hitler's distrust insofar as he sought to gain time for France by delaying tactics. As I have mentioned before, I was the only German there whom he had known before and I enjoyed talking to him; I always believed that despite his tactical manoeuvring he was just as honestly concerned for a Franco-German rapprochement as he had been in Brüning's time, and I also felt a certain sympathy for him in the infinitely difficult position in which he found himself. Besides, he was often fearless in what he said to Hitler, and did not hesitate to express his opinion openly.

Laval often advocated the calling of a big conference, even during the war, of all the States of continental Europe, to deliberate upon their common interest and common action. No doubt he hoped on such an occasion to be able to improve the position of France to some degree. I still recollect a very telling remark he made to Hitler in this connection: '*Vous voulez gagner la guerre pour faire l'Europe – mais faites donc l'Europe pour gagner la guerre!*' he exclaimed emphatically. ('You want to win the war to make Europe – but make Europe to win the war!')

Naturally Hitler saw nothing in such an argument, having absolutely no use for many-sided discussions, feeling no doubt that he was not at his best in diplomatic interplay. He was a dictator: he could not negotiate. His mental rigidity made it impossible for him to reach a compromise and it was his uncompromising nature, of which he always boasted, which finally proved his downfall.

Three weeks after this Munich Conference I went to Rome again with Göring. The Axis position in North Africa seemed serious, and Göring wanted to stimulate the Italians to greater activity. At the sessions with Italian officers he ranted and threatened. He showed very little psychological insight, for he alienated all the Italians by his crude insensitive behaviour and it was my impression that he left them still less inclined to make an effort than they had before.

On this same problem of the defence of North Africa, later I interpreted at a conversation between Göring and French General Juin in Berlin. Juin offered to defend the Italian-Tunis boundary at the Mareth Line using French troops against the British pursuing Rommel from the east but declined to carry out his defence jointly with the Germans. 'As long as there are still French prisoners of war in Germany,' he explained to Göring, 'I cannot ask my officers to fight with the German army.'

Towards the end of December 1942 there was another 'three powers' discussion between Hitler, Ribbentrop, Göring, Ciano and Laval, this time at the forest FHQ in East Prussia. Laval came in for very harsh treatment again. The interesting feature of this discussion was Ciano's urging that peace be made with the Soviet Union. Obviously on Mussolini's instructions, he stated: 'At least we could abandon any offensive operations in Russia. We could build up a defensive line to be held with relatively small forces.' All the Axis forces, he went on, must be available for the battle in the west, particularly of course in North Africa. Hitler ignored these arguments and confined himself to reproaching Ciano for the conduct of the Italian troops on the Eastern Front, saying that it was their lack of staying power that had made the Russian break through near Stalingrad possible. I need hardly add that the whole list of the French offences was recited to Laval again. More fantasy in the dark woods at Rastenburg'

Scarcely a month later, on 23 January 1943 Roosevelt and Churchill met at Casablanca. We had had a report from Spain some time before on the impending conference, and in translating the Spanish text too literally the Languages Service made a dreadful howler. They had not realised that Casablanca was a town in French Morocco and translated it as the White House. Our Foreign Office spokesman thereupon boasted at a press conference that we had certain knowledge of an imminent meeting between Roosevelt and Churchill in Washington, and it was an unpleasant surprise for our press chief when the conference took place a few days later in North Africa.

I was dismayed when I translated the fateful declaration announced at that conference about there being no terms available to Germany except unconditional surrender to all the Allies jointly. I realised immediately how immensely it would strengthen Hitler's position at home and abroad, and weaken much of the opposition to his policy, such as I had heard recently expressed by Ciano. It was quite clear to me that the German resistance to Hitler had received a very severe blow by this declaration that all they could work towards was unconditional surrender.

At that time, of course, I did not know that considerable criticism of it was also expressed amongst the Allies. Cordell Hull writes in the chapter of his memoirs devoted exclusively to the demand that he was just as surprised as Churchill when for the first time his president stated it suddenly in Churchill's presence to a press conference during the Casablanca talks in January 1943. He says he was told that Churchill was left speechless. So Roosevelt had also surprised his Foreign Minister. Cordell Hull goes on to say that he was basically opposed to it for two reasons, as were his associates. One was that it might prolong the war by solidifying Axis resistance into a battle of sheer desperation. The second was that logically the victor nations had to be ready in principle to take over the defeated enemy's national and governmental activities and properties. In his view, the Americans and their allies were in no way prepared to undertake that vast operation.

During an excited debate in the House of Commons on 21 July 1949, Churchill stated that he heard the formula of unconditional surrender for the first time when the US president announced it. 'The statement was made by President Roosevelt without consulting me,' he said, 'I have not the slightest doubt that, if the British Cabinet had considered that phrase, it is likely they would have advised against it but, working with a great alliance and with great, loyal and powerful friends from across the ocean, we had to fall in line.'

We learn from Cordell Hull that not only were the American Secretary of State and the State Department in agreement with Churchill and Eden in their disapproval of the formula (which Roosevelt, as he stated, took from the American Civil War), but also General Eisenhower's advisers and even Stalin disapproved of it. In December 1943, Stalin stated at the Tehran Conference that the principle of unconditional surrender was 'bad tactics in the case of Germany.'

In spite of all the objections put forward, however, Roosevelt refused to retract: over this question he was just as uncompromising with his allies as I had found Hitler to be in his discussions with his Axis partners. When the Italians or Antonescu advised him to conclude peace with the Western powers or the Soviet Union, I was often asked to translate this reply: 'You can see for yourselves that we would get nothing but a demand for unconditional surrender if we tried to come to terms with one of our opponents.' To Keitel, Ribbentrop and others of the entourage I often heard Hitler say, 'Now that the enemy threatens us with unconditional surrender, the German people will follow me with all the more resolute determination to final victory.'

Shortly after the Casablanca Conference, at the end of February 1943 I went with Ribbentrop to Rome to explain away the Stalingrad disaster. The came the Salzburg Season in April, which I have already described, and in May there were more empty conversations between Hitler, Laval and Ciano's successor Bastianini.

The last meeting between Hitler and Mussolini before the collapse of Fascist Italy was a memorable one. It was held at a small country house at Feltre near Belluno in northern Italy. Mussolini was taken severely to task by Hitler before the assembled Italian generals. Moreover during the session exaggerated reports were received of the first big air raid on Rome, which the city suffered that same afternoon. This meeting of 20 July 1943 was one of the most depressing I have ever taken part in. Mussolini himself was so overwrought that on his return to Rome he asked urgently for my report: we were told that he had not been able to follow the conversation and could therefore only consider the defensives measure agreed upon when he had my text before him. After Hitler had gone through the report at FHQ *Wolfsschanze* it was despatched to the Duce by special plane.

One of the most remarkable meetings at which I was ever present was that between Ribbentrop and the new Foreign Minister of the government formed by Badoglio after the fall of Mussolini. They convened in August 1943 at the Italian frontier town of Tarvisio. There were not many people in Germany at that time who knew that Ribbentrop was actually prepared to negotiate with an envoy of 'the rogue Badoglio' as the new head of the Italian government was called by the Goebbels press.

'We must leave all our secret papers and cypher keys on German soil,' Ribbentrop said when we left Velden on the Wörthersee in his special train for the discussion. 'It is by no means impossible that these brigands intend to kidnap us on Italian territory, on British and American instructions,' he added darkly. For this reason, in addition to myself, there was only a small staff: some Waffen-SS men sat by us in the train with loaded Schmeissers. When we arrived at Tarvisio the SS detachment immediately threw a protective cordon around Ribbentrop's saloon coach in which the negotiations were to be carried on.

The Foreign Minister, Guariglia, who had recently been ambassador at Ankara, asserted that Italy would continue the war; at the same time Ambrosio, the new Chief of the Italian General Staff, aroused our suspicions by endeavouring to restrict the transport of German troops over the Brenner. Ribbentrop stated that we were sending these troops 'for Italy's protection'. After two hours of futile discussion, in which both parties seemed to be attempting to trump the other's lies, this fantasy also came to an end.

We were not kidnapped, but when our train left the station our Italian Foreign Office counterparts, who had bade us farewell on many a triumphant occasion with the Fascist salute, just stood to attention by our coach wearing embarrassed smiles. This final act brought home to us more than anything else that the Fascist regime in Italy had ceased to exist. That moment revealed to us the menacing background to the fantasies that had been enacted on the political stage during the last two years. The omission by those Italians to give the Fascist salute at that little frontier station presaged Italy's defection.

This defection followed shortly afterwards, on 8 September 1943. It came as another heavy blow after a succession of catastrophes; the capitulation at Stalingrad on 3 February; the Tunisian collapse on 7 May; the British landings at Sicily on 9 July and the fall of Mussolini on 25 July, only a few days after the Feltre meeting. Whilst the storm clouds massed ever thicker over the military sky, the conversations that I had had to interpret had been carried on in tones that sounded ever more hollow.

NINE

1944 AND 1945

A week after the capitulation of Italy, so clearly foreshadowed in Ribbentrop's remarkable conversation with Guariglia, there occurred one of those unexpected switches that characterised foreign policy under Hitler's regime. On 15 September 1943, Mussolini was freed and proclaimed leader of the Fascist Republic. A year after the Feltre conversation, which I had thought would be the last between the two dictators, I was again present at a meeting between them. This took place only a few hours after the attempted assassination of Hitler on 20 July 1944 at FHQ *Wolfsschanze* at Rastenburg.

Whilst there in the autumn of 1944 I saw the culmination of the political drama in a form that could not have been more typical of Hitler's self-delusion.

When I had to translate parts of the annihilistic Morgenthau Plan I realised that even in the Allied ranks there existed deluded fanatics devoting themselves to destructive projects. The Plan was initialled by Roosevelt and Churchill in September 1944 at the second Quebec Conference. The details as I translated them seemed to me exactly on a par with Hitler's fanatical destructive mania. I know now, as I did not know then, that the US Foreign Secretary – how different from his German opposite number! – brought all his influence to bear against the adoption of this murderous plan dreamed up by the then US Finance Minister. Appropriately he called it 'the Goat Pasture Plan' because the intention was to rob Germany of her entire heavy industry and turn the country over to grazing. Cordell Hull was more successful over this than he had been over opposing the unconditional surrender formula and the Plan was finally dropped, although the Morgenthau spirit persisted for quite a time. Cordell Hull devoted the whole of chapter 113 of his book to the departmental wrangles about the Plan. Even Roosevelt finally decided against it. Cordell Hull wrote: 'Stimson informed me that the President was obviously horrified when I read him these sentences [from the Morgenthau Memorandum] and declared he could not imagine how he had come to initial that memorandum; he must have done so without much reflection.'

Churchill told a more than usually attentive House of Commons on 21 July 1949, 'If this document [i.e. the Morgenthau Plan] is ever brought before me I shall certainly say "I do not agree to that and I am sorry that I put my initials to it."' Throughout the time I interpreted for Hitler I never once heard him make a similar admission of error, even to his closest friends. This seems to be a noteworthy difference between Hitler and the statesmen of the West.

In 1944 the fantasies produced by Hitler's self-delusion continued on their routine course. I still made frequent trips to collect Hitler's visitors at the frontiers, and then conducted them back again. I liked this occupation, not only because one could sleep better in a train than at home, but also because the journey from FHQ to the frontier and then back to Berlin gave me an excellent opportunity to dictate my accounts of the conversations in peace and quiet. Conditions in Germany were already such that fairly continuous work was only possible in an office on wheels; at the end of such a journey it was always with regret that I left the private couchette in which I had lived and worked for about a week undisturbed by air raid sirens.

It was in the course of these duties that, towards the end of October 1943, I awaited Prince Cyril and members of the Bulgarian Regency Council at the German–Hungarian frontier. As host, twice daily I sat opposite the prince

in our banqueting saloon coach a
with him. Especially in his manne
of his brother King Boris, who ha
who had met Hitler frequently. Usu
conversations between King and Fü
Hitler did not seem to want a recor
sometimes when they met, howeve
diplomat, knew how to handle Hitle
if not shyness that I had observed in
Victor Emmanuel of Italy and Leopol
unconstrained with Hitler, speaking
delicate matters as though it were the n
unassuming ease was his great strength

his wishful thinking. He ere
premises, quite convinci
they collapsed like a
many visitors be
On his retur
he exami
got

travelled in the special
train, sometimes Boris rather embarrassed the Foreign Office representative
accompanying him by saying that for an hour he did not wish to be a state
visitor. 'I'll look up my colleague on the engine,' he would say, for he had
passed the express-train locomotive driver's test in Germany. He would go off
and return some time later – to the relief of his German escort – somewhat
sooty and with a pleased smile.

His unassuming manner made a good impression of Hitler and his
entourage. While confidence in the 'sly fox' was not unqualified, Boris was
congenial, at any rate for a monarch. In his negotiations with Hitler this king
had achieved a short-term success of an unusual kind: realising Bulgaria's
territorial ambitions without firing a round. He was promised Macedonia
and his boundary extended to the Aegean. He might even have got Salonica,
but a Soviet minister remained accredited to him throughout the whole war,
and when Hitler sounded him out about entering the war on Germany's side
it was his stock answer that 'The Bulgarian people would never go to war
against the Russians, whom they regard as their liberator from the Turkish
yoke.' As events turned out, his policy had he lived could have brought him
no more than a short-lived if brilliant success.

Prince Cyril was given the standard pep talk just like the ones of which
I had translated dozens. I always felt that Hitler himself actually did believe
what he told his foreign visitors. He seemed to apply a sort of autosuggestive
Coué system to himself and to his visitors, except that he spun out Coué's
brief statement 'Every day and in every way I get better and better' into an
interminable monologue adorned with a wealth of technical detail. I noticed
that Hitler based his argument on certain false premises that fitted in with

...ted a completely logical structure on these false
...ng to those who did not see their falsity. Naturally
...house of cards once they had been perceived. Cyril like
...ore and after him seemed to fall prey to Hitler's illusions.
...journey he too found that the edifice began to crumble when
...ned its foundations, and saw it fall completely into ruins when he
...ome and learnt the true facts in all their bleak reality.

I never saw the collapse of this capacity for self-deception in Hitler. The last
I saw of him in person was in December 1944 when he and Szalasi, head of the
new Hungarian puppet government had, to quote the official communiqué,
'a long conversation on all questions affecting the political, military and
economic collaboration of Germany and the Hungarian nation united under
the revolutionary Hungarian movement.' The phrases 'firm determination of
the German and Hungarian peoples to continue the defensive war by every
means' and 'the old, traditional and proven comradeship in arms and friendship
of the two peoples' were typical examples of such self-deception. Hitler's Coué
mentality had not changed even though the enemy had already advanced far
into Reich territory. Moreover, in this last conversation, a few months before
the collapse, I saw no sign that Hitler had lost any of his facility in argument.

I was told after the war by acquaintances near to him up to the last that
Hitler's illusions were shattered only just before the end when he suddenly
realised that he was giving orders to an army that no longer existed. He sat
for two hours in complete silence in the Chancellery bunker, his map spread
before him, gazing into space. Then like a bad captain he left the sinking ship,
abandoning the passengers to their fate.

Auto-suggestive treatment was tried once more at the Salzburg Season
of 1944, but by now some of the patients had begin to rebel. Antonescu's
remarks had for some time been more and more critical and challenging.
This old pupil of the French Staff College ruthlessly laid bare the weakness
and errors of Hitler's strategy. Fine words no longer availed with him and
I was interested to observe that Hitler gave up any attempt to conduct a
conversation with him on Coué lines. With astonishment I saw that the
overbearing dictator was consulting the Romanian marshal. 'I do not know
whether I should evacuate the Crimea or defend it. What would you advise,
marshal?' he asked. I had never before had to translate such a sentence
for Hitler.

'Before I answer your question,' Antonescu said rather condescendingly,
'you must tell me whether you have finally given up the Ukraine.'

'Whatever else happens I shall recapture the Ukraine next year,' Hitler replied, referring to 1945, 'since the raw materials there are indispensable to us for carrying on the war.'

'Then the Crimea must be held,' was Antonescu's verdict.

Another miracle occurred. 'I suggest a compromise,' said Hitler, who would have liked to evacuate the Crimea. 'We shall draw up two plans, a plan for its defence and a plan for its evacuation.

'Agreed,' said Antonescu in a brusque military tone.

Hitler took it all quite calmly. Indeed, on this and on future occasions he was more friendly to Antonescu than to any other of his visitors. Perhaps the Romanian marshal had found the right technique for dealing with dictators.

Hitler was less amenable over important political questions. Especially in the spring of 1944 at Klessheim, Antonescu constantly advocated coming to terms with the Western powers. Hitler would not hear of this. Perhaps he would have been more ready to consider an understanding with Stalin, and although he refused any hint of this possibility made to him in my presence, I was struck by the fact that he did not turn down the idea with anything like the fanatical emphasis he showed when speaking of the 'plutocrats'.

I was very interested to see Hitler's reaction to the peace feelers put out by Russia at this time, of which we were informed by our Stockholm Legation. I happened to overhear a conversation between Hitler and Ribbentrop in which Hitler decided against going any further into this matter because the confidential agent (a so-called V-Man) attached to our legation was a Jew and because 'Stalin is certainly not in earnest, but hopes by such a manoeuvre to incite his Western Allies to open up the second front.'

Towards the end of 1944 and early in 1945 the Germans themselves put out peace feelers to the Western Allies through their embassies or legations in Sweden, Switzerland and Spain. At first Hitler was against this, but finally he permitted Ribbentrop to launch this inefficient peace offensive. 'Nothing will come of it,' he told Ribbentrop, 'but if your mind is set on it, you can make the attempt.' The whole operation was code-named 'Gold'.

'A preliminary condition for any peace talks is that the Führer confines himself to his position as Head of State, and hands over the government to a Herr X,' I read in a telegram from Madrid.

'I would also lose my post,' I heard Ribbentrop say when he saw it. 'There can be no question of that.' Not a word was heard from Berne or Stockholm.

I also escorted the Hungarian regent Horthy to Salzburg in the spring of 1944. He was becoming increasingly more fractious. Once again I was dismissed when Horthy arrived, and so I do not know the details of his discussions with Hitler.

Having nothing to do I was standing with some colleagues in the hall of the great castle at Klessheim when suddenly the door of the conference room flew open and to our surprise the aged Horthy came rushing out, very red in the face, and began to climb the stairs to the first-floor guest rooms. Hitler, looking angry and embarrassed, came running after him and tried to call his guest back. Showing great presence of mind, the tall *chef de protocole* Freiherr von Dörnberg placed himself in the path of the runaway Hungarian regent, engaging him in conversation until the other runner in the race, Hitler, could catch him up and accompany his guest to his room. Then, still angry, he returned downstairs and disappeared with Ribbentrop into the council chamber. We soon discovered the cause of all this. Hitler, alleging the unreliability of the Hungarian government, had put demands that amounted to instituting something like a German protectorate over Hungary. To this Horthy had responded: 'If everything here has already been decided, there is no point in my staying any longer. Therefore I shall make my departure at once,' and with that had made his startling exit.

The castle now became active like a disturbed beehive. Horthy sent for his special train (there was a special station near Klessheim Castle for guests of honour), Ribbentrop contacted Stojai, the Hungarian Minister in Berlin, a most convincing fake air-raid was staged, even including a smokescreen over the castle, as a ruse to prevent Horthy's special train from leaving. The telephone line to Budapest turned out to be 'badly hit' so that the regent was cut off from home. By the use of these diplomatic and military devices, another talk was finally arranged between Horthy and Hitler.

'If Horthy does not give way, you will not be accompanying him back to the frontier,' Ribbentrop informed me. 'He will have no guard of honour, but will travel as a prisoner under guard.'

In the end I escorted Horthy back to the frontier that evening with full honours, for he had said he was willing to replace 'the unreliable government', of whose contacts with the western powers we had been informed, by a new government under Stojai. I was much struck by the contrast with Antonescu's behaviour in similar circumstances: Hitler had shown him documents from which it appeared that his Foreign Minister Mihai Antonescu (no relation) was in touch with the western powers, but the marshal refused to act and Mihai remained in office.

On the return journey we were invited to dine with Horthy in his coach. In spite of his troubled day the old gentleman was once again a grand seigneur of the old double monarchy, and as such I always found him very congenial. He made no reference to the embarrassing scenes of the day but entertained us with delightful stories of old Austria–Hungary, memories of the First World War and the time when he had led the operations of the Austro-Hungarian fleet in the Mediterranean. Later I found it particularly painful to recall that delightful evening, for Hitler forced Horthy to return to Germany as a political prisoner, kidnapping his son rolled-up in a carpet to extort the father's presence.

From the Hungarian frontier I returned to Salzburg as further visits were in prospect. Before these occurred I paid a visit to the Berghof when Eva Braun was staying there.

I had heard rumours linking her name with Hitler, but had not thought much of them since Hitler seemed to me to take no interest in women. I knew better when I saw them in the large hall at the Berghof one evening holding hands by the fireside. At dinner she sat next to him, enabling me to observe her more closely. Tall, slim and good-looking, her dress and general style were typical of Berlin's West End; not at all the type of German womanhood featured as the ideal of National Socialism. She was very well made up and wore valuable jewellery, but somehow she did not seem to me to feel quite at ease in her role. I did not get to know her well, for I did not form part of the intimate circle at Obersalzberg. Her presence there was concealed carefully from outsiders; Hitler's permission was obtained before I was admitted on that occasion.

The next visitor whom I was sent to collect was Mussolini, who then ruled the Fascist Republic of North Italy from Milan. His daughter, whom we had liberated as we had his wife and children, remained in Germany.

I interpreted conversations between Countess Edda Ciano and Hitler on two occasions. Each time the tall, elegant daughter of the Italian dictator raised political questions with Hitler, and did not hesitate to express views opposite to his own vehemently and with great ability. 'You can't punish someone just because his grandmother is a Jewess,' she said once, her large brown eyes flashing like her father's. She advocated passionately more humanity in the treatment of the Jews. At her second visit, which occurred after Mussolini's downfall, she put forward a long series of complaints about the treatment of Italian prisoners of war in Germany.

Hitler was obviously impressed by the force with which Edda Ciano expressed her views. He tolerated her saying things which he would have taken ill from a man criticising his policy, but he remained obdurate on the question of Ciano and his wife going to Spain. 'I fear you would have only unpleasantness there,' Hitler said, 'You are better off with us in Germany.' This refusal cost Ciano his life.

As I have said, I was meant to fetch the temperamental Edda's father from the Italian frontier at the end of April 1944 as he too had been invited to Salzburg, but fate decreed otherwise.

The head of the Fascist Republic naturally no longer possessed a special train to which in the ordinary way my two coaches would have been attached at the frontier and so I was entrusted with most of the coaches of Hitler's train, which was to go to Milan to collect Mussolini. When I was leaving, Dörnberg said, 'Now please don't make yourself too comfortable and stay in the train until Milan. The guard of honour gets off and on at the Reich frontier, and if the Italians in their present sensitive mood hear that you travelled from the frontier to the destination they will start saying that the German Foreign Office has now extended the Reich frontier to Milan.'

I arrived at Lienz on the River Drau in the Führer's special train at 3 p.m., and here the guard of honour and I de-trained to await the return of the train at 3 a.m. for the journey back to Salzburg. When the train came in next morning not one of us was there – we were all in Lienz hospital suffering from concussion and fractures. While on the way to Heiligenblut the NSDAP district officer driver had swerved to the side of the road as the result of a puncture, the car had crashed down the bank, toppled over and landed upside down in the Drau, trapping us inside.

For the time being there was to be no more travelling or interpreting for me. When I was discharged from hospital the Foreign Office sent me to Baden-Baden to convalesce. I stayed in an attractive suite of rooms at Brenners Hotel occupied by an interned US diplomat before me. Later when interned by the Americans I was interested to compare American and German hospitality as shown to interned diplomats.

At Baden-Baden I had my treasured portable wireless set by my bedside; it had enabled me to listen to Roosevelt and Churchill throughout the war. It was always a literary delight to hear Churchill although by no means did I always agree with what he said. This wireless was largely responsible for my battle vocabulary whose extent often surprised my listeners when I held forth on the situation at the front. 'The longer the war lasts the easier translating gets,' I told a colleague once; by carefully listening to and comparing the texts of both sides I observed that each combatant said very much the same thing in a similar situation. This parallel was especially marked in the appeals made in Germany in connection with the formation of the *Volkssturm* towards the end of the war: I told the Languages Service when they translated these appeals to use the texts of the English-language broadcasts made when the Home Guard was raised in 1940; with these texts beside them they would find the translation much easier. That was not by any means the only occasion on which the Languages Service consulted their opponents, so to speak, for valuable assistance.

I was still recovering in hospital at Baden-Baden on 6 June 1944 when I learned that the Atlantic Wall had gone the same way as the Maginot Line and later the Westwall. 'Bad times for impregnable fortifications,' a colleague wrote to me from the Foreign Office.

After I had convalesced sufficiently I was ordered to report to FHQ in East Prussia for a meeting between Hitler and Mussolini on 20 July 1944. On the early afternoon of that day my car drew up at the first barrier. I was to be on the platform of the small station that served the FHQ at 3 p.m. on the dot. This station served a single branch line and had a narrow, unpaved low platform with an open waiting room fronted by a kind of veranda. For security reasons it was named 'Görlitz', also the name of a station in Berlin. At this small railway 'halt', as no doubt the railway authorities classified it, many important visitors had come to FHQ.

Much has already been written about the unsuccessful attempt to assassinate Hitler on 20 July 1944, but not much mention made that only two hours after the attempt Hitler met Mussolini for a political discussion at the scene of the explosion.

'No! Not even you can go to HQ today!' the sentry at a barrier told me.

'I have been summoned to a conference between Hitler and Mussolini. You must let me through!'

'The conference will not take place,' the sentry said.

'Why not?'

'Because of what's happened.'

This laconic answer was the first intimation I had of the attempt of 20 July. I finally succeeded in getting past the sentries and reached the little station where I was told what had actually happened by Hitler's physician Dr Morell, who had not himself fully recovered from the shock of the explosion. He told me that miraculously Hitler had escaped practically unhurt while other people in the room had been seriously wounded. He expressed great admiration for Hitler's complete calm; he found his pulse quite normal when examining him for injuries.

While Dr Morell was telling me this, Hitler appeared at the platform to welcome Mussolini. There was outwardly no evidence of what had befallen him except that his right arm was rather stiff. When the train came in I noticed that he held out his left hand to Mussolini, and that he moved much more slowly than usual and seemed to have difficulty in raising his right arm. Over the few hundred metres walk between the station and the bunkers and barrack huts of the encampment Hitler told Mussolini what had just happened, quietly and almost in a monotone, as though he had had no part in it. Mussolini's naturally prominent eyes seemed to start from their sockets in horror.

The three of us entered the conference room, which looked like a bombed house after a British landmine had exploded nearby. For a while the two of them inspected the damage in silence and then Hitler related some of the details. He showed Mussolini how he had been bending over the table to see something on the map, and was leaning on his right elbow when the explosion occurred, almost exactly beneath his arm. The table top had been blown off and it was this that had hurt his right arm. In a corner of the room was the uniform that Hitler had been wearing that morning, and he showed Mussolini the tattered tunic, ripped to shreds by the air pressure, still draped over a wrecked chair, and the back of his head where the hair was singed.

Mussolini was absolutely horrified; he could not understand how such a thing could happen at FHQ; his face expressed utter dismay. They spent a while in silence letting it sink in, Hitler then sat on an overturned crate and I had to fetch Mussolini one of the few still serviceable chairs and the two of them sat amidst the devastation.

'When I go over it in my mind,' Hitler said in a strikingly quiet voice, 'while others in the room were seriously wounded and one man was literally blown through the window by the air pressure, my wonderful escape shows that nothing can happen to me. It is by no means the first time that I have escaped death in a miraculous manner.'

These sentences visibly impressed the superstitious Mussolini. Then Hitler spoke the notable words, 'After my escape from death today I am convinced more than ever that it is my mission, even now, to bring our joint great cause to a successful conclusion.'

Mussolini indicated his agreement with a nod of the head. 'After seeing all this,' he said with a sweeping gesture of the hand, 'I absolutely share your opinion. It is a sign from heaven!'

They sat together for some considerable time until Mussolini had recovered his composure sufficiently to congratulate Hitler on his escape. Then they both rose and continued their discussion in one of the bunker rooms. Neither of them said as much, but there had been a breath of adieu in their quiet and fairly aimless talk, and this actually was the last time they ever saw each other.

Hitler now believed more firmly than ever in 'his' providence. His confidence was fortified. His revenge took on inhuman forms. His policy led to truly grotesque contrasts between self-delusion and irrationality. One of the most remarkable examples of Hitler's complete lack of touch with reality following the providential intervention to save his life on 20 July were the negotiations conducted at FHQ Wolfsschanze over a week in October 1944.

I refer to Hitler's attempt to form a new French government. The head of this government was to be a French ex-communist, Jacques Doriot, who had founded a party of the extreme right in France. The France that this new government was to represent was now mainly in the hands of the Allies, and so it was proposed that its seat should be at Sigmaringen in southern Germany, where the local *Gauleiter* had already protested at the raising of the French tricolour.

The prospective French ministers were characterised by their personal rivalries in the operatic style of the pre-war film *Les Nouveaux Messieurs*, and 'Prime Minister' Doriot was so much disliked by his compatriots that he lived with us Germans in the Sports Hotel on the Schwenzeitsee, so that I had many opportunities of talking to him. Doriot was a highly intelligent man who seemed to know exactly what he wanted. As a communist he had been received by Stalin, and he knew the east, particularly China, very well. He dominated the other Frenchmen of the 'government delegation'. He was a far superior as a negotiator to Ribbentrop.

The unreality of the whole thing was underlined impressively by the thunder of the Russian guns at Augustov, only 50 miles from Hitler's headquarters, and at night one could see the whole south-eastern horizon lit by the muzzle flashes of the artillery.

After a semblance of unity had been obtained, with great effort, amongst the French, Hitler received the 'new French government', and after a long discourse on Calais and Dunkirk bestowed upon them his blessing with his old eloquence. The incident involving the Hungarian regent Horthy in December 1944 at Klessheim to which I referred earlier was a sequel.

This was the last time I saw Hitler. FHQ Wolfsschanze was abandoned and by December had long been in the hands of the Red Army. Thus ended my work as an interpreter. It had begun on 1 August 1923 and had caused me to play for almost a quarter of a century a modest but not unimportant role in diplomacy, closely linked to political events in Europe and the rise and fall of my own country. My experience led me to the conviction that certain principles hold good for all peoples and determine events regardless of the will of any individual, however powerful. My work in the Foreign Office was terminated with the unconditional surrender of 8 May 1945, but my activities as interpreter and translator were to continue.

EPILOGUE

1945
TO
1949

Soon after Whitsun 1945 I passed Klessheim Castle at Salzburg in a crowded lorry guarded by two US soldiers with rifles at the ready. This journey reminded me of something I had not seen since the Röhm purge in 1934. A short while before, I had been taken into custody with other colleagues by the US Counter Intelligence Corps, a kind of political police. After my arrival at the Augsburg internment camp, for the first time in my life a cell door crashed shut behind me. I was treated correctly and sometimes with friendly consideration by the Americans.

'In the Languages Service we racked our brains trying to find the English equivalent of *Sippenhaft*,' I said to a colleague on our first round of the prison yard, 'and since yesterday one can see that it means 'automatic arrest', treating all German officials from senior administrative officer upwards as being related by blood.' It was not the first time that a term from the recent past had shown its meaning with a rude awakening in the present.

Over the next few years I had a unique observation post and could follow the liquidation of the past and become acquainted with those who dealt with this work on the Allied side. Escorted by a very kind French officer I was taken to Paris in August 1945 in what had been von Rundstedt's car. We passed through Verdun, just as the verdict on Pétain ('Defender of Verdun' in the First World War) was announced there, so that I was too late to give to be called as a witness at his trial as had been intended. The associates of de Gaulle, then head of the French government, were very interested in other matters of which I had knowledge, particularly the conversations between Molotov and Hitler.

Coming from an internment camp in devastated Germany I felt as though I were dreaming when, practically at liberty, I walked along the boulevards of intact Paris where I did not see a single broken windowpane. With my police inspector escort, I sat on the café terraces I knew so well, or walked up and down the Boulevard Saint-Michel, even ate at Fouquet on the Champs Elysées amidst elegant British and Allied society.

This dream lasted ten days, and then I was returned to an internment camp near Mannheim. The next three years were spent alternating between solitary confinement and lodging in a villa, between witness detention in a prison at Nuremberg and nominal house arrest at Tegernsee; and to complete the experience I spent three months at Dachau concentration camp under very strange circumstances.

My experiences during this period were little inferior in historical and human drama to those of earlier years. I appeared at the main trials at Nuremberg for the defence and for the prosecution, but also worked as interpreter and languages 'maid-of-all-work' at the Nuremberg 'witnesses' prison', an arrangement typical of the period after the conclusion of hostilities. I was the only German working in the so-called Prisons Operations Office, was employed briefly in the American Languages Division and appeared at court martials occasionally as the official interpreter, taking evidence from German witnesses in cases brought against US citizens serving in the Wehrmacht.

The night when those condemned in the main trials were executed, I was lodged in a wing about 50 yards from the gymnasium where over the last few nights I had heard the gallows being erected. I interpreted for the American psychiatrists, accompanying them on their visits in the prison, and witnessed human dramas of great tragedy.

In my professional capacity I took part not only in the liquidation of the past, but also in the political and more especially the economic developments of the immediate future. I had to translate for the Americans many memoranda by German officials. The problems and their phrasing often bore a striking resemblance to papers on which I had worked in the 1920s, and my old vocabulary of the period of reparations conferences and trade negotiations stood me in good stead. I started again from the beginning as a one-man languages service, translating as I had in 1923 about trade balances, levels of trade and industry, pressures of taxation and unemployment. A rather inferior portable wireless, successor to my old friend, kept me up to date with the vocabulary of the post-war period – the distress of refugees, the Iron Curtain, dismantling and stripping, and the Berlin Airlift.

My experiences during this post-war period were no less varied than during diplomatic events from 1923 to 1945, but since I was no longer concerned with the diplomatic stage, although the work was similar, and I had been relegated from the stage to the auditorium, those experiences do not come within the scope of this book.

INDEX

If you enjoyed this book, you may also be interested in...

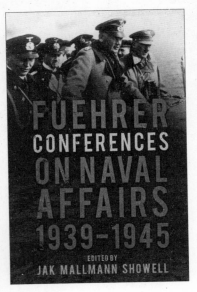

Fuehrer Conferences on Naval Affairs, 1939-1945

JAK MALLMAN SHOWELL

978 0 7509 6438 8

As the Allies made their inexorable last assault upon Germany in 1945, Adolf Hitler ordered that every official military document be destroyed. Admiral Karl Dönitz, then supreme commander-in-chief of the navy, felt differently. The navy, he believed, had waged an honourable war, and posterity would prove the fairest judge. Accordingly, the records fell into Allied hands. Were it not for Dönitz's singular decision, this remarkable book would not exist.

Fuehrer Conferences on Naval Affairs is the faithful first-hand account of Hitler's meetings with his navy commanders-in-chief – Grand Admiral Dr Erich Raeder until January 1943, then Admiral Dönitz – and a handful of other highranking officers. Such was the nature of these meetings that even secretaries were excluded, and both Raeder and Dönitz personally checked the typescripts of the meeting notes before approving them.

The conferences concerned either subjects upon which Hitler requested information or topics that the commanders-in-chief wanted to bring to the Fuehrer's attention. This is, therefore, an authentic and intimate account of the views of Axis high command upon naval strategy and its execution throughout the Second World War, covering such key events as the invasion of Norway, plans to invade Britain, the sinking of the Bismarck and the Normandy landings.

Visit our website and discover thousands of other History Press books.

www.thehistorypress.co.uk